The Selected Letters of
BERNARD BERENSON

BERNARD BERENSON, 1865–1959

The Selected Letters of
BERNARD BERENSON

edited by
A. K. McCOMB

with an epilogue by
NICKY MARIANO

HOUGHTON MIFFLIN COMPANY · BOSTON
The Riverside Press Cambridge
1964

Acknowledgements

IT IS my agreeable duty to thank those who have been so kind as to provide me with letters written by or to Bernard Berenson.

His Majesty the King of Sweden has graciously permitted me to publish some letters written to him. I am further under obligation for letters appearing in this volume: to the Biblioteca Marucelliana; to Mrs. John F. Kennedy, Miss Gisela Richter, Miss Natalie Barney; to Mr. Harold Acton, Mr. Walter Lippmann; to the late Judge Learned Hand, and to his executor and son-in-law Mr. Norris Darrell; to Mr. Lawrence Berenson, Bernard Berenson's attorney; to Mr. Henry Coster, Mrs. Alfred Barr, Mrs. Norbert Muhlen; to the former American Ambassador to Italy, Mr. William Phillips; to Mr. Philip Hofer, Custodian of MSS at the Houghton Library at Harvard University; to Professor Hugh Trevor-Roper, Regius Professor of History at Oxford; to Professor Paul Sachs and to Professor Richard Cary of Colby; and to Miss Margaret Perry for letters given by her to Colby College. I desire to thank Mr. George Stout, the Director of Fenway Court, for allowing me to examine and use the collection of letters to Mrs. Jack Gardner which are in his care, and Mr. Walter Whitehill, the Director of the Boston Athenaeum, for letters to the late Arthur Kingsley Porter and Mrs. Kingsley Porter which are in his charge, and the Executors of Mrs. Porter for their kind assent to this permission.

For permission to use two letters from Vernon Lee (Violet Paget) I am indebted to Miss Irene Cooper Willis, Miss Paget's executor, and for knowledge of one of them to Miss Sybille

Pantazzi, Librarian of the Toronto Art Gallery. Similarly for the right to publish the long extract of a letter from George Santayana to Mrs. C. H. Toy, I desire to thank Mr. Daniel Cory, editor of *The Letters of George Santayana* (Chas. Scribner's Sons, 1955), and the publishers themselves. This last-named volume is of course of the greatest interest and charm in its own right.

The actual copies of Berenson's letter of 1897 to Vernon Lee, and her reply, were given me by Mr. Peter Gunn who had had them made at Colby College (where the originals of both are preserved among Vernon Lee's papers, these papers being a gift to the College from Miss Cooper Willis) while he was at work on his (now, I understand, completed) book on Vernon Lee. I desire to thank through Miss Nicky Mariano who was instrumental in securing letters from them a number of Berenson's correspondents with whom I have not been personally in touch. These are Miss Edith de Gasparin, Mr. Arthur Waley (for letters to Beryl de Zoete), Dr. Axel Boethius, Mr. Roger Hinks. Finally, in verifying various facts for the footnotes, I have found Sylvia Sprigge's biography of Berenson most useful (*Berenson*, Boston, 1960).

For typing a great part of the Ms. and for useful suggestions I cannot sufficiently thank Mr. Robert Lynch and similarly I desire to thank Signora Fiorella Superbi for transcribing many of the letters which happened to be preserved at Florence, in I Tatti or at the Biblioteca Marucelliana. Finally, for what Prince Bismarck, in greater connexions, might have called the "imponderables," I remember most pleasurable conversations on the subject of this book with Mr. David McKibbin, Mr. George Watson, Mr. George Kaftal and Dr. Richard Offner.

For valuable help of all sorts, including the securing for me of many letters from contributors I did not personally know and their transcribing, as well as permission to use letters in the collection at I Tatti, which include those to and from Mary

Berenson in the nineties, I particularly desire to thank Miss Nicky Mariano, Mr. Berenson's secretary over many years and his literary legatee. Miss Mariano indeed was my collaborator throughout and the stereotyped phrase which comes to mind has in her case a literal and genuine application. Without her aid and constant interest it is hard to see how these letters could have been put together.

A. K. McComb

Boston
June, 1962

Table of Contents

Introduction

I

BERNARD BERENSON was born in Lithuania in 1865, hence a subject of the Emperor Alexander II. His family migrated to America in 1875 and settled in Boston. They were in humble circumstances, but the brilliance of the boy inevitably attracted patronage and after attending the famous Boston Latin School, he went to Harvard spending there the years 1884-1887. He was one of the early editors of the *Harvard Monthly,* succeeding Santayana who was a friend and a contemporary. Indeed his first interests were literary.

Berenson went abroad for the first time — if we discount his Russian early childhood — in 1887 and the first letter of this collection is perhaps the earliest one preserved of the many which he was to write from Western Europe, where indeed he spent the rest of his life. It is addressed to his chief patroness Mrs. Jack Gardner who with others helped Berenson financially and enabled him to go abroad. The later letters to Mrs. Gardner here reproduced will indicate what proved to be his life profession — namely the "expertising" and attributing of Italian Renaissance pictures and drawings. In this matter "B.B.," as he was known to his friends, was a pupil of Giovanni Morelli who had devised a revolutionary method of attribution based on the careful comparison of the rendering of minor repeated physical characteristics in figures and, by extension, also of aspects of landscape, etc. This system took the place of attributions based on general style-impressions and the results were embodied in four small volumes on Italian painting which Berenson published between 1894 and 1907.

In 1890 Berenson met at her family's house in England Mary Costelloe, the daughter of Philadelphia Quakers who had settled in Sussex. She was the wife of Frank Costelloe, a barrister by whom she had two daughters. In 1891 Mary Costelloe went to Italy where she from then on spent most of her time. Much later, in 1900, a year after the death of Costelloe, she and Berenson were married. As Mary Berenson's previous marriage had been a Catholic one, there could have been no question of a divorce during the period 1891-99.

In 1899 B.B. purchased a villa, I Tatti, at Settignano which for the rest of his life was inseparably connected with him and where he subsequently built up a collection of Italian Renaissance paintings — although he did not think of them as a collection but merely as decorations for his house — and a valuable library on which perhaps he set even more store. Here the Berensons lived in the fashion of so many expatriates of their period and here Mary Berenson died in 1945, Berenson surviving her by fourteen years. Here they stayed even during the war of 1939-45 except for a brief period when during the German occupation Berenson went into hiding in the house of a neighbour which was diplomatically immune. The story of this disturbed time is revealed in some detail in the letters. The Berensons had no children but in later years Mary Berenson became much wrapped up in her grandchildren who were then growing up. Mary's brother, Logan Pearsall Smith, the distinguished writer and critic, as well as her sister Alys, the first wife of Bertrand Russell, had settled in England and become Anglicized; her own daughters were of course English and had married Englishmen, and therefore her grandchildren were likewise English; B.B.'s relations continued to live in America and to remain Americans. One of his sisters, Rachel, married Ralph Barton Perry, the philosopher, and there were several cousins, one of whom, Lawrence Berenson, his attorney, figures in the correspondence which follows. Berenson himself always remained an American citizen.

Berenson first made a competence from buying pictures on commission for Mrs. Gardner's collection. Indeed he was largely "responsible" for the collection. Later he also collaborated with other great American collectors, such as Walters, Johnson and Widener. He had a long association with the dealer Duveen. His word as to authenticity and authorship carried overwhelming authority and was in the highest degree financially remunerative. B.B. enjoyed a commission of 10 percent on the net profit of every painting which Duveen sold and which Berenson had attributed. After 1927 this arrangement was replaced by an annual retainer. Later he had a connexion with Wildenstein and before his death had accumulated a fortune which brought him an income (in 1939) of ca. £8,000 ($40,000) a year.

In later life he seemed to regret having become an expert and developed a wish to have led what might be called a Goethean life. After the purchase of I Tatti at the turn of the century and perhaps particularly between the wars he entertained a great deal. Many frequenters of the house were also his correspondents as the collection in this book will show. He was a social and gregarious man and had a vast acquaintance which extended far beyond his professional interests. Berenson's tenor of life has been compared to that of a Prince in a small court. One sees what is meant but the objections to such a view are in detail formidable. A rather closer parallel to the life of I Tatti which perhaps will make its nature clear, must have been that of Ferney. Both were well appointed houses lying just outside what Spengler calls "cultural cities." There was the same cosmopolitanism, the same coming and going of celebrated persons from all parts of the civilized world, the same atmosphere of esprit and "enlightenment" and the same centring of attention on the Master of the House. Now, in the Villa as a Harvard institution, one feels the lack of his presence. So might some eighteenth century visitor feel who returning as a ghost to Ferney failed to find Voltaire.

II

Bernard Berenson was an indefatigable correspondent. Following the courteous custom of his generation, all his numerous letters are in long-hand, though written after the invention of the typewriter. A complete collection of the letters would fill a number of volumes and a great part might of course be interesting only to specialists, colleagues, art critics, museum curators, dealers, and so on. Such a collection would certainly be of interest considered from the point of view of the history of taste; the present selection has however another purpose. It is to present to the general educated public an *aperçu*, through his letters, of a great connoisseur, expatriate, and cosmopolitan of the turn of the century. For this is the time to which Berenson essentially belonged, though he lived until 1959. Berenson was a rich man and led a life of some style. In this aspect, too, he was a representative of the last stage of classic capitalism. His interests and attitudes all reflect this moment in typical fashion. We are told, e.g., that his attitude to the welfare state embarrassed some of his younger, more "socially conscious" English visitors but equally these attitudes were pleasing to those who were older or took a more traditionalist, conservative or classical view of the world. In addition Berenson was a very well-read man not only in fields tangential to his own but in those widely separated from his professional interests. One gets the impression that he somewhat consciously "cultivated" his mind, as one might a garden, and that this process had its acquisitive side, so that he was at once pleased with the look of the garden and proud to be its owner. As Santayana has said when comparing Berenson with Charles Loeser, his neighbour *oltr' Arno* and also a rich collector: Loeser seemed to enjoy the Renaissance while Berenson had the air of displaying it. Such psychological

questions may be left to the reader, who will gather a good deal
directly and indirectly from the letters.

Berenson was very much interested in politics and in questions of the day and his letters are full of topical allusions. The
most interesting reflexions to a later generation are doubtless
those of a general character, as for instance his view of other nations' attitudes to England, his comparison of Nazis and Com-
munists and so on rather than in day-to-day comments on political details. The latter would of course be interesting in the
case of a statesman's letters, but Berenson's comments on this
subject were often merely those of a gifted journalist. His attitude to America (where he spent only twelve years of his life),
to Italy ("a great culture but not a great nation" I heard him
say one day in the presence of Carlo Placci who was understand-
ably not pleased), or again to distinguished persons of his time,
such as Santayana or Edith Wharton, have a special interest. It
is not too much to say that the letters (which to be sure are very
consistent with the living person one knew) add a good deal to
his formal writings and reveal a marked personality. We know
that he was a celebrated one. His friends will derive some pleasure from seeing his figure once more as it is here outlined.
Those who did not know him personally will perhaps feel after
dipping into his correspondence as if they had.

Mary Berenson and her brother Logan Pearsall Smith (whose
English was rather exquisite) did not believe that B.B. had any
great literary gift. I venture to agree with them, and think that
the interest of the letters lies elsewhere. I shall add — for the
amusement of the reader, in case he chooses to make a comparison of his impressions — that I find the earlier letters, let us say
before 1910, fresher, more spontaneous and even more genuine
than the later. The world impinged a great deal on Berenson
— he knew it and gave expression to his regret more than once.
Berenson, who enjoyed being verbally malicious, was fundamen-
tally nevertheless extremely loyal and tenacious in his friend-

ship for those who won his approval. The editor of these letters himself can testify to many kindnesses and much generosity in the estimate placed by Berenson on some of his occasional writings concerning Italian painting. But Berenson was a complicated person. Though very constant in his attachments to the arts, he was divided I think with respect to his life and his rôle. I use the word rôle advisedly for like many persons of his generation, he much of the time, one might say, thought of the world as a stage. To those on the outside of course his life seemed to have great consistency, and from this point of view it was a work of art. Berenson who was charmingly easy of access was not easy to know more à fond than a social contact implies. We may leave these puzzling matters about an interesting man to the reader, who may find he can learn something about them from what follows.

A. K. McComb

Lausanne
October, 1961

The Selected Letters of
BERNARD BERENSON

To Mrs. Jack Gardner

54 rue de Vaugirard
Paris
24 August 1887

My dear Mrs. Gardner,

   . . . I have been here since the day of my landing. For several weeks — was it exhaustion because of the very crowded life I had been living; was it mere topsy-turviness resulting from being plunged so suddenly into the most horrible of solitudes, a great city where you do not know one friendly soul — whatever it was for a few weeks, I barely lived. I kept to my room, slept a good deal, and sometimes I did not sleep at all but analyzed a fever and ague that were playing hide and seek within me. Then about three weeks ago began the delightful weather and since then I have been as happy as I can be away from Boston. I have buried myself with seeing and reading. But travel as travel I detest. . . . I do not like gypsying and worse I find I am moved not at all by what is the cause of so much travel, the historic sentiment. The fact that something happened in a certain place does not make that place in the least interesting to me, unless it has some purely aesthetic merit with it. . . .

Sincerely yours
Bernhard Berenson

To Mary Costelloe[1]

Perugia
3 February 1891
Sunday

He will think about it I am sure. He was so nice really. It's so encouraging to meet people so simple and honest as he even in their bad tastes.[2]

I heard from the Father to-day. I enclose the note. Make all the allowance you please for Italian epistolary styles, and yet there is plenty left to show what a man it is. I am sure there's nothing personal in the note. I mean he probably does not feel a bit more fond of me than of the other people that have come and spent a few days with him. It is simply his way with everybody. I look forward so much just to seeing him again, and I so like his way of taking religion. I suppose dogmas have given him little trouble, and controversy less; nor can I believe that there has been much inward struggle in his life. He is so simple, an uncharitable person would say silly. But to me he has seemed endlessly beautiful, and I love his little faults, and weaknesses. They are so much on the mere outside. He does not know the object of my visit at all, and I really don't know what he will say when he finds out. Whatever he does will be the proper thing I am sure. I wish so he understood English, or French better. I don't altogether like to go to confession in a language like Italian which I don't know so well but that I am nearly always conscious of the mere words. Still this may be all the better. Then I would so like to read to him those hymns by Faber you sent me. He would love them so, and Frank's tract on the Mass too. In some ways I feel so ab-

---

[1] Mary Costelloe was the sister of Logan Pearsall Smith and of Alys, the first wife of Bertrand Russell. Her first husband — Frank Costelloe, a barrister — died in 1899. B. Berenson and Mary were married on December 18, 1900, in Settignano. The obligatory civil ceremony was followed, both B.B. and Mary being nominal Catholics, by the religious ceremony ten days later.

[2] Time has obliterated the identity of the person referred to.

surdly like the Methodists. I could get up, and make "testimonies." I used to loathe those poor people so. I never will
again, I hope. Religion means too much to me from the inside,
henceforth to allow me to despise any person's strivings, no
matter how mistaken. Oh, I have been so narrow, and what is
more absurd, bigoted. It takes one taking a religion as I have
taken Catholicism hitherto to be really a bigot. I really am
making "testimonies," am I not? I don't fear to somehow, for
one reason because I know you will sympathize with me, and
furthermore because I am in earnest about what I say. Tell
Frank that I really "mean business" at last. I almost hated him
the other evening for using that phrase. Words have such a
strange effect on me. But I do mean business now, I have begun
to go to school, and furthermore I long to be enrolled with the
class — to complete the metaphors. Frank was right. What I
needed so much was religion. I hope I have made the beginning, and with God's help the rest will come. To myself
scarcely anything is so significant as the ease with which I can
now use the name of God. It is quite wonderful. Now it is so
natural to pray, to kneel down, to cross myself, and to use many
of the symbols, as if I had done so all my life. What a difference
it is making to me. With this new light Italy itself seems so infinitely more beautiful. Do give my love to Ray. I thought so
much about her through the night. And my love to Frank.

To Mary Costelloe

Milan
13 February 1891
Friday evening

Surely my brief note to you last Saturday was not meant to remind you that you had ever hurt me. I was feeling so grateful

and so loving to you that I could not bear to think I had ever felt less; and as I had I simply could do nothing but confess it, and then human weakness led me to mitigate my own sins by giving a cause for them. Please don't forget that the knife was very necessary in my case; I was myself the victim of words, and it needed sharp words to make me see this. I wish I had thought of telling you about my reception into the Church. Now it will keep till I see you, which will be soon. How glad I am. It was all so simple. I had a letter from the dear Padre this morning. I left him not over well, and made him promise to write to me. I enclose his note. The Gustavo he wishes to be remembered to is Frizzoni.[1] I always have such funny luck in Milan. Frizzoni is always going away, when I arrive, and there is sure to be some overwhelming holiday in the town. Hitherto Frizzoni has been able to put off going away, but this time he had to attend the burial of a near relative, so he left yesterday. Still it is delightful to feel that he was as sorry to leave, as I was to be here without him. We had two hours together in the Brera yesterday, and talked over so many things. He is so funny in some ways, but truly devoted, and far more serious than all the others. I can't really speak to Morelli because he expects to be treated *en maître,* and I can't talk to Richter because he is *trop marchand.* Frizzoni is disinterested, hard-working and painstaking; also not above learning so I am always glad to discuss discoveries with him. He is a trifle obtuse, and I hope you won't think I am too intolerant but I am sure it is due to his being a Protestant. I simply can't tell you how *indecent* it seems to me for an Italian to be a Protestant. I feel as if it put him beyond the possibility of understanding himself, cuts him off from his own past, and if he lives, it is only the life of a branch that has been hacked off from its parent trunk. I see it in Frizzoni, in his "literature" tendencies. He is always discussing whether a Madonna is properly interpreted or not.

[1] Distinguished Italian art connoisseur and collector (1840-1919).

Now I am sure a true Italian would never do this, nor a Catholic of the Italian kind. It takes a Protestant to discuss a given artist's interpretation of the Madonna, or the Neo-Catholic, the Schlegels for instance. A Neo-Catholic is like a Neo-Christian — a Matthew Arnold. I am not thinking of them, or even of vituperating Protestants, but I like Frizzoni so much I can't help feeling sorry that he is cut off from the innermost heart of the very study he is devoting his life to. He was fifty the other day, and his clan presented him with a nice little Lotto, a bust of St. Catherine. He has given me a photograph of it, and you shall see it.

I can't tell you how much I love Milan. You will understand it if you bear in mind that much as I love the past, I love the present more, and here one feels the splendour of both. Milan is the one Italian town where you feel no shrinkage. It is as great, and throbbing, and wide-awake a town as ever. I overheard such a delightful talk at lunch to-day. It was all about Bellamy's *Looking Backward*.[2] The man that spoke roamed away and beyond his subject, and it was all so subtle, and yet sensible. The Carnival is still going on here. It is so gay. Now the piazza is illuminated most gorgeously, and bands are playing, and the crowd is so thick you can't elbow your way through it. But an Italian crowd is delightful. It does not swear, and it does not use elbows. To be in the midst of it is truly to be taking *un bain de multitude*. My dear friend Davies asked me to consider the Italians before I became a Catholic. I have considered them, and although I don't forget their many shortcomings they still seem to me the most humanized race of my acquaintance, and they are so because they are the most truly Catholic. Italy is Catholic, very much more than people think. I, who haunt churches so, and have talked seriously to young men, know. The Milanese churches are delightful from the

2 Edward Bellamy (1850-98), American author. The description of a social Utopia in *Looking Backward* had a great vogue in its day.

Duomo downwards. The Duomo is the least visited. Probably the people feel that it is not right. I spent an hour in it this afternoon. It impressed me overwhelmingly, all that was not Gothic in it. So very little of the matchless, sublime interior really is. The churches always crowded are S. Ambrogio, S. Eustorgio, and the other early churches where the very bricks tell you that Christ is the great Comforter, and not a supreme-Demon. The dearest church, the one I love most to think of bringing you to is S. Celso. There you will see the finest and ripest architecture, the loveliest pictures, most splendid decoration, and such Romelikeness, such an air of peace, and joy. How I look forward to showing you one town after another of my blessed Italy, now more divine to me than ever. I can't tell you how much more *en rapport* with it being truly a Catholic makes me. I am still gathering such delightful impressions, and I hope they will keep *toutes chaudes* throughout my stay in England, so that I may be able to use them at any minute. I want so much to make everybody enjoy life as I am enjoying it.

B.B.

To Bernard Berenson from A—— B——
M.O.M. [Monte Oliveto Maggiore]
11.2.91[1]

Signor Bernardo Carissimo,

La passeggiata, che feci con D. Giuseppe domenica scorsa subito dopo la Sua partenza, mi fu funesta. Al ritorno ebbi a mettermi a letto, bere acqua calda, applicarmi al petto una carta senapata e purgarmi nella notte. Lunedì mattina mi sentivo più sollevato, ma con tosse e dolor di gola. Col riguardo

[1] The date is of course to be read in the European sense: i.e., 11 February 1891.

avutomi, ieri mi andava assai meglio, oggi mi pare di essere rinato e domani del mio raffreddore non ne sarà altro.

La stagione fattasi nuovamente rigida mi tiene in pena per la Sua salute e col più vivo desiderio attendo di esserne da Lei rassicurato.

Il piccolo vetturino, al quale Domenica sera passai l'elemosina da Lei lasciatagli per potersi mettere in migliore arnesi, sta meglio, La riverisce e ringrazia senza fine e pregherà per il suo generoso benefattore.

D. Giuseppe è vispo e sapendo che Le scrivo, m'incarica di dirLa per conto suo le più care cose e che L'aspettiamo qui pel ventuno settembre.

Mi ricordi con sinceri saluti al Sig. Gustavo. A Dio rivolto io non cesso di dirgli col salmista ciò che a Lei, carissimo, ripeto: *beatus, quem elegisti et assumpsisti: inhabitabit in atriis tuis, in saecula saeculorum laudabit te.* Essa a Sua volta gli dica qualche buona parola per me che ho la sorte di protestarmele a tutta prova

devmo e affmo amico vero
A.B.

TRANSLATION OF THE ABOVE LETTER:

[Monte Oliveto Maggiore]
M.O.M. 11.2.91

My very dear Bernard,

The walk that I took with D. Giuseppe last Sunday had some bad consequences. When I got back I had to go to bed, drink hot water and put a mustard plaster on my chest and take a purge. Monday morning I felt a little better but had a cough and sore throat. With the care I took, yesterday I felt considerably better. To-day I feel like a new person and to-morrow nothing will be left of my chill.

The weather having become rather severe again, I am wondering about your health and await your reassurance.

The little cab-driver to whom I gave on Sunday evening the money you left for him so that he could get himself some better clothes[1] feels better and thanks you from the bottom of his heart, and says he will pray for his generous benefactor.

D. Giuseppe is flourishing and, aware that I am writing you, desires me to send the warmest messages and wants me to say how much we are looking forward to seeing you on the 21st of September.

Remember me please to Sig. Gustavo. When I pray, I constantly address God making use of the words of the Psalmist, which I now repeat also to you, dear Bernard: *beatus, quem elegisti et assumpsisti: inhabitabit in atriis tuis, in saecula saeculorum laudabit te.*[2] You too please in turn say a good word to Him for me who have the good fortune to be

your devoted and affectionate good friend
A.B.

To Mary Costelloe

Florence January 1892
Monday evening

It has been a lovely day. I have rarely seen a sky so pure. The mountains of the Casentino, those of Carrara, and the

---

1 This passage might mean in Italian usage metaphorically "to put himself on his feet."

2 Psalm lxv: 4 (King James version); Psalm lxiv: 5 (Douai). Blessed is the man whom thou hast chosen and taken to thee, he shall dwell in thy courts and praise thee forever. The last phrase *and praise thee forever* is not found in either the Douai or King James version.

Apennines of Pistoja, all covered with new snow looked not a stone's throw away. I hope that something like such weather has fallen to your lot to-day. I wonder where you are now — getting toward Reims I suppose.

I had a long read last night after writing a ten page letter to my sister. I read all the text and most of the notes of those two German books. The text was interesting. It contains already many of Vasari's mistakes, and many of his anecdotes, showing clearly that Vasari did exactly what I have supposed he did, — gather up all that was current in his days about the different artists, without giving himself the trouble to examine the sources of his information. The German editor calls Vasari nasty names for this. He, Carlo Frey, tells you in his notes that a Kunsthistoriker should above all things be a trained philologist. I can pass the philology, and not the history. The Kunsthistoriker should above all things be an historian. Such a one would not expect Vasari to do what no other historian of his day did. They were all satisfied with hearsay, or at any rate information already arranged as information. But it's a waste of paper telling you about Frey. Throughout his notes his tone is of a corporal drilling *Einjährige* — all other Kunsthistoriker than himself being the *Einjährige*. I have got a lot out of them. For instance the little Pesellino of Morelli's, the Jerome and Francis is described exactly in the Medici inventory as being in Lorenzo's own chamber. All my theories on the spirit of Florentine art are confirmed by the stereotyped phrase Ghiberti uses in praising an artist: — *"Era gran dottore."*

In the text itself are already all Vasari's stereotyped phrases "Una cosa bella, e veramente rara," "Pare Vivo," etc. Of course such phrases like most stereotyped phrases go back to the Greeks. Reading these documents, written evidently by people as learned in their own day, as a German *Doktor* is nowadays, immensely raises my opinion of Vasari, and makes me thank God that he and no other wrote the history of Italian art. It shows you — these documents — that Vasari himself stands on top, or at the head of a lot of people who were trying to do the same thing. We now can differentiate between the current *balivernes,* and his own appreciations, and this gives us a much finer and subtler critic than we had before in Vasari.

This morning I went to Sto. Spirito; the nave seemed too narrow. The sacristy I enjoyed more than ever. The capitals of the pilasters are perhaps the finest in Florence. Looking at Raffaellino di Carli's picture I had an idea. It is this: — He must have begun under Ghirlandajo, and become the assistant of Filippino, remaining with Filippino until his death. When Filippino died, you remember, he left some pictures unfinished. . . .

I had intended to call on Vernon Lee[1] this afternoon, but at lunch I found a note — "un'ambasciata" the padrone called it — from Costa[2] begging me to come to him. We walked out together to Maiano, in search of the Ridolfos but we found nothing. The walk was charming there and back. We caught wonderful glimpses of the clouds. There was no atmosphere anywhere. The whole landscape stood out with a clearness so sharp that it looked undercut. Costa was very nice. He kept drawing my attention to a thousand tiny effects. French painting has opened his eyes, and his mind too. He is coming fast to our view of the Florentines, and roared at Ghiberti's phrase. He means to do very little but sculpture this winter, and that will make him companionable, for I mean to devote myself to that in particular. I had a nice letter from Michael this morning. How I do hope she is with you!

1 Violet Paget (1856-1935) is to-day a somewhat surprisingly neglected author. She wrote under the name of Vernon Lee. Her half brother was the poet Eugene Lee-Hamilton. She lived at Maiano a great part of her life and was a distinguished member of the English colony in Florence. She is remembered for her *Studies of the Eighteenth Century in Italy,* for her biography of *The Countess of Albany,* and for her play *Ariadne in Mantua* as well as for a good many volumes of literary criticism, fantasies, short stories and novels. She was also the author of some charming books descriptive of places, such as *Genius Loci* and *Laura Nobilis.*

2 Enrico Costa (1867-1911), Italo-Spanish connoisseur, art historian, and a pupil of Morelli, who is spoken of in Berenson's *Self-Portrait,* p. 51.

To Mary Costelloe

Florence 1892
Tuesday evening

. . .

After lunch I wrote to Mrs. Bywater and Michael.[1] Then I went to call on Vernon Lee. She lives not far from S. Gervasio, whence to her house it is a very pretty walk along the heavily shaded Africo. I was received by Miss Thomson,[2] and a little later Vernon Lee came in riding costume. She found us plunged in talk already, and when she joined us, she monologized. I never heard such *spropositi* as she aired for an hour. I was scarcely polite in my stern dissent — when I got a chance to cry out a word. Perugino had a great influence on Botticelli she vowed. I begged for proof. He never would have painted scarves as he did if it was not for Perugino. She did not give me a chance to say that he could have got his scarves well enough from Pollajuolo. She rattled on, and on with her theory that both tried to express the same sentiment which Perugino did well, and Botticelli abortively. Then she came out with a theory that between creative process, and creative process there was greater affinity, than between creative process, and anything that is not creative. Now she was creative. Therefore she knew more what was in Botticelli's mind than I could possibly, for I was not creative. All this was à propos of whether influence was a greater factor in art. She insisted it always was because it is with her now. It is next to hopeless, is it not, to talk to people who use the *argumentum ad hominem* instead of a scientific method. Miss Thomson looked bewildered — not by her friend's *spropositi* I am sure, but by my bold dissent. I fancy she is not used to hearing Vernon Lee discredited. I enjoyed the call *quand même,* for it is a pleasure to talk with

1 Michael Field, the joint pseudonym used by Katherine Harris Bradley and Edith Emma Cooper.
2 Clementina Anstruther-Thomson, who collaborated with Vernon Lee in writing a book on aesthetics entitled *Beauty and Ugliness* (London, 1912).

people who cerebrate, no matter how. It ended in an engage-
ment to meet in the Uffizi Friday afternoon. The walk back
was lovely. There was a faint odour of alcohol in the air, which
was delicious. By the way the reason Baglioni came down that
day to get my card, was to be able to tell Vernon Lee who I was.
Stia bene.

To Mary Costelloe

Florence January 1892
Wednesday evening

I lay abed late this morning. It was so dreadfully cold and I
felt tired, so when I rang for coffee your letter from Basle was
brought in on the tray. It made the coffee taste ever so much
nicer. It is awfully hard for a man to let alone a *dame seule*.
He feels about her as the European powers do about an un-
claimed strip of the African coast. Last night I read Frey again,
finishing his introduction in wh. he tried to give a sketch of art-
history from the earliest times down to Vasari. It was a poor
affair on the whole, very assuming, full of irrelevant matter,
and gross errors, e.g. that the portrait of Aretino first belonged
to Giovio, the humanist. Isn't that German? Giovio mentions
having a portrait of Aretino by Titian, so Frey at once jumps at
the conclusion it is the one in the Pitti, just because it is the
only one he knows. This morning I read Eastlake, and Geymüller, and spent two hours in the Uffizi, where it was bitter
cold. I gave very minute study to the Giorgiones, and the more
I study them, the more Carpaccio do I see in them. The under-
painting for a Pietà puzzles me a great deal. It is too Bel-
linesque to be anything but Bellini, and yet — I looked at Botticelli's Venus, and never before did I enjoy it so much. I
enjoyed it as I expected to enjoy it when I used to dream about

it in Boston, reading Pater's description. In that picture Florentine art touched bottom, created something which invites no
comparison, asks for no explanation, is complete in itself as
Degas, or Hokusai, or our friend who did the door of Spoleto.
To bring us close to life is in one shape or another the whole
business of art, and Botticelli in the Venus does bring us close
to life, not the life in Potapenko or Huysmans, but just as much
life. You have it in the toss of the drapery, in the curl of the
flower, in the swing of the line — life full of power, and not
afraid to spend itself. I must make you appreciate the Venus.
You have never done it justice. After lunch I stared for an hour
at blank paper, in the hope of writing, then walked up to
S. Miniato to look at the Rossellinos. Jeroboam? what a frieze
around the base, unicorns, and charioteers! I returned and had
tea, reading "Revelations." What obscene and obscure drivel!
I turned from it to the translators' dedication to James I. That
is matchless English. Costa came in, and we chatted about
Madrid pictures. He holds, by the way, that the *Paradiso* in
the Louvre is by Tintoretto: — look at it carefully when you
get to Paris. To-morrow is the Feast of the Immaculate Con-
ception. Curse it. I was planning to go to the galleries. Keep
cheery, and make the utmost of your visit to the hyperborean
Babylon.

To Mary Costelloe

Florence January 1892
Thursday evening

It has been a damp, cold day such as befits a holiday, and I
have not felt very enterprising. Thy letter posted at Calais
came a couple of hours ago, and cheered me up greatly. My

padrona knew it was from thee, and begged to be remembered. She chatted as I was breakfasting, about Florence when it was the capital and Victor Emmanuel. She says she used to see him eating, from her window in the Lungarno. He always in shirt sleeves, nothing but beefsteaks which he gulped down with voracity, so as to get back to his cigar. Everybody adored him. He looked so young and rugged. Poor Umberto[1] looks so old, and his son[2] can't find a wife — among Catholic princesses, the only eligible ones.

To Mary Costelloe

Florence January 1892
Friday evening

I received your first letter from London this morning. I was so sorry you were not happier in spite of having your children by your side. I had a letter from Burke at the same time, but as you have probably seen him, I need say nothing about it. The weather is dry again, and still very cold. I stayed in till noon looking thro Geymüller. Then I went out and met Costa accidentally. We went together to the Vanchettoni. The two Donatellos are delicious, particularly the babies. In his treatment of hair he approaches the Greek masterpieces. After lunch I met Vernon-Thomson in the Tribuna. They were there already and we pitched in at once, Vernon Lee talking like a steam engine, and neither of them looking at anything, I can't remember a tenth of their jabber, and most of it is too sickening, and too banale to be repeated. Vernon at any rate could see what you mean, if she could stop to [do] it, but Thomson is

1 Humbert I (d. 1900).
2 Later Victor Emmanuel III.

profoundly stupid. She makes an overwhelmingly bovine impression. I realized that what Vernon wanted was not to see anything, but to get information. There is a man she thinks who has done all the dirty work, all the unskilled labour. Let me use my *real* intelligence in exploiting him. You may imagine I don't feel too much like being exploited. But she is stimulating in a way. We get so far from the element that it is a good thing once in a while to meet somebody who compels you to brush up your declensions, and conjugations. That pictures were repainted had never occurred to them. They had a theory that Andrea had invented *plein air* or the Lord knows what. Finally I understood that what they thought of was *sfumato*. They would not look at the Lotto. For Vernon Manet was a man utterly devoid of brains. Rossetti — that's *the* intellectual painter. You think he is no painter: Oh, never mind, he is intellectual. Sargent told her Watts is the greatest portrait painter there is, and she believes it. She adores the "Fornarina" and I could not make her see it was academic, and vulgar. Yet she knows a lot, but it's all topsy-turvy, cussed — Stenbockian. Fearfully ill behaved. They have a way of turning to each other, and excluding you from the conversation — but she had dropped the wrong end of the telescope, and was flattering, always did her work from five, but would find it profitable to suspend it if I came. We remained till the gallery closed. Going to Vieusseux's[1] afterwards I found Miss Britton there just returned. At six Costa came, and read me his Madrid notice — tremendously well written. Please try to be happy, enjoy your children to the utmost, and come back at least as well as when you started.

1 Lending library and reading room in Florence founded in 1820 by the Piedmontese man of letters Gian Pietro Vieusseux. Now in Palazzo Strozzi but in 1892 in Palazzo Spini-Ferroni, Via Tornabuoni, opposite Sta. Trinita. [In deference to Florentine customs, I have here and elsewhere put no accent on the *a* of Trinità. Florentines, unlike other Italians, pronounce the word in question as if written Trínita.]

To Mary Costelloe

1892
Saturday evening

. . .

I lunched with Costa. Giovanni[1] has already begun his service. They tell me he is well treated. *Ça donne à penser.* In France the volunteers are very badly treated by their sergeants, in Germany of course. The difference comes through the fact that in Italy it is very long ago since the lowest class has felt the oppression of the upper class. The former therefore have no burning desire to revenge themselves on the latter and as Italians they are clever enough to recognize the different metal a *signore* is made of, and so consider it. In France the memory of oppression is still too vivid, if not wholly new, and the lowest class, represented by the sergeants, thinks to revenge itself on the higher classes — the volunteer. Of course circumstances give the sergeants plenty of opportunities for turning the volunteer's life into a hell. In Germany the hatred the "Barbarian" and "Cattle" classes have of the "Learned" has a chance to display itself under the same circumstance. The German "Volunteer," and his sergeant and his lieutenant have a common bond, their hatred of his learning, to unite them against him. *Au fond* the fighting class has cause for suspecting the learned class. The learned have a consciousness of intellectual superiority, and a consequent notion of personality which makes the very idea of submitting to a sergeant, hard to bear. The society man has no such consciousness of intellectual superiority. His social superiority is of course beyond discussion, and rests to great extent on his meek submission to society's demands. At certain occasions good society demands you to be a common soldier submitting to a sergeant — and then it becomes quite the thing, and something to be proud of, instead of being more or less

[1] Giovanni Costa was Enrico's younger brother.

galled by it as the intellectual person would be sure to be in spite of his reason and good sense. That is why dudes and chaps of all kinds make such excellent soldiers when a crisis draws them out. This was the case in our Civil War, and has often been commented and wondered at, but *I* explain it. After lunch we looked at photographs, walked until it began to drizzle, then looked in at Alinari's and Brogi's and finally landed up here, for tea. I read Costa "the blessed Damozel" which he caught on to. What a beauty it is! Then I read him the sketch on literature. It perfectly flabbergasted him. *Comme c'est fort,* he kept ejaculating. He caught on to it perfectly, and went away with a very much higher opinion of me than he ever had before. Vernon Lee said something *worthy of me* yesterday. I asked her had she not noticed how precocious had been all those painters who died young. "Yes," she said, "otherwise we never should have heard of them." I can't get my feet warm these days. . . .

To Mary Costelloe

Florence 1892
Monday evening

. . .

Campanella's *Città del Sole* was fascinating, and far too short. Its chief point is the state without a family, which family according to him is the source of most of the evils in the world. This "City" is governed entirely by what he considered pure reason. Of course he only has an historical value. His intense devotion to astrology rather repels one nowadays. He is interesting as showing how much a clever man could manage to say in the darkest days of the Inquisition without getting himself burned. More interesting still as having already rid himself of all considerations not purely reasonable. Even his astrology is submitted to reason. I find it hard to understand exactly what his intentions were about women. They were to have exactly the same education as men, and were to bear arms. As to voting that is done by all *majori di venti anni*. This might include women, altho' I am not sure he meant it to. No such thing as marriage of course. Sexual intercourse was strictly to be regulated by the state, but entirely from the point of view of breeding. Children were to be brought up to consider all of a certain age as possible parents — an old idea of my own. He is specially interesting about education which is the very basis of his estate. Children are taught in such a way that they do not know they are learning, and yet are learned at ten. His method is object lessons, and the modern Kindergarten method in general. Of course there are no castes or artificial grades in his city, and property is unheard of. All labour is noble. On this point Bellamy has cribbed him from beginning to end even the Kitchens, waiting, and the theory that four hours of labour are sufficient. He foresees steamboats, altho' not steam, and many other modern inventions. In some respects the America of to-day is not so very unlike his "ideal." He knows no difference between science and religion. Everything is a strict science, and the most proficient in all the possible sciences is the spiritual and temporal things of the nation. His system of education is of course founded on the methods then newly introduced by the Jesuits. Everywhere his book shows that it was written by a man on whom Catholicism still had a great hold. The most startling thing about the *Città del Sole* is that it seems to contain no notion whatever of freedom. Such a thing is not heard of in his state. The whole book is his dream of a perfect world, and it is startling that it does not even occur to him to question whether the state has a right to persecute the individual for matters of conscience and the like. Such a thought had scarcely occurred to any one as yet. Campanella writes like an angel, and at times pokes delicious fun.

To Mary Costelloe

Florence 1892
Wednesday evening

. . .

On the way back I saw the Ways, accompanied as I thought
by Loeser.[1] Sure enough, he dropped in while Costa was with
us. He, Costa, came to tell us that he would take us to the Tor-
rigiani collection to-morrow. Now Loeser will come too, so I
wished him to the devil. He has been hobnobbing with Kings
all over Europe, and been very intimate with Henry James in
London, got to be dear friends with Bonnat, etc. He seems also
to have advanced from Loeser to more Loeser. So *we* connois-
seurs and the Ways are all here again. It will require a little
manoeuvring to keep clear of Loeser without mortally offend-
ing him, but I do wish to see as little of him as possible.

Burke has been very eloquent all day, and very delightful,
discoursing about science and finance. He is a powerful thinker
and again and again surprises me with ideas I had never entertained.

Have you written to Mr. Deutsch [a dealer]? If you have the
chance you ought to try to see Richter, and get him to show you
his pictures, and Mond's. The latter seem to have a new Botticelli among other things. Here and now, the mere chasing after
pictures seems a remote, and rather vain pursuit. I am in a
fearfully contrite mood, feeling how overwhelmingly difficult
it is to master one's thoughts, and how very little I have it in me
to do it. To be able to account even to oneself why the Europe
of 1500, became the Europe of 1600 seems to me a somewhat
more serious problem than any in connoisseurship. That reminds me, have you had a chance to see Symonds' book on

[1] Charles Loeser (d. 1928). The owner of Villa Gattaia, a connoisseur, collector
and art critic, was a contemporary and friend of Berenson and Santayana at
Harvard.

Michelangelo? Come back quickly, please. I am not much without thee.

To Mary Costelloe

Florence 1892
Saturday   evening

. . .

I got thy Wednesday letter this morning. I hastened to buy a fiver[1] wh. I sent off at once plus the request for thee to get a Braun of Bronzino's little boy of the N.G. to send at once to my sister. I hope thee will attend to this. The same post brought me a long letter from my sister. There is nothing about thee even by implication, but it made me deadly sick and very miserable for a few hours. She seems to have got about as much out of the long letters I have written as a dog does out of something you shout to him. It does not matter whether you shout Snap, Tap, Yap, Jap, or Gap. All the dog hears is Ap. Most people are just like that when you try to tell them something. They pounce on some strongly accented word, and hear nothing else. It is because this is so true of most people that such as Ruskin, Symonds, and Vernon Lee have their use. They shout a lot of nonsense at the public, and all the public gets out of it is the monosyllable *art*. But once the public get the ring of this monosyllable they will follow anybody who shouts it at them, you and me, if we shout loud enough, as much as Ruskin and Co. But to return to my Jordanized sister [Senda Berenson]. My first impulse was to write her a furious letter. My second was to write a bald one. Then I put on the

1 Berenson presumably means a £5 note, rather more than would have been necessary to buy "a Braun," i.e., a photograph by Braun et Cie.

brakes to my brain, reflected that forces work inversely as the distance, so that I, a much bigger force, am of no account beside Miss Jordan. I reflected further that Senda must live in America, and that therefore it is much better for her to be in perfect sympathy with it, than to long for vain culture. It is better for a plant under the arctic circle to become acclimatized to the sky and temperature, than to be supplied with sap and sunshine from the tropics by means of an India rubber pipe. The India rubber pipe can't work long. Of course my pride was hurt, that Senda should have found fault with my letters instead of standing on her head to praise them. Of course being co-uterine does establish a something between people. But she and I will never be much together again, and she and Miss Jordan probably will. So I leave her to Miss Jordan. I will write to Senda pleasantly although I will not send her any more treatises. Ha, ha, so your father did like that article on Potapenko? That proves his intelligence. Logan won't you may be sure. I always told you your father was the most intelligent member of your family. I sent the Mikes a large photograph of just the head of the Primavera. It is very beautiful by itself. We went to the Uffizi this morning. Walked up to Bellosguardo in the afternoon, and looked over the Villa Brighieri. Burke is dying to take it. How I wish he would. I am getting tired of addressing thee to London, and so tired of thy absence. Remember I am by nature a person who gets fonder of people when they are with him, and less fond when they are away.

To Mary Costelloe

Florence 1892
Sunday evening

. . .

I have been reading Michelet's[1] vol. on the Reformation, and Francis. It is a loosely jointed, and for the most part a dull book. But it contains several pages about Dürer's "Melancholia," and these pages beat everything I have ever seen as interpretation. He connects not only the spirit, the sentiment, but every detail of this engraving, with the history of the times, and in a way that is perfectly convincing. This sort of interpretation combined with science would be wonderful. Alone it often becomes ridiculous, as when he, Michelet, tries to reconstruct Anne Boleyn fr. the fam. portr. by Holbein in the Salon Carré. It seems in Michelet's day this putty-faced, dough-kneaded portrait of Anne of Cleves passed for Anne Boleyn.

Que les jours se passent — *voilà* tout-ce-que je demande. What a ghastly impression of America the Xmas no. of *Life* gives! How Tiepolesque most of the drawings — have you noticed? Take good care of yourself.

To Mary Costelloe

Florence 1892
Sunday evening

Costa has just gone. We have had a boisterous talk in which I insisted that the sort of things that would make bad painting would also make bad literature, all this *à propos* of Historical

---

1 Jules Michelet (1798-1874), French historian. Two of the nineteen volumes of his *Histoire de France* are called *Renaissance et Réforme* and B.B. may be referring to them.

romance. I doubt whether he understood me. We started because he told me he could not get through Charles Demailly, and adores Faustin. Bourget has put his tail under his hind legs, and skulked back to his kennel. He found modernity too big a dog to make a companion so he has retreated to catholicism. Good riddance. He counts no more. I have predicted this for some time. Thy Reigate note came this morning. How happy I shall be to have thee better, and perhaps able to walk. I do so yearn for thee to be back — I read a lot of Ranke last night, and it started me thinking so hard that it kept me awake all night. I wrote to my sister this morning, and then we went to the Pitti. I was immensely struck by Andrea's Trinity with Sts. I am beginning to think that the big St. Sebastian attributed to Pollajuolo may be by Jacopo de' Barbari.

At lunch we talked about the English and their attitude towards the new. They have the dread of it that savages have of a tabooed thing, and such a dread of course is never free from fascination. So they keep away from the new thing, until some person they well know and can trust embarks in it. Then when they see that lightning hasn't struck him, they all rush after him — not from a love of new experience, but from the fascination accompanying the dread of this new experience.

I read the whole of my article on Venetian art to Burke this afternoon. He was duly appreciative. In fact he could not be more so. I had not read it myself a long time, and it struck me again as something remarkable. Reading Ranke last night I came to a passage about the attitude of the individual toward Christianity which I thought of quoting whole in my article. But behold I find that I have put it much better myself. What a pity it seems that the thing should remain unpublished. If only I can get a translation of Ibsen's last play I would rather we wrote about that on your return than about Diderot. I have a lot to say about Ibsen, that even you have not heard, and all with regard to his women. I now see the wire that pulls all of them that he himself is interested in. It is so simple that you will say "Oh, is that all!" when I tell you. But I won't tell you anything until you return. It will be three weeks I fear before you come back, such a long time.

To Mary Costelloe

[Florence] 1892
Monday evening

. . .

I walked out nevertheless to Vernon Lee's this afternoon. She was not at home, but I met her a little way down the road driving jauntily, sandwiched in between Thomson[1] and another female. They had been to the woods to gather herby smelling things which are very nice for the fire. I turned back, and Vernon was excessively affable, seemed very much more natural, or perhaps I have got used to her manner. She pulled out the book of the Suardis,[2] privately printed completely reproducing Trescorre, and insisted on my taking and keeping it until she gets one for *me*. She is sure she can. So she seems to be fair. I brought out some of the Lotto photos and she enjoyed them. She somehow makes you feel that she is intelligent. The other Lady by the way was a Miss Priestly[3] whom I had met years ago, and whom we have seen together at different places. Thomson is stupid. The Todi photographer has sent me a photo. of the church fr. the point of view we indicated.

[1] Miss Clementina Anstruther-Thomson.

[2] B.B. is referring to the *Oratorio Suardi* in Trescorre near Bergamo and the cycle of Lotto's frescoes there.

[3] Flora Priestly (1859-1944) was the daughter of the Reverend W. M. Priestly, chaplain of the English Church at Nice. A portrait of her by J. S. Sargent (who made other studies of her) is in the Tate Gallery.

But it is a little blurred. How I do hope the doctor had good news for thee, and that thee is coming back at once.

To MARY COSTELLOE

Florence 1892
Wednesday evening

. . .

I went to call this afternoon on the Misses Forbes, friends of Mrs. Bywater. They are ageless already, one of them almost wholly blind, and the other wholly lame. The way they live opens out visions of modest yet perfect comfort and quiet here in Florence. They talked a great deal about Florence when it was under the Grand Dukes, and Rome, under Pio Nono. They told me a friend of theirs wanted to copy in the Vatican bits of an MS on a classic text. He had to tell the precise page he was going to work on, and the precise lines he was going to copy. These precise lines they enclosed in such a way in a frame that he could see nothing else of the page. Even then he was only allowed to work a few minutes at a time, the recesses, and holidays being so numerous. They told me that years ago there was a large and beautiful Madonna inscribed to Botticelli, here in S. Spirito. A young wife during a severe illness vowed her wedding dress to this Madonna in case she recovered. She did recover, and then, will you believe it, her wedding dress was nailed on to the Madonna with scores of brass-nails. Aren't you glad we are not living in that generation?

I returned and found Costa. He was in a nice mood, and we had a pleasant chat. He agreed at once to the Monaca being Bugiardini, but does not follow us in ascribing the Louvre portrait also to him — but I have no doubt he will, sooner or later.

"Architecture and manners" — what do you think of this for the title of an essay? I would write this if I wrote glibly. Architecture and manners are perhaps more closely connected than any two other expressions of the human personality, manners being in the van, because closer to the person. Of course we know little about ancient manners; still we have lots of letters, in which manners show themselves so quickly, and in these the style is no less severe than the Roman architecture. Look again at the simplicity of manners in the 15th century, and how elaborate and complicated they get in the 16th and 17th centuries, so that the term *baroque* applies to them even more than to the architecture. Then you begin softly to return to nature even though it be on its least natural side, and last century manners were quite as Rococo, and Louis Quinze as the buildings and furniture. Then through Consular, and Empire manners you finally get to us, finding always the same *forms* in the manners that you find in the architecture. — I hope when you get this, Ray's Xmas tree will be ready to start. Come soon. I really should not be left alone too long.

To Mary Costelloe

Florence 1892
Monday evening

. . .

Signora Favilli and I have long chats. She is very interesting in her reminiscences. She was brought up at Anghiari, just this side of what were then the Papal states. She had relatives at Città di Castello, and every time she went to visit them it took an hour at the custom-house where they searched even her stockings. She told me that a cousin of hers was going to marry a nice young fellow who was rather open in his liberal opinions. One day he was overheard swearing in the street. So he was arrested by the "Sant'Uffizio" and condemned to pass a year in a niche where he could neither sit nor stand nor lie. He came out the colour of death, with his hair down to his waist, and his nails inches long. When his fiancée saw him again she fainted away with fright. What do you think of this sort of thing having happened almost in our own life-time, and what do you think of people who would have all this again? The Favilli says she remembers well the day Pius IX was crowned. She was with her relatives at Castello, and there was great rejoicing over the liberal minded young pope. But her uncle asked them to moderate their gladness. *E un prete. Basta!* She tells me that after the enthroning of the present archbishop here, as they were marching from the duomo to the arcivescovado the crowd rotten-egged them. But she says sadly the young people nowadays find it hard to understand why we hate the Pope so. . . .

To Mary Costelloe

Florence 1892
Tuesday evening

. . .

I have also read L. B. Alberti's treatise on love. He discusses in superb prose pitched in the tone of the *Imitatio Christi,* what sort of man a woman ought to take for a lover. He votes for the literary man, *for he can make immortal,* as Corinne and Lesbia were made. Isn't that the best of all illustrations to the passion the Renaissance had for fame?

I will write again to-morrow, and that I hope will be the last, darling, before I see thy sweet face once more — thou beloved.[1]

---

[1] Mary Berenson was brought up as a Quaker (she became a Catholic at the time of her first marriage), which may account for Berenson's use of the second person singular.

To Mary Costelloe

Florence 1892
Wednesday 11 A.M.

I have just received thy Sunday letter. How I hope thee really has started for Paris this morning. It will be too wonderful to see thee again. Meanwhile thy plans trouble me. The way back by Basle is, from the point of time so much the longer. Of course it is ever so much nicer to have thee arrive at 6.40, than at 12.40.

You get to Milan at 7.42 A.M. — I think. Then you leave Milan with the direttissimo at 11.45 A.M. In that case — you must however make *perfectly* sure at the station — you will have four hours at Milan. Go to Biffi's in the *Galleria* for breakfast. Then take a carriage by the hour and make it take you to S. Ambrogio. You will find plenty to see there, including frescoes by Gaudenzio, Luini, and Borgognone, and the cloister, only one side finished, by Bramante. Before going to S. Ambrogio, I should drive to S. Satiro to see the sacristy, by Bramante. From S. Ambrogio, drive to S. Maria delle Grazie, have a peep at the picturesque outside, and the interior of the cupola, Bramante's. His is the cloister, and therein two grisaille frescoes by Bramantino. Then you could end up with the Brera, or Poldi-Pezzoli as the spirit moved you. *Be sure you have some lunch* before you get into the train, as you have no considerable stop before 3.15 at Bologna.

My insomnia is getting worse and worse. I scarcely slept at all last night.

I would like to meet the author of "Poor Nellie." Her opinion of Gladstone, the Jesuits and British politics is absolutely identical with my own.

I am going to ask you a great favour, and you must not refuse it. You must telegraph to me the moment you get to Milan, or from the Italian frontier station if that is more convenient —

but you had better breakfast there so as to be ready for an early lunch. How long it will seem — thou precious darling . . .

To Carlo Placci

Hotel Hohenzollern
Berlin
21 August 1895

My dear Placci,

Many thanks for your amusing and highly interesting letter. Your impressions of the North are funny, and real I am sure. I *could* have them also but I cannot afford such a luxury. *I must* try to see things *objectively,* ha, ha! But I confess that a week of the picturesque was enough for one. Leaving Cologne, I went to Münster the quietness and picturesqueness of which put me into ecstasy. I enjoyed Bremen almost as much. But by the time I got to Lübeck I was so saturated with the picturesque, that I ran away *quanto primo* — and here I am in provincial, empty, ugly Berlin . . . Well we remained at Fiesole till July 4, and my book was finished alas! not very satisfactorily. The bother is that I seek so much more than I can realize, and I fear I shall never do work which will at all satisfy. I mean no mock modesty by this.

We saw Salvemini[1] once more, but at Munich recently at Obrist's[2] I met a young German named Pölnitz, a boy of 19 whose power of intellect simply took my breath away. He talked to me for three hours quietly, and calmly about the

[1] Gaetano Salvemini (1873-1957), Italian historian, in political exile from 1925-1945.
[2] Hermann Obrist (1863-1927), a German sculptor and designer for applied art and a strong supporter of the *Jugendstil* or *art nouveau.*

desirability of anarchy. I could bring up no argument which he did not meet in an instant, and I had to bow down and worship a superior intellect, an act of homage which really gives much pleasure. I shall try to invite this wondrous boy down to Florence some day for your delectation. On his recommendation I read a book which is rousing interest in Germany just now — Hertzka's "Entrückt in der Zukunft." This is a very able and certainly interesting attempt to hypothesize an anarchic but perfect civilization, and while I must confess that the author's political economy was too much for my understanding, I have found him persuasive and interesting.

Obrist himself I found engaged on embroideries which as decorative art seemed to me quite on a level with the very best the world has seen. And this brings me to Hildebrand's[1] fountain which I admire more than I can say. I have heard much against it, and much of the criticism I can follow, but all the same, all faults admitted, it seems to me a genuine plastic creation, and the most serious that we have had since Michelangelo. By Hildebrand also I have seen a plaque of Bismarck that is a marvel. I shall stop at Leipzig on purpose to see his Adam. Here I remain for a week, then to the 11th — Hotel Weber, Dresden, then here and there, until the 17th when I shall be at Munich again to stay till the 28th, hearing Wagner. Do write again soon; if after the 9th, address Baring Bros. London. I am not going to Biarritz, but I do want to make your friend's acquaintance. It must be at another time. I shall be back in Florence early, about October 1.

Regards to Galitzine
Yours ever
B.B.

---

[1] Adolf von Hildebrand (1847-1921). The fountain referred to is without doubt the Wittelsbacher Brunnen, finished in 1894.

To Mary Costelloe

Fiesole
New Year's Day 1896

. . . Miss Crutwell,[1] by the way, lunched at the Palmerino yesterday, and witnessed a frightful quarrel between Vernon and Kit which ended in latter's leaving the room. Vernon protested that she loathed art, abhorred aesthetics, and that the only thing she really cared about was sociology and economics. You will recall of course that when she talked of my book she preluded her sapiences by declaring that the one steady pursuit of her life, foolishly interrupted but interrupted only by economics, had been and was aesthetics. . . .

To Mary Costelloe

2 January, 1896

The day passed very pleasantly yesterday. Obrist and I walked in the morning, and he enjoyed it, in a combative, grudging way. Nothing to be said against it as plastic beauty, as composition, as monument, but he should find no vegetation on all those hills and the *thought* of that spoiled it all. We talked of Miss Sellars.[2] She is rather hysterical, and he suspects some sexual perversity. At all events she is peculiarly moody, and changing. If she talks one day angelically, the next diabolically. She has taken a flat at Schwabing for two years. . . .

1 Maud Crutwell, the author of several monographs on Italian artists of the Renaissance.
2 Eugénie Sellars in 1897 married Arthur Strong who was later librarian at Chatsworth. He died in 1903. Mrs. Strong became an authority on Roman sculpture and was for a long time assistant of the British School in Rome. She lived most of the time in Italy and stayed on during the second world war. She died in 1944 a few days before the entry of the Allied troops into Rome, and, as an ardent admirer of Benito Mussolini, was unreconciled to the defeat of Italy.

To Mary Costelloe

Fiesole
3 January 1896

It is lovelier than ever to-day, and the all-illustrious Obrist
was pleased to remark that he wondered all humanity did not
gather about here, instead of remaining in the grizzly north.
Yesterday Placci came up before 12, and we had some pleasant
talk before lunch. D'Annunzio had intended coming up but
was prevented by the sudden illness of one of his "nephews."
But Father Fawkes came. Miss C. [Crutwell] was furious when
she heard D'A. was not coming, and sat in a fixed, growling
stare all thro' lunch. I rather enjoyed her disappointment. *Sic
semper snobbius.* The lunch was not a supreme success. I put
O. and P. together, but O. could not resist the blandishments
of Miss F. and talked to her all the time in a loud, all-absorbing
way. However I did my best to keep up talk between Fawkes,
Placci and myself, and eventually succeeded. Later, we men
went out for a walk, and made the round of Vincigliata. There
was a keen North wind blowing which made the skin tingle.
The sun was dazzling, the air invigorating, and finally I at least
ceased feeling like anything of flesh and bone and clothes, but
became a spirit that "outdid the waves in glee." Placci walked
with O. and I with Fawkes. The latter is a very cultured, rather
liberal priest —, and I pumped him on his subject, and enjoyed
his tact, his politeness, and his fencing. He has known you, and
is anxious to meet you again. They all came back to tea, Placci
well pleased with O. who expounded as his own all my theories
about the moral import of decorative art — and O. enchanted
with Placci.

In the evening we talked with the females — pardon my use
of this word, but both of them get on my nerves agonizingly,
particularly Miss C. I am sure she is a lineal descendant of Miss
Bates, but worse than her ancestress she with no brains what-

ever, fancies herself interested in intellectual matters — — All
I ask of you is to be scrupulously honest and sincere with me.
It is my first and last request — and condition.

To Mary Costelloe

Fiesole
4 January 1896

Yesterday was lovelier even than the day before. I worked in
the morning. Obrist and I were alone at lunch, and we spent
the afternoon walking up to and wandering about St. Clemente.
Morello shone out in all his plastic beauty. The mountains on
top of the Senario[1] rose out of the midst of its forest like dia-
monds set in emeralds on a signet ring. The whole valdarno
was filled with mists and looked like a sea of absinthe, the lower
hills seeming like swirls in it, and the distant Apennines rising
up on the other side of it like the shores of Purgatory beyond
Acheron.

The air was soothing, the sun warm. I was in a condition of
diffused well-being which made me feel more faun than man.
From S. Clemente you see the Arno winding southward toward
Arezzo, Camaldoli as if you could touch it, and a feudal looking
rock-tower which they call Monte Loro. We lingered till 4.30,
and walked back in precisely one hour.

In the evening we had a long row. Miss C., and Obrist went
with her at first, insisted that art and ethics must needs be
identical seeing that art is a communication of energy, and that
such a communication is by itself ethical. Well, would you believe it, it took more than two hours for Miss C. to perceive that
this proposition is nonsense, and of course she lost her temper

[1] Monte Senario: about one and a half hours' walk beyond Pratolino.

several times by the way. It ended however in her *copying* down the following: — Art communicates energy; ethics exhorts us to accumulate energy, and teaches us what use to make of it.

We dine to-night at the Palmerino. We should not go, but if we had refused, V.[2] would certainly believe that I had not let her see O. for fear of her discovering that I get all my art ideas from him. Sta sana and mi vuole *bene*.

To Mary Costelloe

Fiesole
5 January 1896

Vernonia was charming last night. Not a word was uttered about art, and she tickled and flattered O. into ecstasy by speaking to him of nothing but German Gemüth, the provinciality of English people, literature and art. He left delighted. But the best was yet to be. The moon lay on her back over the quarries shedding her soft light over the plain and hills. When you looked away from her, the sky looked so pale and clear that you would have taken it for the hour just before the dawn. . . .

To Mary Costelloe

Fiesole
6 January 1896

The letters were handed me yesterday in the piazza as we were starting for the Senario, and for thine I felt thankful and

2 Miss Paget.

happy. I like thee to be thus strenuous. *Continuez.*[1] Fail not to visit Burlington House also, and remember I want a catalogue of each. Cook has written to me, and of course I have given him the "St. John."

We got to the Senario. The effects of mist were not at all so wonderful as on the day we attempted the climb. By the way, we were within an easy half hour from the top. I enjoyed every moment of it, and O. enjoyed it a good deal, altho' in a grouching way. Oh, yes, it really was marvellous — and then came all his sickening *clichés* about the bareness, etc. I was a thousand times right, artistically nothing could surpass it, but it was not S. Remo, and was not Thüringen. And with O. as with any philistine, one or two habitual impressions choke out all others. I do not envy him. However at dinner he declaimed pathetically about his *never* having been told how marvellously beautiful Tuscany was, etc. etc.

But really all day long "the sunlight bloomed, and withered on the hills like any wind-flower."

Do not think I am irritated with O. I am very fond of him. But he is not quite the friend of my dreams, the one who will be different from me, yet at least as sensitive, and as intelligent.

I want us both to help O. to the utmost — thee also to join in if thee can pump all sentiment out of the concern. If thee can I beg thee to do what thee can to arrange for his exhibiting in London. I shall write later just what I wish thee to do in Paris.

Thanks for the B.M. notes. The bill from the Autotype came 5 days ago, but as the photos have not yet come, I dare say they are waiting till thee has paid. I write to Baring to send thee £25. Please pay the Autotype and ask them to send the photos at once. Thee knows how much I need them.

---

1 *Continuez* refers to the story of a French General who had to inspect a regiment and had learned that there was a Negro serving in it. He called him out and asked, "Êtes vous le nègre?"

"Oui, mon général."

"Alors continuez."

It is lovelier than ever to-day, the radiancy of spring, with the sparkle of winter. Poor book — I am sorry.

To Mary Costelloe

Fiesole
7 January 1896

. . . He [Obrist] is going to-night, and fond as I am of him, his going will be welcome. His *idées fixes* have got on my nerves frightfully. *Idées fixes* are dreadful in anyone, but despairing in a man with whom conversation, for mere physical reasons, is difficult. No, discussing with O. is about as much fun as being dragged up a steep hill by a half-dead horse.

And now I shall be left alone with Miss C. [Crutwell] and her stupidity. Yet — stupid as she is, she is in ways more intelligent than O. Last night she insisted on talking about humour, how dreadful it was, and how little she felt the need of it in life. Of course it ended in her acknowledging that humour was the balm and oil of life, and that the lack of it was the source of most evils. . . .

To Mary Costelloe

Fiesole
8 January 1896

Of good weather there promises to be no end. O. did not go yesterday after all, and is going to-night. I am glad he stayed, for had he left last night he would not have left a sweet odor behind him. It happened thus. At lunch he defended Berlin as being built in such wise that it gave a tremendous impression of power. The "Passage" where it goes into the Friedrichstrasse he vowed was every bit as good as the Place de l'Opéra. The photographs fr. the Autotype came, and for every one he had some deturpating, crassly unintelligent phrases. You could not be sure. Masterly of course, but artist had not intended it. And what did it express? I stood by in speechless disgust. But in the evening he anecdotized all about his family, how they went away fr. Paris with the last train that left during the siege, etc. etc., and my fondness for him as a human being came back. But to retain this fondness I must not see too much of him.

Miss C. had been at the Palmerino and at dinner told us all about it. Vernonia is still neighing contempt at art and aesthetics. Poor female to think at 40 of still pulling things to pieces — *er liebt mich, er liebt mich nicht.* Miss C. thinks V. by nature very passionate and that her, V's, sourness is due to her never having had a man's love. As a little girl V. used to stay away when company came for fear people should ask "Who is this frightful child?" . . .

To Mary Costelloe

Fiesole
9 January 1896

Lo, a sudden change! Yesterday it was as sweet as May. Lovely mists filled the valleys, and the grass everywhere was the gayest emerald. This morning I was waked by banging doors, and getting up to shut them tight, I looked out and saw the snow whirled about by a howling wind. It still is falling, off and on, and the terraces close at hand are covered white[1] . . .

[1] Snowfall is not unknown in Florence, but is unusual.

To Mary Costelloe

Fiesole
10 January 1896

I added to my letter yesterday a postscript to assure you that I believed Miss Sellars must have misunderstood you. I trust you, and am willing to trust you. So do not lose courage. I have made some vain efforts to decipher Miss S's letter. I confess it scarcely seemed worth while. I must add thus far in life my unformulated feelings about people have always turned out amply grounded. I have feelings of unease about Miss S. I am willing to try her however, but on the indispensable condition that you do not in the least degree attempt to make of her a friend for yourself. If she can be the friend of us both, well and good. If not, she must remain a distant acquaintance.

It blew gloriously yesterday, and walking was an exhilarating form for peripatetic wrestling. I went to town to the bank where I met Mrs. Benn who greeted me with "Is it not a fine day," which reconciled me to her as nothing else she could have said. I lunched with the Buttles. We discussed Miss Franham against whom they feel venomous. They indeed left her little. Miss Buttles[1] sang "Che farò senza Eurìdice" twice over for me, and a lot of Lohengrin.

In the evening Miss C. and I discussed Miss F. Miss C. is in a condition of mind where she knows not whether to hug Miss F. close to her bosom, or to chase her away altogether. She acknowledges that Miss F. is grossly animal, and becomes a mere *femelle* at the least encouragement from a man; but — she has other sides. Miss F. has been told by men that from her lips nothing should come but kisses. — To-day it still is blowing hard. It is cold, and there are occasional sprinkles of snow, but the sun is out. Farewell, and delay not.

[1] Jeannette Midway Buttles (1854-1947) and Mary Meyl (1861-1956), of Columbus, Ohio, were relations of the Egyptologist Theodore Davis under whose influence Jeannette Buttles wrote a book about the Queens of Egypt. B.B. must have met them through Davis.

To Mary Costelloe

Fiesole
10 January 1896
12.30 P.M.

Yrs. of 7th received. So sorry to hear you are ill and low.
Cheer up to please me.

I write in haste. O. Gutekunst, 13-14 Pall Mall East, knows
of a Velasquez wh. may do for Mrs. J.[1] I am very anxious that
you should see it, as I do not like to deal in such big game without autopsy. Please be aware of your responsibility, but I
should not ask you to do this, if I did not believe you as competent as any living person to have an opinion.

I want you to write to G. giving an appointment — with an
alternative in case the one particular day will not do — for him
to take you to see the Velasquez. At the same time he will show
you a Rembrandt of which also you must give an acute report, a
Cuyp, and possibly some other things.

Il s'agit d'affaires énormes. Therefore "pull out thine eyes,"
and do this for me. It will spare me a trip to London.

To Mary Costelloe

Fiesole
11 January 1896

I am sorry to hear that you are so unwell. Please do see that
doctor, and try to get well.

Miss Priestly came to lunch yesterday, and put herself out to

1 Mrs. Jack Gardner. The painting in question, a portrait of Philip IV, was
at Colnaghi's at the time of this letter, and was in fact bought for Fenway Court
through Berenson. Originally painted for a cousin of the Conde-Duque de
Olivares, it was inherited by the Count of Altamira who sold it in London in
1827, whence it passed into the Bankes Collection in Dorset from which it was
purchased by Colnaghi.

be nice. She was charming. I knew she was determined to make an impression, and I like her. She was inconsequent, vivacious, capricious, smiling, tender, reserved — in short delightfully feminine. She "created and satisfied" a need. I had had a note from Mrs. Wm. Sharp enclosing the card of Mrs. Smithe with whom she is staying. Yesterday was this person's reception day, and it seemed best to call then, and in that case I could make a ready escape if needs were. From what Miss Priestly told me about Mrs. Smithe I formed no high opinion of the treat that awaited me. Mrs. Smithe, an elderly lady of pension-keeping tendencies and Scotch lower middle-class standing, has a villa outside the Porta Romana. I found lots of people there, familiar and unknown faces. Mrs. S. handed me over at once to her niece, Mrs. Sharp. Said person is youngish, fattish, dark, round-faced, uncouth features, — in short she would look coarse if a certain goodness and braininess did not also express herself on her face. She welcomed me, and told me at once she neither did nor would know any of the other people present, and that her aunt was a stupid bore. Avoiding art, I made her happy by talking about the Celtic Renaissance as apostle of wh. in particular she has come here. She has a certain balance through it all, and I liked her so well that I invited her up for Wednesday.

Get well dearest, and love me always.

To Mary Costelloe

Fiesole
12 January 1896

Yesterday was the wintriest day we have had yet. Snow kept whirling down from sky sunless, but almost clear. I went out after lunch for what I expected to be a very short walk. But the sight northward from the Piazza was too much for me, and the wind too inviting. So I began to buffet my way to the Morgans.[1] It was exhilarating for the wind's blows turn to warm caresses when you have conquered him. How I enjoyed the blood in my veins. The pines with their branches hoary, moaned and groaned, and murmured. But finest of all was the view from the Morgans', — a world in black, white and grey with swirls of movement like seething whirlpools. It was a treat! — once, familiar European — nay primly Italian world — suddenly turned into a masterpiece of the greatest Chinese art!

I have finished the *Amber Witch*,[2] and find it the most remarkable book I have ever read from the point of view of tone. The time, the place, the temperament and the language are humanized to sheer perfection. . . .

To Mary Costelloe

Fiesole

13 January 1896

I am exceedingly sorry to hear from your note of the 10th that you are so ill and wretched. Please try yr. best to get well, and in heaven's name do nothing more for me. I shall not forgive myself if you fall ill owing to my straw-breaking your camel's back. So please do not bother about going to the B.M. again, and never mind about any other commissions I may have heaped upon you. I will never do so again. If however you can spare the energy, and will not get ill over it, do go to Gutekunsts and see the pictures I already have written about. But even this I would rather you left undone, if it will be a burden.

1 Morgan was an Englishman who owned a property under San Clemente where he wanted to produce wine as good as French burgundy. The walk along this property went on being called the "Morgan walk."
2 Translation of Meinhold's *Bernsteinhexe*.

I hope you will not fail to let the doctor make a thorough examination of you; and please let me know all about it.

No, you can of course do nothing concrete for O. in England now. So do not bother.

It is lovely again. The peaks of the Carrara lift their silver points over the onyx mists. Yesterday Miss Buttles was here to lunch. She sang a song or two, and then we had quite a talk about music; but I will not burden you with a report thereof. Suffice it to say she got furious and refused to make it a matter for reason. I walked down to the Rosses, who are not receiving which rejoiced me. But what pleasure I took in the walk! The colours were subdued; there was a hush over the landscape; it was an hour of peace and heart's ease.

I want you to make it clear to Z.[1] that if he comes to stay with us it is as a guest and not as a boarder.

I repeat my behest. Get well, cast off burdens, and get well.

To Mary Costelloe

Fiesole
14 January 1896

After being so lovely as a dream yesterday it is pouring to-day. We had "company" in the afternoon. Miss Thomson came bringing with her two Miss Hays. One was red-haired, ill-favoured and apparently an idiot. The younger is almost beautiful, with lovely eyes. We all went up the Piazza to see the Duomo, and to my astonishment I found the younger Miss Hay remarkably intelligent in matters of art, choosing out for herself the beautiful things, and knowing why they were so. It was pleasant, and I want to see more of her. We returned to tea, and were joined by Vernonia who brought Miss Wimbush.

---

1 The playwright Israel Zangwill must be meant.

This lady may once [long] ago have resembled Miss Lowndes, but now she seems like an Oscar *à rebours.* Vernonia was raving over Obrist. It amused me. Being unable to hear more than a fourth of what she said, he never said a word, and sat listening intently. Hence, the admiration. . . .

To MARY COSTELLOE

Fiesole
15 January 1896

. . .

I lunched with the Placcis yesterday. There were no other guests. We talked about D'Annunzio, and the evening he had spent there pontificating over adoring the amorous ladies. After lunch I was shown all over the house where comfort of the most American kind has its home but where taste is known only as this shame-faced Goddess presented herself to the Empress Eugénie. Miss Placci and I went to the Uffizi, and looked at some pictures. She has a good deal of native feeling for art — more than Carlo, and is altogether, I find, a delightful person. . . .

To MARY COSTELLOE

Fiesole
15 January 1896
9 P.M.

I am writing this evening so as to save time to-morrow morning. It has been a delicious day — bright sun, and a fresh cool breeze. Mrs. Sharp came to lunch, and deepened the impression she first made as a coarse-grained, but well-meaning, un-spoiled simple creature. She still is much in love with her hus-band two of whose photographs she brought up to show me — a handsome, sturdy beggar. She also brought a new volume of his which I am to look over. She tried to pump me on art, but I told her I had no tabloids prepared, if she wished though we might go down and look at the olives. At these gnarled beauties we looked, and she was silent. Miss C. took a great dislike to her — rather in Mrs. Sharp's favour. I pointed out the Palmer-ino, and said "Yonder dwells the Palmerina Sibyl." When Vernonia is nice though we shall speak of her as Sibylla Palmerina. . . .

To Mary Costelloe

Fiesole
16 January 1896
9 P.M.

I am glad to understand by the tone of your letter of 11-12 that you are better. I do hope that things so are shaping them-selves that you need not delay.

Last night, directly after writing to you I was seized by a Colic that tortured me thro' the night. I am all right again now, but all this afternoon I felt as weak as a fly. I went down by the 2 tram, and fetched Benn[1] for a walk. We went through the Cascine to the Indiano,[2] passing hoary ilexes some of them held in the grip of the most decorative vines imaginable. Poor Benn is not very well, and as I was not feeling brilliant I had to

[1] A. W. Benn (1843-1916), English philosopher and historian. He and his wife lived for many years in the Villa del Ciliegio near San Gervasio.

[2] At the farthest point of the Cascine where the Mugnone flows into the Arno a polychrome bust commemorates a young Maharajah who died in Florence in 1890 and had to be cremated according to Brahmanic ritual at the confluence of two rivers. This bust is known as the "Indiano."

tug at conversation. We gossiped, and chatted. Finally it turned to spiritualism, and he expressed something like disgust for my taking to it. Finally we came to Gurney.[1] He said he once had asked Vernonia how it was that a man so intellectual as Gurney could take to spiritualism. Vernonia protested it all was the doing of Mrs. Gurney, who was intellectually so over and by far her husband's intellectual and moral superior that she won him over to think just what she did. But Benn had asked, how did it happen that such a miracle of a woman had herself taken to spiritualism. Perfectly simple, Vernonia replied; Mrs. Gurney had been a very diaphanous, spiritually minded girl, and spiritualism was her only way of keeping hold of these qualities in riper years.

This in the light of all you have told me about Mrs. Gurney, sounds delicious. Vernonia's impression of people seem on a level almost with her art notions.

Miss C. has just made me read one of Kipling's poems called "Tomlinson" — a bab-ballad with a Tommy Atkinsy reel. This Vernonia, Hamilton, and Hellen Zimmern uphold as one of the greatest poems in existence.

It has been lovely to-day. It is blowing now, and may turn colder; but all in all we're in luck for weather.

Good-night, darling. Love me.

To Mary Costelloe

Fiesole

17 January 1896

To-day has been perhaps the loveliest of all the days so beautiful that we have been having. The forenoon was cheered by the reception of your pleasant letter of Tuesday. How glad

---

1 Presumably Edmund Gurney (1834-1888), author of *The Power of Sound* and of books on psychological research.

I am for your children and your happiness in them. We had to lunch that nice Miss Hay of whom I already have written, Mary Buttles and Miss Whaling. After lunch I took Miss Hay the rampart walk. Dear Mary she feels more than you and I do, the beauty and power of things, and the words she uses to describe her feelings always descriptive of physical states like ours, are often more poignant. Too bad her voice and features are not what they should be, but she has eyes like brown green stones with gold-thread, wonderful, adorable eyes. How I do hope she will not be gone before your return. Do not mistake. So far as I at present know her she is not at all intellectual, or clever, but a creature with a remarkable sense of beauty. . . .

Miss Farnham arrived this evening to stay till Sunday. She has a good deal of brain, you know, and I am sure she has a history. It turns out by the way that she has studied Latin a good deal, and knows a great deal of Horace by heart. She rattled off some of the odes. In much that she says I find an almost cynical frankness, in much else naïve observation. What makes her queer, I fancy, is that she clearly wants a man. . . .

To Mary Costelloe

Fiesole
18 January 1896
Saturday evening

I received your letter and two post cards and was glad of your more cheerful tone. Here it has been heaven — really I know not how else to describe it; heaven despite the fact that ever since you left I have been peculiarly sleepless and therefore feeling tired mornings. So you have been all the way to Bury St. Edmunds, you poor dear. I knew not I was imposing so severe a task. How I hope that at least it hath been to a purpose!

I have read *The Scarlet Letter* and begun *Esmond*. The latter seems like ploughed fields compared to elastic turf after the *Scarlet Letter*. What prose this — like an emancipated transfigured blank verse! And what an heroic character Hester's! But the great creation in that book — one of the four greatest in art — is Pearl. I know nowhere else such a supreme embodiment of all that in childhood appeals to me as most fascinating.

Yet all in all the *Scarlet Letter* is not quite one of the few greatest books. To be that its atmosphere would have to be more palpable, and more convincing. It does not have that perfect singleness and imperturbableness of point of view that for instance I find in the *Amber Witch*.[1] But with its two characters and its profound humanity, had it also the perfect tone of the *Amber Witch*, the *Scarlet Letter* would be perhaps greater than any other work of pure literature in existence.

How puissant and black the branches of your sumach are, stencilled against the copper tinted pink of the twilight! Few works of art can vie with such an effect of what we call nature.

I had a charming note from Mrs. Jack who seems delighted with my dream of her gallery, and hints at wishing it to be realised.

To Mary Costelloe

Fiesole
19 January 1896
9 P.M.

I have much enjoyed all thy letters and cards of Wednesday and Thursday. Thee is sweet! Well, I have been saying of

1 Translation by Lady Duff Gordon of Wilhelm Meinhold's *Bernsteinhexe*.

every day past that it was the loveliest yet. I have to say it again and it is true. I should have roamed out early this wonderful forenoon, but for my haste to write to Mrs. Jack about the Rembrandt. I dined last night at the Palmerino. Miss Wimbush — whom I have nicknamed *"Oscar à rebours"* — is staying there. Vernonia was charming and sweet as she always is when she comes off her pole or perch and becomes nearly human. The walk back was glorious in the starlight. . . .

To Mary Costelloe

Fiesole

21 January 1896

I can not tell you how lovely it is this minute as I am writing by my desk, and looking out over the golden bronzed plain to the silver ledges of the Carrara peaks! I met Mrs. Sharp in the Uffizi yesterday. The poor dear is as ignorant and as blind as a bat, but simple and willing to learn. I walked home with her, and she furied against Vernon who fifteen years ago must have been a holy terror — worse far than she is now. Vernonia really had no right to run down poor Sharp's verses so — she who thinks alphabet Robinson so very great a poet. Have I written by the way that she swore to Miss C. that no real art-comprehending person possibly could endure Mantegna — because he *has* such tactile values.

Leaving Mrs. S. I strolled up Bellosguardo and enjoyed the view from Donatello's tower and then from the Villa Brighieri. The hill seems nearer there, looks far more plastic and bronzed than from here. I dined with the Buttles, and had a regular romp with them. I now realize why they enjoy me so much — it's because I am perfectly natural with them, relaxed, and un-striving. The result is that I feel rested and happy myself, and in this happy state I talk a good deal of laughable nonsense. They were telling me of a friend of theirs fr. Milwaukee who has been here three days, has already bought 6000 photographs and is having copies made of all the Carlo Dolcis. I walked back as the moon was setting an eery sight, blood-red, and lying low on her back.

Let me know when you are coming and where to meet you.

To Mary Costelloe

Fiesole
24 January 1896

After threatening to change for the worse yesterday, it is very lovely again to-day. I plunged down to town, looked into the library, had a peep thro' the Pitti, and then panted up to Arcetri, and had a pleasant hour with the prim, stiff, but high bred, human and delightful inhabitants of that charming place. The mother and both the daughters had spent the entire spring summer and autumn nursing a nephew back to health out of a frightful malaria. This led us to talk of cures, and this in turn of sensitiveness to pain, and how very differently different people bore it. "Yes," said Mrs. Scott, "the Chinese prove by their insensitiveness that they belong to quite a different creation from ourselves. They are Preadamites, you know." Here Violet interrupted, "Yes mama, Canon McCall says they are Preadamites." Mrs. Scott continued "Of course they have *some* of our blood through Cain who wandered eastward." The dears, you may be sure I did not betray myself.

We then talked of cruelty to animals, and I suggested that it arose from too strong a sense of property in beasts, and how in the past this sense of property extended even to wives and children. "And fathers used to sacrifice their sons for their own sins" Violet burst out indignantly.

Miss Buttles spent the night here, and I was so grateful, being thus saved from Miss C. and then the music. She sang, and sang, and quite as I had never heard her yet. During dinner we talked of Mr. Davis, and I said he would argue with a signpost about the mileage.

This is my last letter to Leysin. I shall now obey whatever directions you may give. If I miss you at the Pisa station go to the Netturno, and ask for me, or await me.

I have cut my left thumb, and am amazed to find how it disables one. It took me at least twice as long to dress. I enjoyed the throbbing of it, and being made aware of its existence.

To Carlo Placci

The Burlington Fine Arts Club
14 July 1896

My dear Carlo,

I have been charmed with your letter, and delighted with the enclosed from Galitzine assuring me I can go to Russia. It would nevertheless not be out of place to make surety certain by doing what you could with Lobanoff.[1] But it must be for the autumn of '97. I shall not have the leisure sooner. What think you I did on arriving here? I went to bed with a fever and chill, and staid there for a week. I am not well yet, altho' just well

[1] Prince Lobanov-Rostovski was at the time Russian Minister of Foreign Affairs. He died on August 30, 1896, a few weeks after this letter was written. Berenson in fact never re-visited Russia. His hesitation in 1896 was doubtless due to questions of double nationality and military service, and not of course to any of those fears to which a person living after the Revolution might be subject.

enough to creep about. It was most annoying as my every hour was mapped out, and as you can imagine I am driven all the harder now.

I rush about and see pictures rarely of the greatest importance. My ambition now is to have done with all but the few great masterpieces of art, and in art as in life to meticulously keep away from the sordid, the second-rate, and pettily personal. Ye gods hear and grant my prayer! I envy your seeing the Duse. She is almost the only person in the world I would have any eagerness to meet. I want to hear her talk about acting, regarding which I have many ideas which she only realizes. About the 28th I start northward and shall spend most of August among the hyperboreans. Toward the middle of Sept. we certainly shall be in Vienna. Join us there.

Have you read Aphrodite?[1] It is worth while. I have seen Balcarres. The poor boy is frightfully driven. Good-bye.

Ever yours

B.B.

To Mrs. Jack Gardner

Fiesole

9 November 1896

. . . A qui sait attendre tout arrive! I am sending you registered the photo of a Velasquez after my heart's desire and of yours I am sure. It is a portrait of Philip IV, infinitely distinguished, every inch a King. It is not the Holford portrait but it is not inferior. As a portrait it is unquestionably grander and profounder than the Holford, the which however has advantages of its own being more coloured for instance. It — the one

[1] By Pierre Louÿs.

I am proposing — is a little earlier than the Holford — in fact it is a replica of the Madrid portrait (No. 1070) than which it is better in execution. It was painted directly after that and avoids some mistakes of the first version.

. . . I tried to get Capt. Holford's but in vain. The Captain will not hear of selling it. Now for a whole year I have with scarcely an interruption tried one Velasquez after another. Excepting Holford's none came up to the one I have now hit on. As to the price £15,000 is asked. I hope to be able to beat it down a few hundred, possibly get it for £14,000. At that price or for a little more it is very cheap. Alas I know too well what Velasquez' fetch — and if by any unhappy mischance, this one does not please you, I should despair of ever getting another of its quality and at this comparatively modest price. You are of course aware that Velasquez both with artists and buyers stands now at the very top and is of all painters the most sought after.

The market being thus I must beg you to decide with your customary despatch and to cable YELAQEZ = yes, Velasquez NOQEZ = no, Velasquez and may the Muses direct your decision.

P.S. I should add that the condition of the picture is perfect and that the photograph does no justice whatever to the exquisite detail in the painting of the dress.

To Mrs. Jack Gardner

Fiesole
29 November 1896

. . . At the same instant yesterday I received your letter from N.Y. and your wire with rejoicing tidings about the Velasquez. As soon as all is arranged I shall cable you to send the cheque.

I most heartily congratulate you on your choice. By the way I know not yet whether the price will be £15,000 or £14,000 or something in between. You will understand that XIVM = 14,000 XVM = 15,000 XIVMVC = 14,500 but I shall telegraph them *cursive* so as to arouse minimal suspicion.

To Mrs. Jack Gardner

Fiesole
6 December 1896

. . . This must be a hasty note to tell you that last night I cabled to you the mystic words BENE, XVM, SUBITO the which, interpreted as you will have, means "Send cheque for £15000 at once." To my great regret and contrary to my expectation I could not get the V. for a penny less and was in fact glad to get it at that.

To Mrs. Jack Gardner

Siena
22 February 1897

. . . I rejoice that you have at last received his most Christian majesty el rey Filippe II [1] [*sic*]. Why did Banks sell him? The poor fellow wanted money, that's all. The picture was one of the most famous Velasquez in England.

[1] Berenson means to write: His Catholic Majesty, el rey Felipe IV. "His Most Christian Majesty" was on the other hand the Papal title conferred on the Kings of France and Navarre.

To Carlo Placci

Villa Kraus
Fiesole
7 April 1897

My dear Carlo,

Thanks for the Idea Liberale which I have read with interest. I am half tempted to take up your challenge about Salisbury[1] and whether he also is "half-educated" because he prays. But what's the use! Arguments are of small avail except where common premises are assumed, and a common method of reasoning. But I may say that by "half-educated" I mean persons who seriously think that religious dogma can be defended as scientific principles can be.

I think a man of (relatively) perfect education may believe anything, but such a man will not try to defend his belief.

With you I have no bones to pick. If it does not estrange from me, or makes unpalatable one of the two dearest friends I have on earth I shall have nothing to say against your religion. I believe religion . . . to be an expression of temperament. Religion is a form of art; taken as objective reality it is the art of the un-aesthetic; but taken consciously as subjective it is perhaps the highest form of beauty.

By the way it is very "half-educated" to distinguish between active and contemplative life. Without either the other perishes. So let us throw stones at neither.

Yours affectionately
B.B.

[1] Berenson is referring certainly to the celebrated third marquess who was at the time Prime Minister and also Foreign Secretary. In view of Berenson's comment it is perhaps relevant to remind the reader that Lord Salisbury was an amateur scientist.

To Miss Violet Paget (Vernon Lee)

S. Moritz
24 August 1897

Dear Miss Paget,

I fully appreciate yr. kindness in sending me the proofs of yr. articles. I am sure you intended to give me a taste of that pleasure which the blessed gods used to take in first fruits. I have just had my "first read off" yr. paper & it certainly will not be the last. For where else shall I find such perfect distillations, such delightful reminders of numerous conversations I have been privileged to have [had] with you at the Palmerino & of even more numerous visits with Miss Anstruther-Thomson to the galleries? And here I must make the *amende honorable*. Do you remember my sustaining[1] that Miss Anstruther-Thomson was quite without a memory, while you opposed that she had a memory super-human, incapable of forgetting? I see from yr. paper that you were right. Her memory is indeed startling. I confess it inspires me with a certain awe; it is too much like conversing with a recording angel, I must add, a benevolent recording angel, one who stores up nothing against one, but takes the whole burden upon his own shoulders.

With your main thesis I can not agree — at all events I should not give it anything like the importance that you do. But with your instances, examples & *obiter dicta* I am simply delighted. They are such familiar, cherished friends. Perhaps I was just beginning to take them too much as a matter of course, as something for the few initiated, already hackneyed & you make me appreciate them afresh. How can I sufficiently thank you!

But it is yr. gift of putting things freshly, with all the illusion of lucidity that I envy. What is insight, experience, thought compared to it? All these & myriads of other qualities are but

1 Presumably Berenson means *maintaining*.

purveyors to the divine gift of utterance. And yet I console my-self, perceiving one fatal drawback to this gift. It is so fre-quently accompanied by unconsciousness; & to people of my stamp, consciousness in every form, even under its ethical aspect of conscience is after all the one humanizing thing — that which distinguishes man from the brutes on the one hand, & the gods on the other.

I was very sorry to hear of Miss Anstruther-Thomson's break-down & anxious for her recovery. I am glad to know that she is better. Pray convey to her my thanks & kindest remembrances.

Four weeks of S. Moritz have apparently worked miracles with my health. Even if the after effects are indifferent I shall have enjoyed days & days of the kind of well being that I had supposed vanished with one's teens. Then as luck would have it a number of our common acquaintances have been here. We have been discussing art a great deal, so that they will be well prepared to appreciate the originality of your method & results in aesthetics. I am sure they all would be sending you their re-gards if they knew that I was writing.

Believe me,

Very truly yours
Bernhard Berenson

I insert here the following rather curious reply to Beren-son of September 1897 as it illustrates the kind of quarrel likely to arise in a small expatriate society not unafflicted with nerves. It is doubtful if Miss Paget would have been so harsh if it had not been a question of her great friend Miss Clementina Anstruther-Thomson.

VIOLET PAGET (VERNON LEE)
TO BERNARD BERENSON

[La Ferté sous Jouarre
on writing paper of
Il Palmerino
Maiano
Florence]
2 September 1897

Dear Mr. Berenson,

I feel obliged, after some days of repugnance, to take notice of certain statements & implications contained in your ostensibly very friendly & courteous letter; lest you should, perchance, misinterpret my silence as much as I still hope I may be misapprehending your words.

First let me thank you for all the fine things you say about my powers of expression. They are the more welcome because, as three quarters of the essay are written, with scarcely a word of alteration, by Miss Anstruther-Thomson, it would appear that she participates in a quality which you find rarer than I do. As regards the novelty of the subject matter, my position throughout this essay (& in my review also of yr. book in *Mind*) is precisely that the progress of criticism & psychology must inevitably suggest such views & thoughts as ours & apparently yrs.; so that I find myself amply confirmed by your assurance that they are quite familiar to yourself & other initiated persons. I might indeed think the expression you employ — "hackneyed" — savours of exaggeration; and I might regret that your sense of their being hackneyed prevented your including them in any of your books, if I thought your vein of sarcastic inuendo [*sic*] at all suitable to this occasion.

For the plain English of your elaborate ambiguities about "perfect distillations of numerous conversations" etc, about "a recording angel who stores up nothing against one, but takes the whole burden on his (*read* 'her') shoulders"; about the divine gift of utterance "to which insight, experience, thought" i.e. those of a 3d person, are only the purveyors; and finally about that "absence of consciousness even under its ethical aspect of conscience" which you connect with the possession of the gift of utterance thus attributed to my friend & myself — the plain English of all this equivocating sarcasm is that Miss Anstruther-Thomson & I have stolen the larger part of our essay from our conversations. I set it down in all its crudeness, because I believe that whatever mean & absurd things your tendency to exaggeration and your pleasure in complicated utterances may have hurried you into writing, you will recoil from acknowledging that a thought so ludicrous and so detestable ever seriously formulated itself in your mind.

Ever since your letter arrived, I have been trying to get over my disgust & indignation & trying to understand by what extraordinary combination of superficial reading, of confused memory & rash & violent expression you can have written a statement so untenable and so slanderous. Thus as regards our conversations on aesthetics (wh: came to an end with my reading you some notes on the proof sheets of T.P.), and those wh: you had in previous years with Miss Thomson in the galleries, I expect that you utterly confuse them with conversations you have had with other persons later and when your own ideas had evolved into a much greater resemblance with ours than would appear from your books & than either Miss Thomson or I have any recollection of. For I remember perfectly not only my own conversations with you, but those which Miss Thomson's splendid memory enable her to repeat to me; and in neither can I find the theory exposed in our article, anything like the twelve or fifteen experiments detailed therein or like the "illustrious obiter dicta and instances" to which you refer; but, on the contrary, a much greater amount of dissimilarity in all detail views than the fact that we were both of us looking for the secret of aesthetics in the same direction & with the same methods would have led me to suppose. Indeed, I always went against the fears of Miss Anstruther Thomson, lest you let out discoveries similar to her own and oblige her thereby to communicate her views to you before they were matured by sufficient experiment & comparison. Nay one of the motives in writing that article in *Mind,* besides the desire that your services to psychology should be appreciated according to their priority, was the wish to have summed up your views before publishing those embodied in Miss Thomson's & my notes, so as to clear either party from any suspicion of plagiarism on the part of the public by showing the appearance of exactly how much of your views we then knew — of our vague project of communication — & how little we agreed with them. For this same reason I read you some elaborate criticisms & you have evidently confused what you may be in the habit of saying now with what you said — with what in the then stage of your evolution as shown in Tuscan Painters, *you must have thought,* at the time that we still talked over these subjects. The appearance of Tuscan Painters decided us not to place our ideas before you before this publication, because the difference between them & yr. own seemed too great to render an interchange in the least useful to either party, while it might have been extremely disconcerting & disheartening to one of them.

You see by the details I have given you about Miss Thomson's & my work, and by the explanations I am trying to find for your confusion of *meum & tuum,* that I as yet decline to hold you responsible for the charge of wholesale robbery which constitutes the gist of your letter; a charge which, had you seriously & deliberately maintained [it], your own manliness & good sense would have couched in the form of a straightforward & specified statement, rather than in semi-jocular ambiguities.

I have the greatest admiration (I have shown it in writing twice about you & in helping you in yr. tongue-tied days) for your talents; I have felt real gratitude for your kindness towards my brother & that generous helpfulness towards Miss Thomson of which alas! you are now spoiling the savour. Moreover, I am sincerely attached to your friend Mrs. Costelloe, & have been glad to find that some of my best friends are among yours; all of which circumstances make me extremely anxious to find that you did not mean to commit the offence of which your pen has been guilty. I shall therefore mention this matter to none of our common friends unless you force me to. For these reasons also, but still more because in her present condition of health & with her unflinching & unforgiving sense of honour the bare thought of the writer of such a letter as a near neighbour would make disagreeable to her, for all these reasons I have communicated neither your letter nor its real contents to Miss Thomson — so the matter rests between you & me. I ask for no explanations or apologies on your part, holding such things as useless; I am writing to forget, if I can, this lamentable manifestation on your part. Only should you feel inclined to repeat any of these accusations viva voce to our common friends, I shall trust to the consciousness & conscience on wh. you pride yourself, to accompany such accusations by a sight (to others) of this present letter, and to myself by a specified account of at least some of the alleged plagiarisms.

I have the greatest aversion to such correspondence as your letter and my answer sometimes lead to; and I therefore request that there may be nothing of the sort. Whatever the attitude you assume, I trust we may neither of us bore or amuse our acquaintances with any unusual behaviour. Meanwhile I hope I may be justified in still signing myself

Your friend
V. Paget

A letter that Miss Paget wrote to Carlo Placci many years later gives her view of this episode from the perspective of 1913:

Il Palmerino
S. Gervasio
Florence
28 May 1913

My dear Carlo Placci,

Many thanks for your letter. It is what I wished; indeed it tallies quite oddly with what I had just put before Miss A. T. as your probable defence.

I have myself long since felt persuaded that just because Berenson was (passez moi le mot) an ill-tempered and egotistic *ass* to mistake us for plagiarists, we, on the other hand, were not very intelligent in mistaking him for a slanderer and a villain. The whole incident was merely a comedy in which the usual (indeed perhaps more than usual!) human incapacity for understanding other people's ideas and the naive human demand that other people should *exactly* understand *one's* own, played the chief and not at all amusing parts . . .

Before quitting the subject let me however say that I believe that my ill will, even when at its worst, never led me to think or speak ill of Berenson either as a man or a savant; indeed I once or twice took up the cudgels on his behalf against friends of ours who thought because I disliked him I should like to hear him abused . . . and as to the Berensons I have never heard that they spoke of me in a different spirit. So though there was foolishness de part et d'autre . . . I don't think any of us have made beasts of ourselves.

And now no more about this foolish matter, which has wasted opportunities of mutual interest and even perhaps of intellectual cooperation. . . .

Your sincere old friend
V. Paget

To T. S. Perry[1]

> Hotel z. Löwen
> Mühlen, Graubünden [Canton Grisons]
> 29 August 1897

Dear Perry,

I am just leaving the Engadine where I spent four weeks with my sister whom I am now taking to Antwerp whence she sails home.

I had three profitable weeks in England seeing a number of collections of such difficult access that I had never seen them before. The "discoveries" will be incorporated in the large illustrated edition of the *Venetian Painters* appearing soon. Of course you shall have a copy.

At the Engadine — S. Moritz — we had a charming time. We were at one of the smaller inns forming a happy family with a small number of the very nicest people in Italy. At walking distances were other Italian friends. We climbed mountains, walked over glaciers, danced, in short frivolled. I have not read three books the while, the nearest approach to a serious work being Mosso's Fisiologia dell'Uomo nei Alpi, full of remarkable results & splendid suggestions. . . .

I turn back soon to Venice for some weeks. Early November will see me at my desk again.

Don't forget me. "Soles occidere & redire possunt" but old friends are rare & departed return no more. With best regards to Mrs. Perry.

> Affectionately
> Bernhard Berenson

[1] Thomas Sargeant Perry (1845-1928), American scholar, author, lecturer.

To Carlo Placci

Old England Hotel
Bowness-on-Windermere
7 August 1898

Dear Carlo,

Your last letter contained too little news about yourself. I was sorry to find that so late in July, and hot as it was, you still were staying on in Paris, exciting yourself about matters which are no business of yours physically and intellectually. After all, though, why should I be putting on this mentor's tone! If you like this sort of thing it is just the sort of thing you like.

I for my part have been pursuing different paths. I have seen a number of friends, done more or less real work, and revisited Oxford and Cambridge. In both places I feasted my eyes on beautiful things, on picturesque gothic, on italian architecture in some respects better understood, and more refined than any in Italy — good talk was also not wanting, on metaphysics and politics, above all on the advance of Anglo-Saxon civilization, and culture. Humanity is at the best a poor and sordid affair, and Anglo-Saxon humanity is human. But it is less poor and less sordid, on the whole than any other whatsoever, and the world can not but benefit by its rule. For the world's sake I would have America and England conquer and control everything. But I doubt whether we should be improved by this Augean task, and so I am satisfied that none of us should take except just what we need, and what we can't help taking.

I do not bother my head too much about these matters. They will fall into shape no matter what you and I say or do. Surely it is much more profitable for each of us to spend our time on things that will make us happy as individuals, that will advance our souls. As for me I know that my own sensations, and my own ideas are to me of primary importance, because it is by them alone that I really live. Without them I should be a phonograph, and I prefer to be a man.

I am in love with the North. Here I am in the famous Wordsworth country, and truly charming it is. Robert Trevelyan,[1] a most delightful youth, who promises to be a real poet is with me. In a day or two we shall plunge into the wildest Highlands of Scotland.

Give my love to Adelaide and your mother, and my best regards to the Malvezzis, and what other friends may be at Caspari's.[2]

Affectionately yours
B.B.

Address Baring Bros. and write soon.

To R. C. Trevelyan

5 Via Camerata
San Domenico di Fiesole
6 November 1896

My dear Trevy,

I fear I am proving myself a worse letter-writer, if possible, than your charming self. The fact is that travelling I cannot prevail upon myself to scribble as much as a note and settled down I have not yet been long enough to feel that leisure of mind requisite for writing.

We enjoyed our trip in Germany particularly after the Russells joined us. Together we visited some quaint small towns and then rambled down to Italy. At Mantua bicycles met us and for a fortnight we spun about on the high dykes over the Lombard plain. We saw many out of the way and beautiful

---

[1] Robert Calverly Trevelyan (1872-1955), English man of letters, poet, translator of classical texts. Elder brother of the historian George Macaulay Trevelyan.
[2] An hotel at St. Moritz.

things. The one drawback was Horne. He certainly was no addition to the party and, between you and me, he as it were dropped his mask and betrayed at once an exceeding incapacity for seeing with his own eyes and an excessive eagerness to gather into his notebook all that he could squeeze out of me about the various galleries we visited. However he was always endurable which in dearth of better things is something in a travelling companion. The Russells left yesterday leaving behind them a very sweet odour. Bertie I have been seeing a great deal and I liked him better and better. His mind is exquisitely active. True it has as yet perhaps not gone beyond picking up one moss-grown stone after the other to see what is under it but that by itself is perfectly delightful. Were I really interested in metaphysics or he in art we should be super-humanly well joined. Mrs. R. improves on acquaintance. She has wit and good intentions and as her shyness wears off — remember shyness often takes the form of bluff — she is charming.

I have not yet got to work and I stand before it like a balking horse. I should be at it now instead of writing rot to you. Mommsen's *Provinces* have been my chief reading since I left you, most interesting, affording answers to all sorts of questions I used to ask myself, indispensable for the knowledge of the origin of the mediaeval and modern world. The *Iliad* I finished and the Homeric hymns — have you read them? The Demeter is exquisite, the Aphrodite delicious and the Hermes amusing. Now I am at Aeschilus [*sic*] . . . I am also reading your father's life of Macaulay!

Yours ever

To R. C. Trevelyan

Poggio Gherardo
Via Settignanese
Firenze
1 December 1900

My dear Trevy,

You see I already have left my diggings and until December 20th, the wedding day, am staying here. Mrs. Ross tells me you mean to come down toward the end of the month. Please do. It would be a real pleasure to see you again and I am of course eager to make your wife's acquaintance. Unfortunately I cannot, as I so much would have liked offer you hospitality, for, besides Logan, Mrs. Smith and the two Miss Costelloes will be staying at the new villa until after the New Year. On our way back however I shall insist on a visit from you both.

My autumn has been divided between hard but enchanted work on Michelangelo and reading Carlyle. Of the latter I was almost virgin. I am going through him and find ever more pleasure in his torrential gorgeousness, in his inimitable points of portraiture and even in his point of view, under different "clothes," exactly Nietzsche's.

To Carlo Placci

Nervi
2 April 1901

Dear Carlo,

The great event has come off and on the whole surpasses my expectations. D'Annunzio as usual begins with a promise almost noble. Then the piece,[1] lacking all real movement, became more and more boring and disgusting — and we were all

---

[1] Judging from the date, it is probably d'Annunzio's *La Gioconda* that is referred to.

happy to get into even the pouring rain once more. The Duse was very mannered — all her usual *clichés,* — but had charming moments. Zacconi conceived his part as that of a convict in a rut, and this brought down the house.

The two uppermost galleries were filled with students who applauded incessantly. A better organized claque there never was. The rest of the house — wh. by the way was a full one, chiefly of Germans — applauded little, and only Zacconi.

The day before the performance Donna Laura — who by the way is perfectly charming — had a note fr. D'Annunzio offering her a box, and the next day, one from the Duse herself. L. can no longer be quite fair to the Duse — who, whatever her charm, is at bottom, to judge by her yesterday's acting, a vulgar soul. . . .

Yours affectionately
B.B.

To R. C. Trevelyan

Abbazia di Fiastra
11 October 1901

My dear Trevy,

I was very much pleased with your hearty and indulgent reception of my Juvenilia. One neither writes nor publishes with the thought of pleasing anyone yet when please it does it is a pleasure.

I am at present staying with [Prince Giustiniani-Bandini], at once a Roman prince and a Scotch earl, whose daughter, the Duchess Grazioli, may now be counted as an old friend. Their seat is an old Cistercian abbey founded it is said by Saint Bernard himself and the magnificent Romanesque architecture thereof is worthy *tanti nominis.* The surrounding country is of exquisite beauty rolling plains with grand mountain ranges, the Majella and Gran Sasso in the distance. There are pleasant oakwoods near the house, streams crossed by wooden bridges traverse the country, the roads are shaded and every hilltop is crowned with a village or castle. We drive about in a four-in-hand and explore. Every church or chapel has something to show. My favourites Crivelli Lotto and Lorenzo da San Severino worked much in this neighbourhood and some of their paintings are still *in situ*. Then such golden weather. One could live it forever. Yet in a day or two I hie myself home to go to work on my monument.

On the way hither I paid my first visit to the operatic Republic of San Marino. It is a very beautiful spot, one of the most jagged pinnacles of which is crowned with what was once the strong keep. Now it serves the humbler purpose of a prison, not of state but of the common or garden type. It has now but three prisoners. You must know that it is quite lucrative to be a prisoner of the Republic. You get a dole of 1.20 a day. You thereupon mess with your gaoler who boards you for fifty centimes a day and that leaves you 70 centimes but I understood that the handsome Gaoler and his *soror pulchrior* win it away from you at cards between meals.

To Mrs. Jack Gardner

Friday's Hall
[9 August[1]]
Coronation Day
Haslemere

Dear Friend,

. . . I have a great weakness for the King who is so jolly and debonair a figure and after all the prophecies that have been

[1] The year is of course 1902. King Edward VII was not crowned in the year of his accession (1901) because of an illness and an operation which he had to undergo.

afloat to the effect that he would never be crowned I rejoice
that the hour has come and that — so far as we here in the
country know — he is safe.

. . . If I live on I must earn a living. With all the experience
I have had in buying and the control I could easily have of the
market, advising about pictures is the path marked out for me.
But you have now nearly had your fill. It is true I have
several other friends and acquaintances who buy on my advice.
But I could sell ten times as much as I do now without taking
more trouble if only I had a larger circle of friends. I know I
can rely on you to help me enlarge this circle, can't I? I want
America to have as many good pictures as possible. You have
had the cream. Other collections will only enhance the merit
of yours. . . .

Devotedly
B.B.

To J. P. RICHTER[1]

La Floridiana
Naples
5 January 1905

My dear Richter,
I was indeed delighted with your "Golden Age of Xian
Art." I do not hesitate to pronounce it epoch-making. I hope
you will go on endeavouring to illuminate that dark procession
of ignorance which now passes for knowledge regarding the history of art in the West during the first 13 Xian centuries. A

---

[1] Cf. the letter exactly fifty-one years later (16 January 1956) to J. P. Richter's
daughter Miss Gisela Richter.

more magnificent task awaits no one & you are the one person capable of achieving it.

What I am telling you about your book I have told & written to many people. But as for the N.Y. *Nation* there seems to have been some misunderstanding. I suggested to Miss Taylor that you should send a copy to that journal. She said you would & begged me to write to the editor to ask him to give it out for review to an historian of early Xianity rather than to an ordinary art critic. All this I did & it would be stultifying my own words to suggest now that I should do it myself. Besides, I am a very bad reviewer & almost never do such work. But if you send a copy to the *Nation* I am sure it will be seriously noticed.

I expect to spend all next week in Rome at Hotel de Russie. If you are there I may have the pleasure of seeing you.

With best wishes

Sincerely yours
Bernhard Berenson

To Mrs. Jack Gardner

Grand Hotel de Paris
Madrid
25 October [1906]

. . .

As the post goes in a few minutes I must be brief. It is about the Velasquez Pope. The lowest possible price is 500,000 frs. I had to use strong language and much plain speaking to get them down to that. They assure me that Roger Fry who has recently seen it will move heaven and earth to get the Metropolitan Museum to buy it and that he suggested 600,000 as a fair price.

All that I cannot guarantee. But what I can tell you as a fact is that Mrs. Potter Palmer only waits for my approval of the picture to purchase it. Please keep this a secret. Still I wish you to let me know whether you want to make the desperate effort to raise so big a sum or whether you prefer to step aside.

Of course I may conclude that the picture though wonderful is not Velasquez. . . .[1]

Ever affectionately
B.B.

To Carlo Placci

I Tatti[2]
27 November 1907

My dear Carlo,

I am glad you like my last book.[3] Your appreciation has always been peculiarly dear to me, because few if any are more than you the audience I have in mind while writing.

As for the rest of your letter I simply do not know what it is all about. We parted last time on the most affectionate terms with the understanding that you were to return in a very few days. You did not appear, and I was disappointed. But assuming you had other things to do I was not offended. I let ten days pass and then wrote, unconscious then, as I am still of

1 In the event Mrs. Gardner did buy the painting referred to — an oil sketch for the head and shoulders of the seated portrait of Innocent X, Doria-Pamfili, which is in the Doria Gallery in Palazzo Doria in Rome. It had belonged to Prince Brancacci. Some present-day critics (Pauli, Ponofsky) have questioned its authenticity.

2 Berenson had rented the Villa I Tatti at Ponte-a-Mensola below Settignano in 1900. He and Mary moved in on 28 December 1900. They acquired it after the death of the owner, Lord Temple Leader, from his heirs in 1905.

3 The North Italian Painters of the Renaissance.

any intention to offend. I do not know what you want of me. If you want me to change my character, my *Weltanschaung*, my manners, my habits, you must surely know that at 42 one *does not*. I am what I am, and as a quality not likely to change much. If this quality, such as it is and inevitably must remain, gets on your nerves, or if you are over-saturated with it, and it cloys on your palate, I shall have to submit to your distaste as one of the fatalities that life is full of. I shall regret it beyond words. You have in the course of the last 13 or 14 years meant more to me than any person in the world except my wife. I have loved you, and still love you, and *quand même* shall love you, as one does the people one has accepted without further chance of change, for better for worse, as one's own for ever. If you go back on me I shall receive a loss that nothing can repair. It will take away much of the pleasure in life. You may imagine that to ward off such a disaster I would do anything feasible. But it is not feasible to change essentially. I could promise, and flatter, and cajole, if I did not love you enough to take you in good earnest. If we continue to frequent one another it can only be on the old terms. I am not an Englishman, not even an Anglo-Saxon. You are not aware how little conscious *parti pris* I have in favour of their ways, but if I have their ways to the extent of being quite unaware that I have them, how can you expect me to get rid of them? And if *per impossibile* it were to be done, it would not yet mean that I could take on yours.

No, that is not to be dreamt of. For me you never have been an Italian, but *etwas Niedagewesenes,* namely Carlo Placci. To you I should be nothing but B.B. a very specific individual standing for nothing but himself. My relations to you have been what my deepest relations have been and ever must be, purely individualistic. It never occurs to me to stand on ceremony with any real friend. I do not expect them to kow-tow to me, to consider my opinions, my prejudices. I do not try to force my convictions, my preferences upon anyone. I hate and avoid subjects for dispute. My attitude is implied, and if it makes itself felt offensively, it is a misfortune I regret, but being unintentioned, and indeed unconscious, it is a thing I can not mend. Why then not continue to take me as you have taken me for so many years? The fraternal friendship between us has brought much joy to me, and simply has not been unpleasant altogether for you? Why end it for reasons I can not even understand? I hope and pray you will allow your affection, if that has not departed, to get the better of whatever grudges you may have against me. We all are full of grudges against our nearest and dearest, for no one meets all our requirements. Yet once we have felt that a person gives us all he can, and that that quality is good, it surely were sad to dwell upon the rest. I protest I am not worse but better, not less but more affectionate, and I trust not less interesting than ever. Then why suddenly turn around and see only the disagreeable side of me? I beg of you not to bring to an end, or to let die down a friendship so rare as ours. And whatever you decide to do, I warn you I shall always remain

Your loving friend
B.B.

To Mrs. Jack Gardner

London
8 July 1908

Dear Isabella,

Just a word to tell you that I saw to-day at Agnew's a perfect jewel of a little picture by Giovanni di Paolo of Siena. He is all the rage now because the collectors not only of paintings, but of objets d'art are after him and paying long prices for him. He is almost the most delightful of the Sienese Quattrocentisti and I have never seen a picture of his more charming in feeling and purer in colour. Agnew is sending you a photo but don't think it gives you anything like an idea of the picture. The price is very reasonable £450 delivered to you free of all charges in Boston. I strongly urge you to get it and in that case to lose no time in cabling YEPAOLO addressing Berenson, 36 Victoria St., London. In a fortnight John G. Johnson of Philadelphia will be here and sure to snap it up. . . .[1]

Yours
B.B.

To Carlo Placci

Hotel Somerset
Boston
18 November 1908

Dear Carlo,

I had supposed until a few days ago that Mary had written to you since we have been here, and I take the first opportunity I find to send you a few words. To write in full would take end-lessly, and bore you stiff, for you are not much interested in Boston and things peculiarly American. When we get to New York it will be a different matter. There are people there you know, and life is altogether more European. Our only common friends here are the Curtises[2] whom I have seen a number of times. We see a good deal of Mrs. Gardner, and her really marvelous collection. Although I got most of her pictures for her, I had no idea what a series of masterpieces they were.

What would have interested you most would have been the

[1] The picture was bought by Mrs. Gardner. The subject was the Child Jesus in the Temple Disputing with the Doctors.

[2] This may be Ralph Curtis who owned the Palazzo Barbaro and may have been in Boston for a visit. Placci knew him well.

centenary of the Catholic diocese that took place here some three weeks ago. I went to the high mass at the cathedral, and as a spectacle function I had never seen anything so fine in Europe. Cardinal Gibbons in his robes looked grander than a Raphael. After the mass there was a procession of 40,000 Catholics passing the Archbishop's home. They marched very well, and it was a curious sight. I hear the present arch-bp[1] is quite a man of the world and very eager to raise the social level of Catholicism.

I have the conviction that were I to live here I should be a stalwart Catholic. My intellectual position would not be changed, but I should find such needs of the strongest possible anchors with the past — and there are none such as the Catholic Church. All partisanship, and beliefs apart, it is the mightiest projection the Greco-Roman past I love so well can make upon the present. And here the present is so obstreperous, so insistent — in fact not unlike a young man who finds he can ultimately outstrip all the world's genius, simply because he does not know the world and has no idea of genius.

Taft during elections was accused of being at once a Unitarian (which he is) and a pro-Catholic. He ignored the first, but defended himself on the second charge by saying that in the Philippines he would have acted as he did toward any church whatever that happened to be in the same position.

The newspapers are horrible and contain almost no European news — and we get but the vaguest echoes of what goes on. But the Kaiser seems muzzled for a few minutes. If his people have really begun to see thro' him we shall all have reason to be grateful. I hear he writes constant autograph letters to Roosevelt, and as Roosevelt does all his thro' a secretary on the typewriter he is bored to death answering with his own hand.

Ferrero[2] is just coming here, and is sure to have a great suc-

---

1 William O'Connell, subsequently Cardinal.
2 Guglielmo Ferrero, a historian of Rome.

cess. Boston is full of intellectual *mi-côtes*. People here love lectures. W. James is talking at Harvard on metaphysics and can not find halls large enough for his audience. I see him fairly often, but he is a moody creature, and not always at his best. I hope he will be to-night. Santayana is a much more fascinating man.

I hear that am'g the Italians here the *padrone* system is as virulent as ever. I am told that the last consul was dismissed in disgrace for trying to put an end to it.

On the 27th we go to Mrs. Hewitt's for 3 days, and then to New York for as many, and then Philadelphia for the whole of Dec. Ray Costelloe[1] has been having a wonderful time making suffrage speeches in the West. Karin[2] is hearing very well. Write at once, take mine and Mary's love, and give some of it to all the Henrauxs.[3]

Yours
B.B.

To R. C. Trevelyan

29 Buckingham Gate S.W.
2 July 1909

My dear Trevy,

We are here for the month and hope to see you and your wife as well.

Do you happen to own the numbers of the Burlington Magazine containing my two articles on Sassetta? I think they were

---

1 Mrs. Berenson's elder daughter by her first marriage. She later became Mrs. Oliver Strachey.

2 Mary Berenson's younger daughter, later married to Adrian Stephen.

3 Lucien Henraux was Carlo Placci's nephew.

in the autumn numbers of 1903. I am going to reprint them for the coming autumn and I wish you would look through them carefully and point out solecisms and over-akwardnesses. If you do not own the articles I will have them sent to you.

To CARLO PLACCI

Hill Hall
Theydon Mount
Epping
26 July 1914

Dear Carlo,

I wonder why you have not written to me for so long, for I wrote you fr. Paris addressing you to the Br. Leg. at Stockholm about 4 wks. ago. You must be at the Bayreuth [festival] now but as I don't know your address there I must send this to Florence. Personally I have fair news. I keep pretty well, and in London particularly have been enjoying the Brit. Mus., the Russian Opera and ballet, and Society and my friends. Just now I am at Mrs. Hunter's along with George Moore and other companions. In a few days I join Mary at Ford Place, Arundel, and until August 5 you can address me there. What I shall do then I have not decided. Perhaps Scandinavia, perhaps even St. Moritz.

It is very exciting here just now what with Ireland on the one hand and Servia on the other. At one of the embassies yesterday I was assured that there would be no peace in Europe until the Balkans had been dipped under the Ocean for 24 Ks. Sympathy here seems to me strong for Austria and I don't believe that in case of war England will support Russia.[1]

1 Though Berenson's prophecy was not fulfilled, he exactly catches the English mood of 26 July 1914.

Let me have your news and your views, as well as your plans
Love to Adie

Ever yours
B.B.

To Professor Paul J. Sachs

I Tatti
Settignano
Florence
31 January 1916

Dear Mr. Sachs,

It was very good of you to send me such a long & delightful
letter. Of course I am greatly pleased that you like my relations.[1] I know that they esteem it a favour of Providence to
have you for a neighbour. I am greatly touched too by your
words on the war & the squalid never to be either forgotten or
forgiven *gran rifiuto* that we have made as a nation. American-
ism has been to many of us & not least to most of us expatriates,
a religion almost more than a patriotism. And our country now
had the chance, risking nothing essential, in taking an attitude
that would have made her the supreme tribunal of the earth.
All we needed to do was to declare our moral horror of Germany's doing at the very start & to excommunicate her. I am
convinced that such a step not only would have given us the
premier place in the world as a people, but would have hastened the Kingdom of Heaven on earth by centuries. Instead
who more despised than we — not even a Greek is so despised.

I am glad to hear that the prospects of the Fogg are so good.
I am of course greatly excited with curiosity to know what pic-

1 Presumably Ralph Barton Perry and his wife, Rachel, Berenson's sister. R. B.
Perry was Professor of Philosophy at Harvard.

tures . . . you are planning to get purchased by friends & I shall be very grateful if you let me know directly you can.

It is good of you to ask me to let you know of any pictures going. The truth, incredible as it may sound is, that as a general rule I hear about them only when I am in Paris & London & the big dealers come to consult me. Here I seldom get word of anything for Italy really is completely exhausted. The last *patrimonio artistico* laws have worked more rapidly than one could have imagined. Then there is another point I must make. Many years ago I was led by experience never to propose the purchase of anything to any person who was not absolutely free to decide on his own individual responsibility. I can have no relations with representatives or committees.

But there is one thing I can perhaps do that may be of some slight importance. That is to give you my opinion on any pictures you think of buying. Needless to say that you could count on mine as I in turn should have to count on your discretion.

A long hand-written letter wh. you must be patient with.

Sincerely yrs.
B. Berenson

To Professor Paul J. Sachs

I Tatti
Settignano
Florence
27 April 1916

Dear Mr. Sachs,

. . .

You will have heard of the death of Mr. Horne.[1] It is a very

---

[1] He left his works of art to the City of Florence where they are now housed in Palazzo Horne.

great loss to our studies, & such a waste. Had he lived the usual span of life he might have done work now which would have been of real value, for he was in his way a living spring. . . .

With kind regards

Sincerely yrs.

B. Berenson

To Professor Paul J. Sachs

I Tatti
Settignano
Florence
21 June 1916

Dear Mr. Sachs,

. . .

Horne's death was a great loss to our studies, & he is not likely to be replaced. Happily each generation gets what it deserves, what it prefers.

I see that the fool policy of our present quadrennial Tsar is bearing fruit. For a war with Mexico, none will be to blame except the ignorant conceit of Pres. Wilson. He must go even if all the German Americans *are* against him. There is such a thing as being worse even than a pro-German. It is to be a Wilson let loose in international affairs. I fear you who have not been abroad of late can not conceive the humiliation we "expatriated" Americans feel & suffer. As a nation we have never been so low in international esteem since the days of Wilson's previous incarnation when he was called Madison.

With kind regards

Sincerely yrs.

B. Berenson

To Miss Natalie Barney
[Postal stamp: 9 janvier 1917]

Hôtel Ritz
Place Vendôme
Paris
Tuesday

Dear Miss Barney,

Many thanks for the letters of Rémy Gourmont. I shall read of them all I can before bringing it back Friday at 4. Mary's voice is returning and she looks forward to seeing you again.

It was delightful meeting you so responsive, appreciative, and zestful. I ought at my age to be more indifferent, but I can not resist *my* good. There are quite people enough to take care that one is not spoiled out of the withering sense of reality. So I bless the gods that brought us acquainted and I pray to them to continue their kindness.

Sincerely yours,
B. Berenson

To Miss Natalie Barney

Settignano
2 February 1917

. . .

Do you know why I like the *Spoon River Anthology* to the extent I do? It is of course not the realism and naturalism and all that in and for themselves, but for the implied background of classic idealism and Hellenic restraint of tenderness which I feel in them. They were inspired by the Greek Anthology and catch not a little of the rhythms and atmosphere of those epitaphs. Of course the subject matter contrasted with the time, as it were, is very fetching. I have just read *Du côté de chez Swann*. I certainly have never come across before anything that came so close to the revelation of my own innermost minutest but all-determining psycho-physical reactions. Since early childhood have I been aware of them, and they have made me, but never before have I found them in books, let alone literature. Do you know Marcel Proust, and if you do tell me about him. Why don't you send me the small volume of aphorisms you promised me? Even though in verse, for remember that I am interested in you, *content* as well as form.

B.B.

To Miss Natalie Barney

Settignano
4 March 1917

. . . We shall both of us be genuinely glad to have you stay with us. You will have to put up with few physical hardships (except what may be due to the lack of benzine) but perhaps not a few of a subtler kind. For I may not be my best self. I am subject to moods, to violences, to black devils. At times I know not what savage Semite or Tartar or Slav ancestor takes possession of me. But I seldom bite, although perhaps occasionally I bore. Be it as it may, you shall not find me masked to impress you. Such as I am you shall see me and I trust to take and not to leave. . . .

Apart from being a no mean stunt — which however would not impress me — as an exercise in self-transsubstantiation, your verses strike a singularly vibrant chord of my own lyre. For though in French they are essentially due to the impulse of the passionate pilgrim come from America home to beauty. Your inspiration is of that quest, and your expression gains therefrom a directness, an eloquence, and a glow which nothing short of an un-Latin need of self-revelation can create.

I wonder how many people there are who can enjoy you as I do. In the first place one must know English as well as French. Then one must be an American. Then one must enjoy the artistic effort of a person who enjoys the illusion of attaining to a less hackneyed form of expression than is possible with the worn out [coin?] of one's mother speech. And finally one must sympathize with the point of view, and it is one which can be entertained by a very few renegade Americans and no others.

Am I all wrong?

I want to read all you have written, because you interest me. I dare say I shall be again rewarded beyond my expectations. Come soon.

B.B.

To Miss Natalie Barney

Settignano
6 May 1917

. . .

Then you have for me a great advantage over most versifiers, and it is that you always have something to say that cogs in with the wheels of my own life. Even when your form is ungracious you always appeal to my experience, and that, by the way, is why you must send everything you have written, whether printed or in manuscript. You must omit nothing, for all of it is sincerely you, and it is you I wish to get to know. . . .

D'Abro came yesterday. To my great regret I had but little private talk with him. I charged him with many messages to you.

Yours as much as you will

B.B.

To Carlo Placci

Paris
22 November 1917

[postcard]

Dear Carlo,

So you want me to go on with *inni ed elogi,* and the whole
pack of swindling lies that has brought so low the country I love
best on earth, and its people whom I regard as a marvellously
gifted one. If Italy had among her own sons *one hundred* who
loved her and her *real* people as I do, much that has happened
would not have. I do here all I can for the *real* Italy and not
the pseudo-Prussia of the last 30 years. I have joyous hopes for
that real Italy, but of course I don't expect to be appreciated
for my confidence and my pains.

Mary returns this evening. Come back and represent Italy.
You are needed.

B.B.

To Carlo Placci

40 Avenue du Trocadéro
[Paris]
22 December 1917

My dear Carlo,

I understand fr. Mary that you have declared war ag. me for
speaking ag. Italy. It is true that on arriving here I felt so
bitter ag. yr. pro-Boches on the one hand and ag. yr. Nationalists
on the other that I did speak ag. them. And if you think that
these two parties are equivalent to the whole of Italy, then
your accusation against me is perfectly justified. But in mo-

ments when your optimism rose as high as mine with regard to your own people I thought you as able as anyone, myself included, to realize that these two parties were Italy's worst enemies. I supposed that in accusing them I was defending and exonerating the Italian people. Unfortunately you seem to share the opinion of the wretched gang who would demand of me acquiescence in all the miserable offspring of Crispi-Giolittism, of the whole Triplice, of the *sacro egoismo* and *nostro-guerrismo* and accuse me of being an enemy of Italy if I don't.

If your representatives here had a grain of wisdom they would instead of conspiring ag. me, and muttering threats, attempt to use my knowledge, my authority, and my possible influence for the Italy we all love together. Their conduct is not only stupidly undiplomatic but I fear confesses that they find nothing in common between their Italy and mine.

As for you, my dear Carlo, we have been friends for half a lifetime, and quarrelled often, but there is in my heart under much annoyance and exasperation a profound affection for you.

I should be greatly distressed if this could never reach you again owing to your hardening your heart against me.

With all good wishes to you

B.B.

MARY BERENSON TO CARLO PLACCI

I Tatti
28 December 1917

My dear Carlo,

Fancy our not speaking if we met! Or even not being really delighted. I am quite sure you would feel au fond as happy as we!!

My proposal is only to avoid recurrences of friction by having no intimate visits till the War is over. I honestly do not think talking would do any good. I have not acted as buffer between you and B.B. all these years without *understanding the situation perfectly.* But according to my code and practice there are lots of things, even between friends, which are better not formulated in words.

I have explained to the Salveminis all my grounds, outside B.B.'s promise which I trust absolutely for being SURE he will not do or say anything to embitter Italy's relations with *any* of *her* Allies. Although they cannot tell you these grounds, you know they are reasonable people, and I think you will trust their judgement and tend, if you hear anything fresh, to believe that B.B. *did not say it.*

I was so sorry to hear Mme Henraux had been ill. You did not tell me that before.

Better luck for us all in 1918!

Yours always affectionately, but till the end of the War, from a distance

Mary Berenson

To Professor Paul J. Sachs

Hotel Ritz
Place Vendôme
Paris
26 August 1919

My dear Sachs,

I returned yesterday fr. a 12 days' trip into the 12th century. I am getting almost as familiar with it as I am with later phases of art & revel in it. In Spain that century too was my chief delight. You know we spent May, June & July there & we saw wonder upon wonder. If I were in less wretched health I should devote myself henceforth to the art of that last refuge of ancient culture.

And now to yr. letter. Of course I shall be not only delighted but most grateful for every photo of whatever art object you send me. Until further notice address here & fear not that you may fail to interest me. *Aestheta sum. Artis nil a me alienum puto.*

Sincerely yrs.
B. Berenson

To Professor Paul J. Sachs

270 Park Avenue
New York
26 November 1920

Dear Sachs,

Here we are installed in the Aladdin home of Carl W. Hamilton.[1] So do look us up if you come here before Xmas. On Dec. 23 we mean to transfer to Boston & there to remain a fortnight or so.

Please let me know what there is to see here that might escape me. Also, it would be very nice if you gave us words of introduction to yr. relations & friends who collect.

Remember me to Forbes & other good fellows.

Sincerely yrs.
B. Berenson

1 Mr. Carl Hamilton had formed a (rather temporary) collection of paintings which he had secured from Duveen and installed in his luxurious Park Avenue apartment. The "Aladdin" apartment seemed to me to be conventionally, if expensively, furnished in the New York manner of 1920 and had when I saw it a rather "unlived in" air, so that Berenson's adjective is surprising.

To Miss Natalie Barney
[Postmarked 5 January 1921]

The Copley-Plaza
Boston

Best and deepest wishes, dearest Natalie, for a thoroughly satisfactory 1921. I hope it will bring us together a good bit. Remember me to Valéry. I hope to find you in Paris when I return at the end of March.

We are here for homing reasons, and return in a few days to New York. It would be delightful if we were well enough to enjoy our opportunities. But neither of us can any longer stand the fun. And when all is said and done I don't desire to be in it, and yet slightly resent being out of it. I like the men well enough, but the women! When the sex-attraction is over, how few of them attract. I remain faithful to old loves however, and I truly revel in Isabella Gardner, although she is 85 and immobile.

I kiss your feet.

B.B.

To Professor Paul J. Sachs

270 Park Avenue
New York
21 January 1921

My dear Sachs,

Ever & ever so many thanks for the three photos of Miss Brownie's Funeral of St. Clara. Please try to have the inscription reproduced & deciphered. It would oblige me.

We shall be here till Febr. 20 & you must try to drop in before we leave. I want to show you a Botticelli portrait that Hamilton has just acquired. He brought it back under his arm the other night.

Tomorrow we spend with Platt at Englewood. Saturday 29th we shall be at New Haven to inspect the Jarves pictures. Febr. 20 we shall go to Bryn Mawr, whence to explore Philadelphia & its coast. Then Baltimore a few days. Washington & Boston again toward March 10.

With best regards to Mrs. Sachs as well as yourself fr. us twain

Ever yrs.
B. Berenson

To Professor Paul J. Sachs

New York City
10 February 1921

Dear Sachs,

I know Parmelee[1] very well.

Thanks for offer of service in case I have difficulty in procuring passport.

Yours
B. Berenson

1 Professor Sachs had offered to give Berenson a letter of introduction to Mr. Parmelee, a collector of Italian art who lived in Washington.

To Professor Paul J. Sachs

The Deanery
Bryn Mawr
Pennsylvania
22 February 1921

Dear Sachs,

You hinted in a note that Parmelee might be useful to the Fogg. If that is so I shall give him more time than I should, seeing what a bore he is.

N.Y. was delightful but I could not have stood another week of it. I had got to the end of my tether.

We are here till the 28th. Then at the Stafford Hotel, Baltimore, till the 5th, & at the Wardman Park Lane, Washington D.C., till the 11th. If all goes well we shall reach the Copley-Plaza on the morning of the 12th.

Ever yrs.
B. Berenson

Mary Berenson to Professor Paul J. Sachs

The Deanery
Bryn Mawr
Pennsylvania
27 February 1921

Dear Mr. Sachs,

Mr. Hamilton had some slides made & I gave a Magic Lantern lecture on his pictures. It went off so well that B.B. thought you might like me to repeat it at the Fogg, especially as Mr. Hamilton is now getting some color slides made. The blk. & white looked very well, but of course the color wd. be better.

Probably you will be able to manage it, but B.B. advised me to write about it.[1]

We shall be in Boston from the 12th-16th of March. Mr. Hamilton says he wd. come on for the lecture if I gave it.

We are looking forward very much to seeing you & your wife again.

Believe me
Yours sincerely,
Mary Berenson

MARY BERENSON TO MRS. KINGSLEY PORTER[2]

Luxor
24 February 1922

My dear Lucy,

Your letter of the 29th Jan. & p.c. of Feb. 2 have just come & there is also another train letter to answer. I've been disgracefully but very luxuriously lazy since Nicky[3] came & we started in the Great Adventure of the Nile. I've scarcely written or read a thing, just looked. There's simply nothing to

---

1 Carl Hamilton had recently bought a number of Italian paintings through Duveen. This small, choice assemblage was hung in the owner's flat in Park Avenue. The lecture was indeed given in the (old) Fogg Museum, and was well attended and long remembered. Slides of the very fine pictures in question were shown. I attended the lecture and remember that Mary Berenson praised Mr. Hamilton's instinctual grasp of excellence in painting. She also recalled her own days at "The Annexe," as Radcliffe was then known.

2 Wife of the distinguished archaeologist.

3 Miss Elisabetta (Nicky) Mariano joined the Berenson household as librarian in 1921. As in later years Mrs. Berenson became somewhat of an invalid, Miss Mariano took over the management of the house. The letters of B.B. and Mary Berenson are full of expressions of gratitude, and indeed dependence on, Nicky Mariano. Her sister, Baroness Alda von Anrep, was for many years Librarian at I Tatti.

equal this trip. But one would rapidly become a prize bore if one began to describe it!

B.B. has towards Egyptian Art all the coquetry of a woman *sur le retour* towards the charms of her youth. He works like a demon to prove that he can grasp & retain it with the same ease & tenacity that he had for Italian art 30 — ahimè! 35 — years ago. But anno Domini is too much for him. Dear Nicky remembers it all much better, no detail escapes her & she has become an animated History of Egyptian Art. Whereas B.B. & I muddle up places & things & names with the inevitability that belongs to what we always have called "Middle Age." The only difference is that I feel no responsibility at all towards 4000 B.C. & forget as easily as I enjoy & without vain regrets; whereas B.B. is striving to show he is still young enough to learn new tricks.

In any case it is all really Great Fun — we had no idea there was so much positive amusement left in life for us. It is, indeed, the Greatest Fun we have ever had. You must do it some day!

What is this about your not seeing your way to travel again? Aren't we to meet in Constantinople in September & go on to Greece in October? *We* mean to be there at any rate, with Nicky, and I hope you aren't going to fail? I understand how much you must both find to do, how distractingly occupied your lives must be, but all the same we *do* want you there with us.

We did not mean to take Egyptian politics to heart, but it has been too exciting. Lord Allenby, after successfully dealing with the riots, rushed off to England & is now returning in truimph, a characteristically British triumph, consisting in degrading himself from High Commissioner to Ambassador & handing over Egypt to the Egyptians. It may be the best course since the world got so thoroughly poisoned by Wilson's "Savagery for the Savages" rhetoric but it is very distressing. Not an Englishman among them but *knows* that the Egyptians will govern rottenly, with corruption & inefficiency & oppression of the fellaheen. But as they are all Egyptians they must be allowed to have it their own rotten way. Well, well! [1]

B.B. isn't able to judge Rivoira, but Cresswell thinks his work is positively dishonest & Patricolo (head of the Arab Monument Restoration) thinks poorly of him. B.B. says however bad he is he can't be quite so poisonous as Strzygowsky in his recent utterances.

I have a thousand things to say, but no ability to write them, as I am LAZY.

We all send much love & our hope of seeing you in Constantinople. And do write again. Better address to I Tatti.

Yours always aff.
Mary B.

To JUDGE LEARNED HAND

I Tatti
Settignano
Florence
15 December 1922

My dear Hand,

A madder man than Mr. B. there never had been seen when he received yr. letter of Sept. 14 & discovered that you had been to Florence and he not there — to speak Irish. How dard (*sic*) you! Had he not looked forward to gloating on yr. first impressions the way an old man saves up a small boy to take for the first time to a circus!

It made me so cross that I took all this time to recover & to

---

1 In 1922 "anti-colonialism" had of course not become the obligatory intellectual fashion which it is to-day.

write of my disappointment. Now I combine the confession with wishes to you both for a very Happy New Year. I shall be grateful to 1923 if it brings us together again. I doubt whether it will be on yr. side of the Ocean. I have become a very poor traveller & besides for me America is nothing but dissipation. I cannot afford it too often. Of course I am coming but not yet a while.

So the Cis-Rhenan Super-Boches persuaded you that they were frightened of the *ci-devant Boches ordinaires,* commonly called Germans! You bet! Haven't they been practicing being afraid ever since armistice day & Couéing themselves *à rebours?!?*

And yet they succeed badly. In their heart of hearts they fear not the German. Their narrow souls can hold no other great passion than the one that dominates them to the exclusion of other sentiments. That passion is hatred of England.

If you want to understand affairs in Europe never lose out of mind that under & behind everything is France's crazy hatred of England, Italy's stupid envy of England, Germany's fury with England, Holland's rage with England, Scandinavia's dislike of England, Spain's distaste for England & the Vatican's neverceasing plotting for England's downfall.

So many & so dead-in-earnest are England's enemies that I should fear for the life of that one island in the sea of political misery if the Vatican did not infallibly bring about the opposite of what it was plotting against.

Laugh & call me a crank but read out these priceless words of mine to the one American besides myself who shows first rate aptitude for international affairs, I mean Alvin Johnson.[1]

One of the most appalling fatalities of history was first England's & then our interference in the race between France & Germany as to which should be Boche-iest. It has produced a dis-equilibrium that it will take generations to right. And of

[1] Alvin Saunders Johnson, American economist.

course it can end but in one way. In this paradise which would be a heaven but for the snakes who tempt its Adams & Eves to eat of the apple of Bocherie, here we are, all "pretending" like five year olds that Santa Claus will bring us all things — yes all things, prosperity, peace, perpetual Sunday within, prestige, profit, first-super-ultra-prime-great-poweriness without. And all by believing in Mussolini & the *Stellone d' Italia.*

If you find time read Gogol's "Dead Souls" which has just been translated by Constance Garnett. It is slightly archaic, *doch bleibt es immer neu.*

And I have told you nothing about Germany. You don't deserve to know my impressions & besides they now are antiquated. The mark was 6000 when I left & now it is 35,000 to the pound.

With best regards from us both to you twain

Ever yrs.

B. Berenson

MARY BERENSON TO MR. AND MRS. KINGSLEY PORTER

I Tatti

Settignano

Florence

8 January 1925

Dearest Lucy & Kingsley,

It is just a month since you wrote a most depressed but to us very sympathetic letter about standardized Babbittania — standardized where standardization is death — in Education! Awful it sounds!! We thank God we live here like Cyclops "knowing no law"!

To have left your interesting letter unanswered so long is

accounted unto me for unrighteousness by B.B., & rightly, although one or two things have conspired to delay me.

First of all your Aegean Yachting trip is *awfully* tempting for you are *the* people we like to travel with. I waited to write to Logan, but he wants to know how large a yacht, what price, etc. And then, with his illness, he is no longer in the yachting world as he was, he has even sold his own yacht. But to go back to us, we dread the heat of July & August on the blazing sea & the furnace rocks. Then came an invitation from Mrs. Wharton[1] to take the same trip with her from April 15 — June 15, a better time of the year. But we dread her not wanting to see things with the thoroughness that B.B. and you like.

Over & above all this he says he hasn't the time at present for such an Extra, especially as he does not think we could even land on the part of Asia Minor belonging to the Turks. He wd. rather wait till it cd. be combined with things on that coast & inland. All this was not clear at first, under the stress of the two temptations, but I think now we must definitely not do it. I doubt even if we get to Constantinople, for once BB begins the work of revising his lists, he will find he has months & months of work ahead of him. At present he has finished an article he promised to give Dr. Swarzenski on the Trecento Tuscans at Frankfort, and now he must do an article on some Oxford miniatures. Meantime a nice girl from Chicago, Miss Rickert, works for 3 or 4 hours a day to get the photos into some sort of order for us when we get round to those lists.

I am the more for finishing it now, as I want to go with BB & Nicky in 1926 on the Raymond Whitcomb Co. trip *de luxe,* Round the World. Why don't you come on that? Cambodia, the S. Pacific Islands, India, Burmah, Ceylon, Java, Cochin-China, Japan, China & way stations — 5 months from N.Y. back to N.Y. Everything perfectly arranged. Of course not as slow

[1] An amusing account of Mrs. Wharton and the yachting trip is to be found in Logan Pearsall Smith: *The Unforgotten Years,* Boston (1939), pp. 269-275.

as we should like, but still not hurried & perfect comfort, wh. BB needs.

We do wish you had been in Rome with us. We saw nearly everything Early Xn, Mediaeval, & the miniatures in the Vatican Library. People were most helpful. AND the motor excursions — 10 solid weeks of golden afternoons in a country *as beautiful as Greece* & crammed full of interesting things. O what a pity you don't cut free & come over here to live!!

. . .

If you didn't join the "Society for Pure English," will send you Logan's last pamphlet on "Four Words." [1] But I daresay you have it. We had, by the way, a visit from Mr. Ivins of the Metropolitan & he talked such Pure American that we literally understood only about half of what he said. At last I lost patience & went for him! It was catastrophic!! He got on the defensive & made out a sort of case, too. But it seems a pity, all the same, to lose the capacity for direct speech. This consisted of highly coloured metaphors & slang. However, we liked him *immensely,* so far as we could get at him.

Nicky & BB both send love. I'm full of apologies for the delay. Do write again. We live & breathe your letters.

Lovingly
Mary B.

1 Tract XVII, SPE. Clarendon Press, 1924. The four words are: Romantic, Originality, Creative, Genius.

MARY BERENSON TO PROFESSOR PAUL J. SACHS

I Tatti
Settignano
Florence
14 February 1926

Dear Mr. Sachs,

The five photographs came today and we have found them most interesting. Thank you so very much.

The other day someone telephoned from Florence, and I understood the name "Sachs" and with great pleasure begged the owner of the voice to come up to lunch. When he appeared, his name was Sessions,[1] and we were very disappointed, although he is a very nice young man, a musician abroad on a fellowship and hoping to get the Guggenheim scholarship for another year or two. They say he has a lot of talent.

We hope, however, to hear sometime the voice of the authentic Sachs and have the pleasure of seeing you here again.

Believe me,

Yours sincerely,
Mary Berenson

To T. S. PERRY

Grand Hotel
Naples
2 June 1926

My dear Perry,

Yrs. of the 17th finds me at Naples where on the way back fr. Sicily we are spending some weeks exploring. I have found two

[1] Roger Sessions, the American composer.

Titians that none of us had ever paid attention to in the museum & a great Signorelli in the Royal Palace & any number of valuables in the churches. There is plenty to be discovered as you see. And in this deliciously cool, brisk weather Naples is a paradise. The surroundings are even more wonderful, but hard to explore owing to the impassableness of the roads & the murderous tendencies of the loafers.

I have at last made the acquaintance of B[enedetto]. Croce. Like most philosophers except Balfour, Santayana, Russell, W. James & Whitehead that I have known, he is very stupid or at least one-tracked in Wilsonian fashion. Also he is very ill kept altho he is rich & occupies the whole floor of a great palace in the heart of the town. But he is patently the most candid, innocent & goodest of Italians. . . .

Have you read Waley's transl. of the *Tale of Genji?* I am finishing the 2d vol. & I could read a hundred.

In Sicily I cleared up many questions & enjoyed Greek antiquity & Byzantine Art, mediaevalism & reading the ancient classics. . . .

> Devotedly
> B.B.

To T. S. PERRY

> Consuma[1]
> 13 August 1926

My dear Perry,

I got back fr. my trip south with my insides in misery & I have been in poor shape ever since. It is becoming doubtful whether I shall be able to continue travelling as I have hitherto.

---

[1] From 1923 on it was the custom of the Berenson household to move in the heat of summer to Vallambrosa where a house, Poggio allo Spina, had been rented near the village of Consuma.

I am doing it as comfortably & as carefully as I can, sparing no expense & delegating all the material troubles to others. Nevertheless the shaking about, the hotel food, the energy spent on people, added to all I give out on my job, always reduce me to a rag after a couple of months.

It was so cool all July at I Tatti & indeed is so still, as I hear, that one could easily have stayed on there. I am glad we came up here, for the quality of the air is most vivifying & the quiet unattainable in a place that is already so much of an institution as I Tatti has become. And it is so *waldeinsam.* Here we are over 3000 ft. above the sea & in the midst of beeches, firs & birches. A little [further] down are great chestnut & oak forests & *auf allen Gipfeln ist Ruh!* And we are just one hour from I Tatti.

Have you ever read Moritz's *Anton Reisner?* Moritz was no genius like Tolstoi, but his impressions of childhood & boyhood are better remembered & more sincerely recorded. Add that he must have been most self-aware & loyal to life. We are reading it now in a 2s. transl. that the Clarendon press has just brought out. That press by the way is publishing most sumptously a vol. of mine entitled "Three Essays in Method."

All good wishes to you both & affectionate greetings

B.B.

To T. S. PERRY

Hotel Cavour
Milano
24 October 1926

Dear Perry,

No, I do not expect to be present at the opening of the enlarged Fogg. I never attend such functions if I can help it. The very few times I have I felt like a cheap clown. I cannot stampede myself & for the life of me I cannot let a crowd emotion sweep me away. So I avoid all occasions where conceivably I might be expected to appear as other than the petty biped that I am so painfully aware of being.

I am doing this part of the world for the revised edition of my list whereof I must have written more than once. And I am taking advantage of the occasion to see the early mediaeval things as I never did before. My greatest self-indulgence is grubbing in libraries, poring over very early illuminated MSS. You should have seen me at the Ambrosiana here, where 35 years [ago] his present Holiness[1] used to fetch & carry for me as his successor does now. I shall have been here three weeks & day after tomorrow turn eastward. If only the wet & the cold don't drive me home.

Have you read Thérive's *Un Voyage de M. Renan?*

Ever yrs.
B.B.

To KINGSLEY PORTER

Hotel Bellevue
Dresden
8 July 1927

Dear Kingsley,

Thanks for the batch of succulent photos from every region of Spain. I smack my lips as I suck their marrow, singing your praises in my heart.

[1] Cardinal Ratti, subsequently reigning as Pius XI, had for many years been Librarian of the Ambrosiana.

You see we already are well up in the north & day after to-morrow we go to Berlin. On the 17th we leave for Sweden, Grand Hotel Royal, Stockholm till about Aug. 3 then a few days at Oslo, a week or ten days in Copenhagen & N.W. Germany & you somewhere.

Niver[1] appeared again before we left Settignano, & I liked him much better this time, BUT. I caught a glimpse of him again in Vienna BUT you can't take the flaming walls of the kingdom of art by force & mass attack. On the contrary what is chiefly wanted for that conquest is cultured great-great-great-grandfathers. Creative artists may like lotuses grow from Nile mud or any other muck. Humanistic criticism can spring only from a cultured "background."

O the joy of seeing mature, complete, absolutely competent works of art like the Titians, the Veroneses, the Raphael, the Dürer, the Rembrandts one sees here!

Much love to you both

Devotedly
B.B.

To HENRY COSTER

Consuma
6 September 1928

Dear Harry,

. . . We leave in three days for I Tatti & on the 13th we motor to Forlì, dine with Pellegrina,[2] get into the train for Brindisi & sail the following day for Constantinople. I don't

---

1 Charles Niver, an art historian.
2 Pellegrina del Turco Paolucci, who was married to Raniero Paolucci. They were established in Palazzo Paolucci and also owned a villa, Landino, near Forlì.

feel secure yet, for who knows what the "dengha" will do in the matter.

I have worked hard here & have done most of the job I had before me. I have read a good bit but rather minute stuff in connection with Byzantium. I am ploughing thro' Ernst Stein's *Geschichte des Spätromischen Reiches,* just appeared (1st vol. only). It is not [well?] written but informative & fresh.

Mary got back three weeks ago in poor enough shape but is recovering. Nicky left the same day for S. Lucido where she & hers seem happy enough. Here I have had my brother-in-law Ralph Barton Perry of Harvard & Rachel my sister. Ralph & I have had endless talk about the universe in general & Harvard in particular & as a future part of Harvard, the academy for study of art that I mean I Tatti to be when Mary & I are gone. He entered most intelligently into my world & its dreams & has not only helped me clear up my own mind, but at Harvard on his return will tell them what I mean better than I could. By the way he remembers meeting you & expects to see you at Harvard. You will find him worth while, eminently.

Cecil Pinsent,[1] who is here for the day, gave us a most vivid account of *Everyman* at Salzburg. And yet there is something of the *faux bon* in such things, something of the *Bridge of San Luis Rey* & when I try them I somehow suffer rather than enjoy them.

Address Pera Palace, Constantinople. . . .

Love to Byba.

Affectionately,

B.B.

[1] The English architect who built the libraries and laid out the garden of I Tatti.

To Henry Coster

Péra Palace Hotel
Constantinople
3 October 1928

Dear Harry,

Deus otium dedit in the shape of an extra half hour & I begin a letter. Leisure for writing is scarce. For I read till I have to dress & then incontinently we go out. We return at one, lunch & I go to bed. At three we are out again & I return so tired that I go to bed again, to read it is true, but only periodicals & narratives. After dinner again I am too somnolent for more than small talk & hearing Nicky read aloud. This all but liturgical function has however in the last ten days been exercised by Eric Maclagan, the director of the South Kensington Mus., who has joined us here, but leaves, alas! in two days. He has been intoning Gibbon & I am half horrified at my present "reaction." The old periwig strikes me this time as at once too smart, too monotonous & too mannered. Tell it not in Gath. All the same he possesses the supreme English gift of clear narrative & there is a sumptuous rutilance about his texture that hypnotizes the listener & onlooker. For you look as well as hear, so vivid are his evocations.

I was delighted with yr. letter of Sept. 11 which I found here. All that you say about politics in our country as well as abroad meets the witness in my own mind. I like particularly yr. clear grasp of the fact that the present instant is but a moment of a history which reaches back into infinity. We must willy-nilly act impulsively & too often without conscious reference to the past, but if it is understanding we are after the past cannot be too widely swept, too.

As I read the future from my acquaintance with the past, I take it that for two or three centuries at least we shall hold the central position in the world & be to a degree unknown since the better days of the Roman Empire the arbiters of the earth.

I am so sure of this & I am at the same time so sceptical about our fitness for the task that it seems to me as if the highest duty of our governing classes is to educate themselves for their terrifying responsibility so as to come out of it with no worse stains & no worse corruption than has overtaken the British aristocracy. Unhappily I see few signs of preparedness & the burthen may be piled upon your shoulders in your life-time, Harry.

No sign of yr. sister Salm. She can count on us if she appears.

Yes, S. Sophia is all you say. It is perhaps the most sumptuous building interior I have ever seen. But as a space-effect several mosques of Sinan[1] & his pupils here & in Adrianople seem far more successful achievements. I cannot begin to give impressions of this place for I could not stop. I wish life were so long that I could spend years here.

Write here till the 25th. We may stay till Nov. 6th & then Salonika & Athens.

Love to you both from all of us

Affectionately
B.B.

To Professor Paul J. Sachs

I Tatti
Settignano
Florence
17 March 1929

My dear Paul,

It was a pleasure to get your letter of Jan. 12 & to learn about some of your activities. How different from my contemplative

---

[1] Sinān (1489-1578 or 1588), the most celebrated of Ottoman architects. He was a builder of mosques and palaces and was appointed court architect by Sultan Suleiman in 1539.

dreamy life which sometimes seems more like a mirage than a career! I do not complain, I am distinguishing.

We leave in ten days for Syria & Palestine. We are to be there two months & the program I have made should take two years. There is scarcely an area of that historical region which is not sacred to a humanist like myself. June, July, Aug. & first half of Sept. we shall be here & at Vallombrosa. In the autumn we expect to go to Spain for two or three months. Need I tell you how glad we should be to see you here or even to come across you on our travels?

Now let me comment & answer yr. letter.

I am so glad to hear of all the good things yr. brother Arthur is doing for our studies. Tell him I am deeply grateful for his reference to me in his offer of fellowships. If any come to me I shall do all I can for them. . . .

Affectionately
B.B.

To T. S. Perry

Hotel Reina Victoria
Ronda
Spain
10 November 1929

Dear Friend,

My memory, which is full of things concerning the Tom Perrys, tells me that this place was a favourite of yours. Was it so long ago as the autumn of 1887 that you were here or was it later? On our way to Spain we passed thro' another place that I connect with you. It was Les Eaux Chaudes. Did you not spend the summer of '87 there? How I envied you & how I missed you while I frowsted a solitary in piping hot Paris.

Perhaps you would not be flattered but you certainly would be surprised if you could look into my brain & see what a place the Tom Perrys take up there. Few days go by without something connected with them is flashed upon the screen of awareness from the depths of memory.

So I was inordinately glad to receive the letter that reached me somewhere in the south of France when I was on my way hither. It was good to learn how much zest you retained for life & how you were enjoying your work. I loved to hear of it & I hope you will feel the inclination & find the leisure to tell me more.

How often I have articulately regretted that the necessities of my career separated me from the enjoyment of the society of both of you, & of your friends.

I assure you it was with a thrill of affection that I saw Mrs. Grew[1] a year ago. I took great care not to show too much & alas she went away so that I was disappointed of the expectation of seeing more of her.

As for myself I am again in Spain for the fifth or sixth time. Who knows whether I shall get back! Not that I do not expect to go on travelling, but there is so much else to see & I am greedy for it all & to see over & over again. And I have given up all expectation of seeing India or the farther East.

You would find a different Spain from what you knew. The inns are clean, the food tolerable & the communications fair. When one recalls the horrors of Medina del Campo or Bobadilla forty years ago! [2]

We expect to linger on here into Dec. & then to return to

---

[1] Mrs. Joseph Grew, wife of the American diplomatist, was the daughter of T. S. Perry.

[2] The two most celebrated railway junctions in Spain. I do not know to what "horrors" (an exaggeration?) Berenson was referring as existing ca. 1890. I can testify personally that they were excellent and interesting junctions in 1919 when I first saw them — i.e., ten years before the date of B.B.'s letter.

Florence. But if you write please address me to Baring Bros. London.

Affectionate greetings to Margaret.

Ever devotedly

B. Berenson

To Mrs. T. S. Perry

I Tatti

Settignano

Florence

21 January 1930

Dear Friend,

I got back three or four days ago & found the letters of T. S. Perry. I began to read them at once & have just finished them.

How playful, how genial, how delightfully written. They remind me of Chas. Lamb's.

And Mr. Robinson's introduction is a beautiful bit of work. A friend could scarcely be more truthfully & yet more affectionately presented, or in more charming phrase.

T. S. P. has been very lucky in both the volumes that commemorate him. Both are literature in the sense that I should have read with pleasure without being acquainted with their subject. . . .

With affectionate greetings

Devotedly yours

B.B.

To Professor Paul J. Sachs

I Tatti
Settignano
Florence
16 February 1930

Dear Paul,

. . .

I am not very happy about Kingsley. I regard his settling in Ireland with alarm.[1] I wonder on how many blarney stones he will sit, & Lucy with him. He, like myself, may not be made for teaching or administration, but he is made to be a student. I cannot understand this shrinking from everything classical & his longing for the backwashiest puddles & stagnant pools of civilization. I suppose he too is a tree that the gods will not allow to pierce the sky.

With cordial greetings from all of us to both of you

Affectionately yours
B.B.

To Henry Coster

Sainte-Claire Le Château
Hyères (Var)
23 December 1930

Dear Harry,

This is not a letter but a greeting. I send you both my good wishes for Merry Xmas & a Happy New Year.

[1] Kingsley Porter had bought a nineteenth century castle in County Donegal. (He died there in 1933.) He had become more and more interested in Celtic remains, and this, like Chandler Post's interest in Spanish primitives, seemed rather to distress Berenson, who felt that one should have "one foot on the Acropolis and one in Florence," as he once told me.

I expect to be back about Jan. 18th & look forward to seeing you. We must meet oftener than last winter.

Here it is enchanting as weather, Eden-like as landscape & Mrs. Wharton is at her best in her own house.

When not driving, walking & talking I am reading Bülow's Memoirs.[1] They are particularly interesting to me as I followed at the time the events he chronicles & mythicizes.

Affectionately

B.B.

To HENRY COSTER

Kairouan

3 April 1931

Dear Harry,

I am sending you an article by Ch. Saumagne, an acquaintance we made at Tunis, on la Paix Vandale. You see he goes as far as Fustel [de Coulanges] or Dopsch in refusing to credit the northern invaders with the destruction of Ancient civilization. In talk he told me that the Vandals revived literature at Carthage & had a court of men of letters about them.

Return this pamphlet to I Tatti when you have done with it.

Our first fortnight here has been thoroughly satisfactory & everything well beyond expectations. The landscape is lovelier, the hotels are better, the "Roman" remains more interesting & more important, but most unexpected of all is the unspoiled Orientalism of a town like this where even in the European quarter there is scarcely a jarring note & in the Arab town not the least touch that one would have different. Everything here

---

1 Bernard von Bülow, the fourth Chancellor (1900-1909) of the Bismarckian Reich and Imperial German Ambassador to Italy in 1914-15. His Memoirs have been translated into English (4 vols. Boston, 1931-32).

is as much early Romanesque as it is late Baroque in Italy & Empire in France & I dare say their souls — I mean of all peoples — match their clothes & their architecture, both vestures of the spirit.

The Vandal does not seem to have been a Vandal at all but the Arab was one to the extent at least that he wrenched capitals & columns from their places & carted them hither by the many hundreds to construct this town & its great mosque. In that mosque there is not a capital that is not interesting & few that are not late Antique.

As they are overwhelmingly fourth & fifth & sixth century they witness to the prosperity of this country at a time of supposed distress. It looks as if we shall have to re-write the history of those centuries in the teeth of lying Church Fathers & their parrot-like copyists.

It would have been great fun to have you with us on this tour to discuss matters as they came up. Someday perhaps.

Ask Alda for our address when you feel like writing.

Love from all of us to both of you.

Affectionately
B.B.

To the Crown Prince of Sweden[1]

Hotel Aletti
Alger
4 May 1931

Sir, I have just got here from the borders of the desert where posts were infrequent and newspapers intermittent. We have

[1] Prince Gustaf Adolf, the present King, who succeeded to the throne on October 29, 1950, as Gustaf VI Adolf.

been wandering about east and south for the last seven weeks, impelled by vague curiosity and the desire to see sites like Kairouan and Timgad. We have been overwhelmed with surprise at the beauty of the ancient remains, at the splendour and variety of the scenery and the abundance of material for my own special studies. I do not mean Italian art, which in a sense is now behind me, but the pathology of form which led from the Antique to the Mediaeval. Nowhere else does the disease begin so early, offer such an abundance of material and prove so conclusively that it is not attached to any given epoch but to all declining civilizations and to all civilizations that have not been able to assimilate civilizations superior to their own. Deformations, distortions of early Greek, of Punic, of Hellenistic and of so-called Roman tell the tale.

Then you can study here better than almost anywhere else the arrested development of styles. Everything tends to get crystallized or mummified in what we should call proto-Romanesque, and in native hands remains so till to-day. They still are making "Merovingian" or "Visigothic" jewelry, still carving and decorating in a rustic Byzantine mode.

But how enchanting to find oneself as at Kairouan a thousand years back, with people living, dressing and building as simply, as unconsciously and with as much unstudied dignity and largeness, as they did then.

I must thank you for your letter of January, mostly about Cyprus. It has decided us to follow in your footsteps next autumn and your letter will be our guide.

Bernard Berenson

To HENRY COSTER

Hotel Transatlantique
Micmelet
Algérie
12 May 1931

Dear Harry,

Yrs. of April 20th was a delight. What you suggest about the bad name of the Vandals, that it was chiefly due to their piracy, had never occurred to me. I shall try to see Saumagne again before embarking at Tunis on the 21st, & hear what he has to say about it.

The disappearance of Romanity, including of course the Xian wing thereof from N. Africa, remains a puzzle. It must be that it was urban merely & with the decline & total ruin of these nothing of it was left over. It remains an amusing speculation as to what kind of community would have emerged here had Islam not intervened.

I am finishing vol. 8, the last that has been published, of Gsell's book on North Africa in antiquity. It is neither an inspiring nor suggestive work but encyclopedically informing, The picture you get of the Romans is not pleasant. The nearest approach to a decent trait among them was state-worship another aspect of the Molochism they are credited with destroying. When they are individually worthy you feel that it is as a *stunt*. Of course I do not mean to imply that they were worse than others. I doubt whether they were better in the mass & whether there were not ever so many more civilized individuals among the Hellenistic populations of the same ages.

Of course I am interested in what is going on in Spain.[1] Revolutions have a way, particularly the young Turk[2] & the

[1] Don Alfonso XIII had abdicated in April 1931. Berenson is referring to the advent of the second Spanish Republic.
[2] 1908.

Russian ones started out almost angelically. So I do not feel re-assured about the way it will go on in Spain. It is all a question of what grip the present rulers will have & what good will there is on the part of their opponents. My sympathies however go out to a people whose chief grievance against their King is that he sold them to a dictator.[1] Of course no little will depend upon the results of the revolution in Spain.

No need for such here. There is no display of force, no stunts of any sort but so far as the wayfarer can see Algeria seems a paradise. Perfect roads, flourishing towns, well tilled fields, plenty of timber, excellent inns, not over-populated — in short a perfectly run & running organism. And it is enchant-ingly beautiful. We hope to continue next spring with W. Algeria & Morocco.

We shall be at Hotel Excelsior, Naples, from the 27th. I want to see you before you leave for America.

Love from all of us to you both

Affectionately
B.B.

To Judge Learned Hand

I Tatti
Settignano
Florence
24 October 1931

Dear B.,

I am glad you had a favourable impression of Ascoli.[2] I hope he will learn conversational English soon enough to profit by it.

[1] Miguel Primo de Rivera, Marquis de Estella, who was in office from 1923-30.
[2] Max Ascoli, now editor of *The Reporter,* an American weekly.

It is one of the serious handicaps of international relations that so few European intellectuals speak any language but their own. It is no less unfortunate that diplomats, dreamers, disreputable "Counts" in search of rich wives do speak other languages than their own. So between those who have a lot to say & can't & those who have a lot to lie about & can, misunderstanding between nations is not diminishing.

I have been living here some forty years & I have never yet encountered an Italian intellectual whom I felt to be at all himself when speaking any other language than his own. And I know very few who catch all the natural spontaneity of expression when I am conversing with them in English.

So my instinctive course is to get French, German & Italians to speak their own language & put up with my misuse of it.

What a curse the confusion of tongues has been. If there were but one language aphasia would be confined to relatively small & therefore harmless groups or even to individuals, whereas now I fear that the more people of different speech meet, the less they understand each other. The nearer they are to each other in speech the more dangerous the misunderstandings.

I need not tell you that I was startled & distressed by the death of Morrow.[1] When I saw his picture I was amazed to see how much he had aged in the ten years I had not seen him. Ten years ago he was barely middle-aged in looks & in this picture he looked like a worn out old man. How he must have burnt.

Mary is at the nursing home recovering from an operation.

Love to you both & to Walter. What splendid homilies he is writing!

Yours
B.B.

[1] Dwight Morrow, the American Ambassador to Mexico.

To Professor Paul J. Sachs

I Tatti
Settignano
Florence
4 July 1933

My dear Paul,

I enclose a statement of what it would cost Harvard to run this place, if we handed it over but kept on living here ourselves to the end.

When we left it would cost perhaps a fifth or even a fourth more; for while we are here ourselves we pay for all sorts of odds and ends that you, i.e. Harvard, would have to provide for.

As you see, I have left the items unchanged into dollars for obvious reasons.

This wobbling but ever declining dollar may play the mischief with fixed incomes like my own. Already I am getting only 14 instead of 19.75 Italian lire for each dollar and I don't need to tell you what a difference it makes.

In other respects we are getting on tolerably. Mary is very happy going over my early letters to her and putting them into shape for eventual publication, although not in my life-time. She has at last found the proper channel for her activities, and I hope it will give her more zest for life than she has had for a long time.

As for me, I have finished the revision of the Verrocchio-Credi-Leonardo chapters for the new edition of my Florentine drawings. I next take up Michelangelo. Before doing that we are going to Ferrara, Milan, etc., etc. for ten days or so, if the heat, come at last, is not excessive.

If you can spare the time write and tell me how the world looks from Cambridge and what prospects there are for the continuity of our kind of civilization.

With love to you and Meta from both of us,

Ever yours,
B.B.

[Enclosed in Letter of 4 July 1933]

Upkeep of Library (including Italian books and magazines, photos, bindings, Librarian's salary and lighting) roughly	Lire it.	75.000
Upkeep of Garden		35.000
Heating		16.000
Insurances of house, garden & estate		6.500
Taxes		16.000
General repairs		10.000
Insurance for books and works of art		£340
Books, magazines & photos from England, Germany, Austria, Spain, Holland, roughly		£350
Books, magazines and photos from France, roughly	Fcs.	12.000
Books, magazines & photos from U.S.A., roughly		$500

To JUDGE LEARNED HAND

Gratz
Styria
24 September 1933

Dear B.,

Thanks for yr. dear letter which reached me in Vienna yesterday. I left it this morning, lunched half way here with Werfel,[1] who besides being almost a great writer, is an angelic & enchanting human being & am now pernoctating in this little provincial capital, nestling in the midst of its beautiful heights.

No, you were no burden to Mary. On the contrary it did her a world of good to have you to think of instead of her own miseries. She wrote every day full & lyrical accounts of you both all your utterances & ideas & joys & sorrows.

1 Franz Werfel (1890-1945) Austrian (Bohemian) dramatist and poet.

How much I regret that I missed yr. visit I will not attempt to tell you. I can only say that there is none I could have missed more.

Yes, the outlook at home is not pleasant. If the New Deal succeeds I should not feel happy over it. I distrust every type of soterism & every kind of messiahism. I do not believe in the new economic doctrines of getting prosperous by overspending etc., etc.

You know what I mean & probably think as I do. The same impatience is probably the bottom reason for Hitlerism & every kind of fascism & indeed of Bolshevism itself.

The tide is with all these materialistic mysticisms. The like of us are powerless & can but grin & bear it.

Culturally it is even worse than Xian Science which has the same roots.

I leave Austria after nearly four weeks, in despair over the wallowing voluptuously in the irrational that I have encountered among most of the people I met.

History may be best studied perhaps in the records of man's attitude towards the irrational — whether he abandons himself to it without a struggle as people younger than ourselves are doing, or whether they fight against it to the last ditch, as our generation was brought up to do.

I suppose it would be cruel to expect you to write to me out of the depths of yr. life in New York. I wish you could. And I cherish the hope of seeing you soon. Am I too abandoning myself to the irrational?

Miss Mariano sends her best remembrances to you both & I affectionate greetings

Yours

B.B.

To HENRY COSTER

I Tatti
Settignano
Florence
19 November 1933

My dear Harry,

Thanks for your letter about my sister Rachel.[1] And will you thank Byba for having written as well.

My sister's death has reduced me to a numbness which makes it hard to say anything about her. Even to her husband I have found no words, not even halting ones.

I envy you feeling that you can perhaps cope with the present situation & emerge with assured leisure for study & writing.

By the way Mrs. Wharton, who is here, spoke with pleasure of your sketch about the cats.

Of ourselves there is little to say that is cheery. Mary's health seems worse rather than better & keeps me in a tremor of anxiety. Only less worrying are financial questions. I feel helpless & indeed am helpless. I have been for many years the spoilt child of a favouring accident. Now I suppose I shall have to pay for it.

And pay I should if I had my Mary in good health & I Tatti off my hands. The problem of what to do with it, seeing Harvard won't take it without adequate endowment, is not one I can easily cope with.

But these hours of St. Martin's summer[2] are lovely with the alcoholic fragrance of the decaying leaves & the amber foliage on ground & trees. And with Nicky's powerful help I get forward with my work.

Mrs. Wharton wishes you would write about Calabria. I wish you both would come back soon. You are the only country-

[1] Mrs. Ralph Barton Perry had just died.
[2] In America known as Indian summer but Berenson uses the English term.

man I have here that counts. Even if I see you little your presence in Florence comforts me.

With love to you both

Always yrs.

B.B.

To Professor Paul J. Sachs

I Tatti
Settignano
Florence

Private and confidential
[n.d. but undoubtedly November 1933]

Dear Paul,

In the first place let me thank you for having thought, you & dear Meta, of cabling to me about Rachel's death.

There is nothing to say about death. But the living, for poor Ralph one cannot do too much. I know you will do all that is possible to comfort him.

Then I want to thank you for your loyalty & devotion in forwarding my intentions with regard to I Tatti.

The dollar has already sunk lower than I expected when I wrote from Vienna less than two months ago. I still hope however to get thro' 1934 without troubling you. As for later that is as our Procrustean Dictator decrees.

Now I want to say a word about another matter & I hope I am not indiscreet.

I understand Hendy[1] has left or is leaving the B.M.F.A. Two days ago Joseph Lindon Smith was here & asked why Sachs &

---

1 Sir Philip Hendy, as he later became, was at this time Curator of Paintings at the Boston Museum of Fine Arts and later became Director of the National Gallery, succeeding Kenneth Clark (now Sir Kenneth Clark) who is alluded to in this letter. Mr. John Walker, also alluded to, became the Director of the (American) National Gallery in Washington.

Forbes could not produce a curator of pictures for the B.M.F.A. My answer was that they could but that Boston is still so colonial minded that it is grateful to England for giving her one of her sons whom she has no intention of using herself.

So to get to business why not try to get Johnnie Walker III for the post of curator or director of pictures at the B.M.F.A. Of course he may not want to accept the offer, salary presumably being no object to him. But let not the trustees flatter themselves that they can import an Englishman or Continental European who will do as well. The only charge that can be brought against Johnnie Walker, besides of course that of being a real & not a pseudo gentleman, is his age.

But he is as old as Kenneth Clark who has recently been appointed director of the National Gallery. By the way every serious paper announcing his appointment stated as his chief title that Kenneth Clark had studied for two years with Mr. Berenson. So has Johnnie Walker.

After Walker I would propose Dan Thompson.[1] But let us live on our own hump.[2] It is time that we tried American trained men for our museum posts, even if they stumble a bit at the start.

Affectionate greetings to you & Meta.

Yours

B.B.

[1] Daniel V. Thompson is the author of *The Materials of Mediaeval Painting* (New Haven, 1936), for which Berenson wrote a Foreword.

[2] Berenson lived only twelve years of his long life in the United States but had some of that perhaps exaggerated patriotism so common among voluntary exiles.

To Judge Learned Hand

I Tatti
Settignano
Florence
13 December 1933

Dear B.,

My congratulations on the marriage of yr. daughter Frances to such a delectable young man. I wish I too could see him & make the acquaintance of her as well.

I write to tell you that I know far worse handwritings than yours, mine for instance. I absolve you in fact from reading further, for I have nothing to say worth deciphering. I just want to send you my good wishes for a Merry Xmas & a Happy New Year. It sounds almost cynical to do. But that is or would be flippant. The less likely a wish is to be realized the more reason for wishing it *fortiter*. And besides are we not back in the magical universe where miracles are as common as inventions in our recent geometrical world? And so the miracle may happen allowing us to be merry at Xmas & happy on the New Year. Only it is difficult for old habitués of geometrical seeing & thinking to behold the vision mirific even when it radiates all around us.

Jesus of Nazareth passeth by & we take no notice. All over central Europe — from Greenland's icy mountains to India's coral strands — babes & sucklings are getting impatient. They are telegraphing to their various *Führers* for peremptory declarations as to just what day & hour of next week they are to be led in martial array to the conquest of the cosmos. This is not parabolic but literal. For such is the education the little children of both sexes are receiving.

Do you know Elizabeth Ellis née Wardour? Of course you do. She was here for some time & we had much talk & she made a noise as if but at my back I always heard a voice telling me to put not my trust in princesses. She told me Felix Frankfurter might be coming this way soon. I wish he would.

How strange it is that I who lived in America from my eleventh to my twenty-second year only, yet feel so much more at home with an American of our kind than with any other biped whatever. I have lived now for 46 years with Italians, with French, with Germans, with English people & despite all temptations I still prefer the American. It must be the effect of one's plastic formative years when one was moulded & given cardinal points for life. How much more of my self seems to find satisfaction when I am with you or aforesaid Elizabeth Ellis or Mrs. Wharton. This last mentioned lady spent a fortnight with us just now. I got such a comfy feeling just being in the same room with her. We have known so many people together, travelled together, gossiped together, discussed together, that now it seems quite enough just being together. She is such a Tory & I the last almost of would-be aristocrats.

By this time you either have stopped deciphering or learned to read me like a book & discovered it as little worth while.

We are reading a long & fascinating one, a chronicle of Jew life in Russia just before the war. In English it is called *The Three Cities* by Schalom Asch.

Affectionate greetings to you both

Yours

B.B.

To Henry Coster

Poggio Allo Spino
Consuma
(Prov. di Firenze)
3 September 1934

Dear Harry,

For weeks I have been expecting a letter but no word from you has reached me. I am sorry for you are often in my thoughts & I should like to know how you are faring & what you are thinking.

After several days of Byronic weather it is contritely pure & clear this morning. Even in one's 70th year mere living would be a joy in normal conditions. But one worry swallows up all others. It is Mary's condition. Ever since we came up here, now more than six weeks ago, she has been getting worse. She seldom comes down & then sits bundled up, a huddled mass of misery. The worst is that there seems to be no adequate cause for so much distress. We fear it is mental. Apparently no organ in our bodies seems so subject to suggestion as the bladder & the psycho-analytical reading to which Mary has abandoned herself for years never strays far from that part of our anatomy. She pins her hope to a cure at Fiuggi & is going there with Logan[1] in a day or two.

But for that worry we should have had a delightful summer. Ralph Perry my widowed brother-in-law was here with his son Bernard & Logan & Desmond MacCarthy, all these for long stays. Eric Maclagan for a few days. We had just the kind of talk that I most enjoy & often the Serristori & Riri Visconti joined us.

In a day or two Nicky (who has but returned from Sorrento) & I will be left alone & without plans. If I don't dash to Moravia I may linger here if it does not get too cold, stay on & work. I must be back at the end of the month to receive the

1 Her brother, Logan Pearsall Smith.

Walter Lippmanns. When they are gone & Mary can be left, Nicky & I may join the Doro Levis in Crete. I fear that our future absences will have to be brief.

Only a chronicle. Repay me with interest & tell me more. Affectionate greetings to you both

Yours
B.B.

To Judge Learned Hand

Poggio Allo Spino
Consuma
(Prov. di Firenze)
26 September 1934

My dear B.,

Thanks for your letter from Windsor. It was a real letter & one receives few nowadays. You made me wish I were with you all, with you both, with Dow, with Littell. I should have enjoyed your presence, your essence, your talk. I should have loved yr. landscape background. I know it & recall it with such pleasure that occasionally when out walking here at 3000 ft. above the sea, when glades & hillsides & whiffs of woody odours recall the New England hill country, I feel transported to the days of early youth & all its dreams & yearnings.

It would have been fun if we could have joined forces in your or this Arcady. Here I had my two brothers-in-law, Logan Pearsall Smith & Ralph Perry (with his son Bernard), Desmond MacCarthy & Eric Maclagan. The last two are as agreeable & satisfactory Englishman as you will find nowadays. They are game for any talk & good on their legs.

By the way, you were here in very bad weather & can have

no notion of the variety & beauty of the walks. There are so many that we always are discovering new ones.

But to return to company, we talked literature & people incessantly. We all have read & all are old enough to have known men & women of all sorts & what is important we either have known the same lot or known of them. We seldom touched on events or principles. One takes the second more & more for granted as one's age increases & events are too raw to be touched.

You do not write words of comfort about what is going on in our distressful country. How could one? I suppose the optimist could only say with Moses during the Exodus, "Have forty years of patience & you will reach the promised land." You were such an accurate prophet three years ago, that yr. vaticinations alarm me. But what can one do! For instance. In the last two years every time I have sold out holdings or changed money I have lost — invariably. One's income dwindles & what remains loses daily in purchasing value over here.

I wish you were here to look over the landscape. The early morning air is sweet. The sky is serene without a fleck. *Auf allen Gipfeln ist Ruh'*. The temperature is 65° at the open window where I sit. It is pleasant & I have had mornings like this for nearly a month, left here alone with Nicky, to work, to walk, to read. It is a life that suits me for months together. I linger on & wish I could stay another month. The cold would drive me down, & besides Mary & Logan return in a day or two from Fiuggi, a cure to the south of Rome.

They went there because Mary has been very ill ever since her return from England. Always the same bladder. You would think it was a Zeppelin from the place it took in my worries. She finally got it into her dear head that Fiuggi would cure her. It has not & there we are.

I can only fancy that her pains are largely mental & that its attacks are of an intermittent or recurrent nature. I hope that the present fit will soon be over. I can only hope. The doctors seem to be helpless.

Ralph & Bernard Perry were full of stories, all to your credit, all whetting one's appetite for your talk whether grave or gay.

I have read some bogy books worth recommending. Harris's *Hitler Over Europe* is a gruesome story of German preparation for what has at various intervals of history wrought them up to terrible deeds — the insatiable lust for empire, *die Herrschaft der Welt* of the Wagner Trilogy. Much better literature is the so-called "Berlin Diary" (published in Engl. by Jerrold, London) in which Gen. Bredow tells from the inside what led up to Hitler's triumph.

I fear you do not read Italian so I cannot recommend the best book of any sort that has come my way in months & by far the best about Russia & its (& our) problems that I have seen at all. It is Scarfoglio's *Russian Tour*. If it gets translated into English or French I shall send it to you.

I suppose you are back in N.Y. & will not have the leisure to write. Get Florence to do so, if you can persuade her.

Affectionate greetings to both of you.

Yours
B.B.

To Henry Coster

I Tatti
Settignano
Florence
30 October 1935

Dear Harry,

Yrs. of the 12th was worth waiting for. It was sweet of you, but just like you, to look up my mother & write me such a charming & vivid account of her. Yes I owe her a great deal, in fact all the zest & even the gayety & a certain ease of throwing off care which now that I am 70 I realize I possess more than most people. The ravening curiosity both in breadth & depth I get from my father. It would be hard to exaggerate what he & his friends did for me when I was in my 11th year.

To turn to more interesting matters, namely yr. own affairs. In the first place let me urge you not to submit to an operation. Our doctors are fanatics about the use of the knife. Quite natural in descendants of Yankees whose only relaxation consisted of whittling either on a fence or in the village store. Consult the best diagnosticians on this side before you submit to an operation.

While on the subject of health let me tell you that Mary is home again & although feeble enough, she has no pains & sits up at all meals & hopes to get stronger. She got back four days ago.

Nicky & I left Consuma Sept. 28th with Johnnie [Walker] & went to Rimini where Truelle[1] joined us. Together we visited Urbino & Ravenna & Nicky & I ended up at Venice where we remained nearly three weeks. It was the most leisurely stay I made there in years & I enjoyed every minute of it, particularly the dawns & sunsets. Venice itself . . . remains the greatest artefact of our race. The individual works of art, the masterpieces of a Titian even are comparatively negligeable. And yet, how I did enjoy this. An exhibition of some of his pictures was going, placed most splendidly in the sumptuous surroundings of Palazzo Pesaro. Some of the pictures one saw almost for the first time. I had been scores of times in the presence of the Martyrdom of Lawrence but at the Gesuiti you could see bits only at a time. Now I could enjoy the whole of it & apart from its great poetry, so heroic, so majestic, it turned out to have all the paint qualities of the late Rembrandt.

1 Jacques Truelle, French diplomatist, who was twice attached to Embassies in Rome, first to the Quirinal and at the time of this letter to the Holy See.

So I had a good time in Venice despite public & private anxieties. I have never been able to take the Italo-Abyssinian dispute tragically. I still remain convinced that a *combinazione* will be found. You need not plan to remain away. I hope you can not only come but stay.

I have no idea what learned news reaches you. Pirenne is dead to my great regret. There was still work in him although he was 78. That E. Stein, the Byzant. historian has gone to America you may know already. I have forgotten to what institution. I fervently hope it is not to that *bouillon de culture*, the German-Jew refugee University. Jews like all "races" with an inferiority complex do not enjoy each other's society & make their best effort when with others.

Breasted [1] came to see me in Sept. A nimble, keen, utterly unpedantic Yankee scholar, one we can wholeheartedly be proud of & at the same time a delightful *Unsereiner*.[2] We had a splendid time together & became real friends.

Morra, Giuliana Benzoni, Johnnie Walker & Alberti have been with us off & on. Alberti turns out to read aloud as nobody.

My best to you both.

Affectionately

B.B.

1 James Henry Breasted, American archaeologist.
2 Berenson was fond of rendering "one of us" by the single German word.

To Judge Learned Hand

I Tatti
Settignano
Florence
17 November 1935

Dear B.,

. . .

Now as for news — the great news is that my Mary got back some three weeks ago from Vienna. She is out of pain & for the present her troubles are dormant at least & perhaps gone. But they have broken her down, she is low spirited, discouraged & weak.

Luckily she has the great-grandson with her & his jests & miracles entertain & keep her going. Despite her own protestations to the contrary she is getting stronger & in fact comes down to meals. In a way it is hard on her, for our friends are more & more Continentals & she is so very Anglo-Saxon. She is lazy about conversing in Ital., French or German although she could an she would. And way down little interests her but the fruit of her womb unto the nth generation.

As for myself I am still at my Flor. Drawings — this time so nearly ready that I am plunged in the agony of coming to terms with the publisher. It is the Clarendon Press & they are so frightened that I almost pity them & am sorely tempted to tell them to go to Heaven.

The weather is as perfect as it always seems to be when mankind is quaking. I remember just about this time of the year in 1914 remarking to Edmond Gosse on the glorious autumn we were having. He agreed & recalled it had been just as fine in 1870.

By the way, the most creative young writer of Italy, Alberto Moravia is going to New York. He remembers meeting you at Consuma & would be grateful if you & Frances would hold out a hand to him. He wants to see all kinds of people. Write when you can, but never doubt of my affection.

Love to you both
B.B.

To Judge Learned Hand

I Tatti
Settignano
Florence
17 January 1936

My dear B.

I enclose one of the letters I sent you early in Sept. It has just been returned to me.

Thanks for yr. interesting letter. I fear I agree only too much about not "monkeying with the buzzsaw while in motion." Big communities have grown too heavy & too complicated for our brains & should be treated like forces of nature & not like Swiss watches. More than some chance invention that may smash us in a moment, I fear the probability that we are getting too huge & unwieldy to survive & must perish in consequence as the antediluvian monsters did.

O for a talk with you & our kind! What a spectacle of panic, mass emotion & unmanageableness our fellow bipeds are offering, each boo-hoo-ing at the other.

My best to you both

Yrs.
B.B.

To Henry Coster

Sainte-Claire Le Château
Hyères (Var)
28 February 1936

Dear Harry,

I received three copies of yr. book. I enclose the receipt of
the Florence library. My friend Tisserant of the Vatican must
be away for I have not heard fr. him, having with yr. book
sent him a letter saying I hoped before long to introduce you
to him.

Let me thank you for the way you speak about me in yr. preface. I have not been spoilt that way.

Knowing that I was coming out of Tophet to spend some days
at Mrs. Wharton's I put off writing in the expectation of having much to say that I should not feel it expedient to utter in
Mussolinia. On reflection it occurs to me that probably you are
far better informed than I am, that my comments would have
little savour & less originality & that cursing & fuming would be
unsuitable to pen & ink. So I forgo. Much as I, for my own-
self, regret yr. absence, you do well to keep away fr. the eu-
phoristic hell that Italy seems now to be. The impending
economic consequences will inevitably be so disastrous that
they, the Mussolinians, seem frantically to turn away. As you
must have read they seem almost eager for a *Catastrophen-
politik*.

Personally our own friends are what they were. Most of them
including Ojetti[1] think & talk as we do. One gets tired of re-
peating the same things & yet it is hard to talk of anything
else. I read a good deal & have finished my *Drawing* book. The
Clarendon Press grew so annoying & I must add so prevaricat-
ing, that I jumped at the unsolicited offer of the Chicago Univ.

---

[1] Ugo Ojetti (1871-1946), Italian man of letters, stylist, literary critic. Founder
of several periodicals of art and literature.

Press to bring out the *Drawings* with all the illustrations I wanted & at the accessible price I demanded. Now there is still the burthen of proof-reading but I hope to turn soon to the next book.

Mary clings more & more to her bed & complains of aches & sleeplessness. Her great-grandson (who is a pet) consoles her for a great deal of suffering.

Nicky is here with me & we return to I Tatti in ten days at most. She & I may summer out of Italy but not necessarily in England where Mary will probably be.

Write about yr. present work & how things seem to be drifting & whither in our own country. What a world!

Love to you both
B.B.

To Henry Coster

Settignano
7 April 1936

Dear Harry,

I forward this & thank you for your most interesting letter of March 17. You make me feel as if the situation at home were intrinsically more alarming than over here & that our problems are more difficult & that we are not going toward a solution. About matters over here I am relatively calm. I do not expect war in a predictable time. I do expect the triumph of evil & barbarism, but if war can be staved off we may recover from both ever so much sooner than communities used to [do] when likewise overwhelmed in the past.

I envy you Charleston wh. I know from German (!) publications only. I am going to Rome to-morrow for some three weeks to begin my book on the Decline & Recovery.[1] Mary has her daughter Ray Strachey for my absence.

This is no letter, but an appeal for one from you.

Affectionate greetings to you both

Yours

B.B.

To HENRY COSTER

Grusbach, Moravia

28 August 1936

Dear Harry,

It was a great pleasure to read yr. letter, to get yr. news & to learn yr. opinion of the situation at home. I got more out of it than fr. all I read in various dailies, weeklies & monthlies. You would make a valuable political writer & it is perhaps a pity you don't.

Here the situation is not reassuring. After the triumphant reassertion of brutal force & fraud on the part of the entire Italian people, followed by the entire German people & left unopposed by England, France & the rest of us, what is one to expect! We are cooking up for a desperate series of religious wars betw. totalitarianism & humanism, & I am far from sure that humanism will win out in the present historical horizon. We may be in for a highly mechanized Paraguayan[2] world-state & I cannot imagine what kind of humanity will come out of it, or eventually get the better of it.

---

[1] An old project of Berenson's, long entertained, never completed. *The Decline and Recovery of the Arts* is to be understood.

[2] The reference is presumably to the Jesuit period in Paraguay.

Nicky & I are having a few days of rest here with the Khuens, dear friends wh. you may have met at I Tatti. She is the daughter of the Lützows. It is in this weather enchanting & real country. No scenery, just forest & field. There still are fine horses to drive about with & to ride. Everything still the good life, but furious nationalism is constantly drawing nearer.

You have perhaps heard of our wanderings in Yugoslavia. They were interesting, profitable & altogether delightful. At the very end Nick & I spent a day with Prince Paul.[1] Hearing him talk for hours together did one's heart good. He took such a European & human view of politics & as regent he has a certain power; he may just possibly help to avert or at least defer the threatening horrors.

Have you ever read Delbruck's *Geschichte der Kriegeskunst?* I am enjoying it not only as an intellectual treat but for all the information it gives me about a question that has always interested me, the number of inhabitants in various periods & countries.

I am due at 16 Fitzhardinge Street, London W.1., Sept. 8 & shall probably stay there till Oct. 12 when we shall go to Paris for three or four weeks. Baring Bros., 8 Bishopsgate, London E.C. 2, always finds me. I look forward so much to seeing you & if you come via Paris early in November you still may find me there.

With love to you both fr. Nick as well as myself.

Ever yrs.
B.B.

1 Prince Paul of Yugoslavia, the then Prince Regent.

To Judge Learned Hand

I Tatti
Settignano
Florence
23 December 1936

My dear B.,

My best wishes to you & Frances for a Happy New Year & a 1937 that will not be worse than 1936. There is plenty of room for improvement.

I cannot say that it looks as if we were in for anything better. The plot cooked up in Berlin last winter against Spain is one of the most sinister & Satanic events in history. I know of nothing so deliberately planned to drive the extreme elements in a country crazy & to destroy this country's treasured up civilization. It is a monstrous deed & utterly discouraging spectacle. And perhaps it is only the herald of far worse.

Few see as black as I do & let us hope they are right. Meanwhile it leaves me to stew in my own juice with nobody to talk to. The worst is that in the 50 & more years that I have followed international matters closely, my pessimism has never been disappointed & my optimism — my general attitude — very often.

Write & tell me what you prognosticate for America now that Roosevelt is in again with a mandate to do as he likes. I hope it will not mean crippling culture so as to raise the standard of life for the masses by a degree that will bring them up to the level where men sit & yawn & are bored & bored till they do anything for a change.

Leisure is the problem of the not remote future. The masses will take it for a stone given them in place of the bread they have asked for.

Tell me how you are faring & what prospect there is of seeing you next summer. Plan to pay us a long visit at Consuma. It would make us happy. . . .

Affectionate greetings

Yours

B.B.

To Reginald Nicholson[1]

Paphos
[Cyprus]
14 May 1937

. . . My own impression of the situation here is that given human nature both in governors and governed, the English are running the place invisibly, inaudibly, with no pomp, no display, to everybody's advantage. And yet the articulate Cypriote is really dissatisfied, or pretends to be so. Some go so far as to deny any superiority to English rule. They say the oppression is not so manifest but just as great as under Italy in Rhodes. When you come down to concrete cases they are of the kind that are inherent in human situations everywhere.

Behind it all is the feeling that they have always formed part of the Greek community whether as a church or a state and that they should continue forming part of it in word and deed. That quality of government does not matter. Economic advantages neither. It is not a question of politics but of religion. It is what is now in Latin countries called a *mystique,* by which I take it they mean to confess that the more an aspiration is irrational the more it is imperative.

1 Reginald Nicholson (known to his friends by the nickname Simon) was a member of the British Colonial Service. He was known to the Berenson circle through Mrs. Wharton, who had a letter of introduction to him at the time of her yachting cruise in the Mediterranean when R.N. was *en poste* in Cyprus.

TO JUDGE LEARNED HAND

Limassol
Cyprus
16 May 1937

My dear B.,

This will be no letter but an urgent request that you & Frances come & stay with me this summer at Consuma. I expect to be there till Sept. 20. At any time before that I could put up both of you & for as long as you could stay. The resources of the place you know, even tho' you were there in exceptionally bad weather. At all events you can have quiet there. As for me I should greatly enjoy your company. I should enjoy it with heart & mind.

I have been in Cyprus just three weeks, sight-seeing, charmed with the landscape, mildly interested in its romantic past & curious about its present. I doubt whether foreign rule could be made more palatable as well as efficient & inexpensive as the British make it here. Yet the articulate part of the community expresses its eagerness to get rid of the English & to join up with Greece. The fact seems to be that people care little for invisible, inaudible, undemonstrative rule but enjoy show, parade, buoyant catchwords & above all to be ruled by their own people. What that comes to is that the lawyer, the usurer, the venal journalist remain free to exploit the rest of the population with no impersonal, disinterested foreign power to interfere. And such is the hypnotic power of words that they always succeed in getting their victims to fight for them. That in a nut-shell is the case in India, in a small way here, & has been in Egypt, & in a somewhat complicated way in Palestine. And of course this recalcitrant class takes every advantage of the free speech, free institutions & the legal procedure of the British.

Free countries cannot have subject lands & rule them with their own institutions. And ruling them with others must end by submitting them ultimately to the same ruled condition as was so conspicuously the case with the Romans. . . .

Mary has gone to the nearest place by the sea from Florence, Viareggio. It is hard to tell how ill she is really, at all events not well enough to travel as I still do. Her life is now projected almost entirely upon her great-grandson aged about thirty months. There never was a more fascinating live toy. She reads a good deal, chiefly books about psychoanalysis or the triumphant progress of feminism.

As for myself I have had a poor winter at first too tired for serious work & then knocked down by an influenza from which after three months I have not quite recovered. It has left me with a catarrh so troublesome that I shall have to take strong measures to get rid of it. An alleviation was the visit of Ralph Perry. Evenings he read aloud to us his life of Wm. James. What a delicious book for us old enough to have seen & perhaps heard the heroes of the first volume.

Do try to come. You would do me a good turn. Mary will not be at Consuma, for she will leave for England. Nicky will keep house.

Affectionate greetings to you both

Yours
B.B.

To HENRY COSTER

Poggio allo Spino
Consuma
(Prov. di Firenze)
14 Aug 1937

My dear Harry,

Thanks for the note about Atlantis that would have excited poor Haven.[1] I regret him & shall miss him.

[1] J. E. Haven. American Consul in Florence from 1923-1937.

It was naughty of you not to write. In fact I was expecting a letter.

My personal news rather poor. I have been pretty low myself, on the brink of a breakdown. The news fr. Mary most depressing. Great anxiety over Mrs. Wharton & now her death has stunned me.[1] Yet physically I am beginning to feel better thanks to the very quiet life & the sweet air.

I have not been up to writing but have enjoyed reading. Among things to interest you are reviews & articles in Byzantion & Byzantinische Zeitschrift, particularly one in each on the "people" in Cple [Constantinople].

Internationally the situation seems to be quieter thanks to England's immovable will to stir no finger & to ignore that sooner or later the sectarian question must be settled. I dare say she may go to the extent of buying off the *trouble-fête*.

I expect to remain here till Sept. 20 at least. I heartily wish you were here where there is so much leisure for talk.

Love to you both,
B.B.

To Reginald Nicholson

Poggio allo Spino
Vallombrosa
28 August 1937

Dear Simon,

Thanks for all you tell me about Edith's[2] last days. No written word can say what I feel about her death. Indeed I do not

---

1 Edith Wharton had died at her villa, Pavillon Colombe, at St. Brice-sous-Forêt near Montmorency, not far from Paris, on August 11, 1937.
2 Edith Wharton.

feel it yet as I shall realizing day by day that she is no more there as a term of reference, as the focus for so many wishes and the object of so many thoughts.

It will take much adjustment to get my bearings again in a world where she is no more. May I tell you that of all the band that clustered around her none seem to me to have so genuinely, so disinterestedly felt her as you and Molly have. For which reason among so many others I want to see you both as much as possible. You must let I Tatti, or this spot, take the place so far as possible of Hyères.

The climate of Florence is not unlike that of Hyères, a trifle more wintry no doubt but on the other hand more reliable. I Tatti is fairly comfy and has resources. The country would delight you. It is far less pretty than Hyères but ever so much more linear and more plastic. I should expect you to find your pencil even happier there.

To HENRY COSTER

Hotel Bristol
Wien
19 October 1937

My dear Harry,

Yr. last letter was worth waiting for. It reached me at Cagnolas' [1] where Nicky & I went for a couple of days after leaving Consuma. I have come on here to submit my tiresome nervous system to a famous Dr. Neumann. He does something to nose, throat & ears every day & as he is a very Dr. Johnson of a medico, I rather enjoy the treatment although it leaves me, thus far at

[1] Guido Cagnola (1862-1954), Lombard art connoisseur and collector. One of B.B.'s earliest friends in Italy. Owner of a sumptuous villa, La Gazzada, near Varese.

least, sceptical. I am more confident of results at the dentist's.
There I spend betw. two & four hours each day.

You see I have little time for anything else, none in fact for
art. I can see people a little & those I see I enjoy. Among
them is Reinhardt[1] whom I like more & more. He learns, gets
& sifts information & is fairly communicative. I asked him
whether what had been reported to me about our last minister
here could be true, namely that he had said "I have been here
6 weeks & have seen no sign of Nazidom nor of desire for
Anschluss nor Anti-Semitism." Reinhardt thought it could easily be but that our State Dept., knowing the incompetence of
some of the appointments, takes care to accompany him by a
consul who is more intelligent.

It is hard to make out whether there are more Nazis or less
than four years ago. More or less who, without being Nazis, yet
want the Anschluss.

All are convinced that Austria's fate will be decided by the
internat. situation.

That perhaps is one of the chief reasons why one hears those
affairs discussed so continually.

The feeling here seems to be that trouble will come fr. & over
the Mediterranean. Musso is determined to attempt to get
complete command over it & to let no one cross it without paying toll. He will try to get the dominant influence of countries
that could make it hot for England not only at Suez but Gib. as
well. . . . He is convinced that he can smash the Brit. Empire
& believes that he has already destroyed England's prestige &
authority. And people are inclined to believe he may have his
way. Nobody here concedes the possibility that England is
standing all she does out of any reason except that she dare not
retaliate.

As for our President's encyclicals they smile affectionately but
do not regard them as of the least immediate effectiveness.

1 Frederic Reinhardt. At present Ambassador of U.S.A. in Rome.

So much for politics. To return to myself, my summer began with a fit of depression that was almost a breakdown. I got better but never got to work. I had a delightful visit fr. the Hands followed by one fr. Walter Lippmann. He inquired about you & expressed the wish to see you a good deal more. . . .

Pickman[1] sent me his *Mind of Latin Christendom* but I have not yet had time to read it. If you have tell me what you think of it & whether it is worth my while to plough or even to sail thro it.

Of course I have read Walter Lippmann's *Good Society* wh. is a book after my own heart.

I regret to read that you mean to stay on yr. side longer than last year. I see very little of you & less & less. I certainly lose thereby.

I shall probably have to stay here another three weeks. Mary is already in Florence & momentarily better than for a long time.

Write again & soon & give my love to Byba.

Affectionately
B.B.

To Ruth Berenson[2]

Advice in a letter of 1937 as to becoming an art historian:

. . . I myself regret having wasted my talents in sowing and tending a field which has reaped nothing but weeds and thorns and brambles.

---

1 Edward Pickman.
2 R.B. (Mrs. Norbert Muhlen), a cousin of Berenson and the daughter of the late Arthur Berenson.

To Judge Learned Hand

Hotel Bristol
Wien
6 October 1937

Dear B.

Thanks for a most entertaining letter posted at Gibraltar that I found waiting for me two days ago.

Most interesting yr. account of the visit to Santayana. I am truly happy to learn that he looked so young & vigorous & serene. Personally I wish him a long life & happy activity. Only I am no longer interested in what he has to say. Leisure fails me for reading commonplaces no matter how, like the chestnuts they are, they pop & smell savoury in popping. For that sort of thing my mind is as *complêt* as the Paris buses used to be that stuck out signs to that effect.

Five & twenty years ago I told him that like a god he was careless of mankind, & his retort was "Yes, an Epicurean God." But that is just what I meant. I could make endless comments on his remarks, but abstain because you are a busy man. . . .

I left Consuma ten days ago and went to stay with a dear old friend in a fairy palace in fairy land near Varese. Monte Rosa seemed to close in his park as it glowed & blushed at sunrise. Then we went to spend three ideal days with the Prince Regent of Yugoslavia.[1] We had him all to ourselves & I only wish Walter [Lippmann] had been there to hear him. He has seldom heard anything so "straight from the horse's mouth."

And now I am here luxuriously comfy but pouring out shillings like water upon a chain of empiricists who submit one to all sorts of so called treatments. I confess they leave me sceptical as a certain gospel left Saul of Tarsus. I pray for conversion.

The world situation is awful. Comic to let a second-class

[1] Prince Paul was a connoisseur of painting. He tried to keep Yugoslavia out of the war but the Regency was overthrown by the war party in 1941.

power in the Mediterranean continue to trouble more & more
& more, when a good strong kick would bring peace in this part
of the world at least. Thank Frances from me for her letter.

Ever affectionately
B.B.

To Judge Learned Hand

I Tatti
Settignano
Florence
26 December 1937

Dear B.,

I have not a thing to say except by way of good wishes for a
Happy New Year & a satisfactory 1938. What has it in store for
us? War — unlikely. Further triumphs of the Devil & all his
hosts — almost certainly. Further devaluation of the Dollar — ??? What would it entail? Incalculable effects.

And I do not trust our rulers — I never have. Ruling vast
communities seems to me to be beyond human ability. Mud-
dling along would therefore be the wisest course provided all
muddled along together. These are the "unsatisfied nations."
They must be met, for if we do not, they will destroy us. True
that by consenting to meet them we end by using their weapons
& growing like them. But still we should not even then be so
far from our ideals as they would be, & we should be nearer the
goal if victorious, & ready to start again.

Therefore we must resist Evil & not yield to it, costly as re-
sistance surely is.

To warm up to personalities. Lapsley[1] has been staying for

---

1 Gaillard Lapsley, don at Trinity College, Cambridge, England.

three weeks & been excellent company. Mary particularly has enjoyed him, for at bottom she coddles up to nobody but "Angry-Saxons" & among these most of all to thoroughly anglicized Americans. Gaillard suits the bill to perfection. He is a liberal at heart, altho' he wants his liberalism wrapped up in institutionalism & not, like me for instance, naked & vociferous. Of course we had Mrs. Wharton to talk about. He has been left her literary executor. He goes tomorrow & already another of Mrs. Wharton's "male wives," as I used to call them to her face, has arrived, Robert Norton.[1] He is an exquisite & free spirit, with as beautiful an outside as inside & you would love each other if only I could bring you together.

Mary is a trifle better & joins us after meals. I am not as well as I hoped to be after all my cures in Vienna. But I am resigned.

Write when you can't help writing, but not as a matter of obligation.

With love to Frances as well as yourself.

Yours

B.B.

To Professor Paul J. Sachs

September [1938? — almost certainly]

Dear Paul:

. . . It has been brought to my notice that the rising tide of anti-Semitism may reach me and sweep me out of Italy. That would be disagreeable for me, but I should hardly feel justified in disturbing you with appeals of any sort. It may, however, concern I Tatti as well.

1 English diplomatist and painter.

Now I have for some time been turning over the idea, that in the present condition of Europe, private property, particularly of foreigners, was not too safe. If I have hesitated to turn over I Tatti in our lifetime (for in Italian law it is as much Mary's as mine) the chief reason on my side has been the fact that Harvard might take a turn unfavourable to my intentions and therefore incapable of carrying them out. I wanted, therefore, to retain the liberty of leaving it to an institution more likely to carry out my intentions. After you talked with me a couple of months ago I feel assured that Harvard would do the right thing by me. And as things look now it would be wise and perhaps urgent that Harvard should take over I Tatti at once, leaving us to occupy it for life. I understand that Harvard would hesitate to be burdened with any financial outlays in this matter. But Harvard would incur none while we occupied it and should I be obliged to leave I would be ready to give every guarantee for the upkeep of the buildings, the purchase of serial publications by the libraries, and the salaries of the minimum staff required to keep I Tatti alive and available to students who would wish to use it. Guarantees could be based on my investments. Exact data about these may be obtained from my cousin, Lawrence Berenson.[1] . . . Of course, inquiries you could make at our State Department might end in giving you the satisfactory assurance that nothing need be done. I fear you will scarcely get such assurance. If I am mistaken and there is no immediate danger then the question can be put off until you all have more leisure to attend to it. When John Walker returns I shall ask him to see our Ambassador in Rome. When answering do so in general terms and above all avoid mentioning our State Department. . . .

[1] Mr. Lawrence Berenson of New York was his cousin's attorney and *homme d'affaires* for thirty-five years and is now one of the Executors of the Estate.

To Judge Learned Hand

Casa al Dono[1]
Vallombrosa
(Prov. di Firenze)
2 September 1938

My dear B.,

Thanks for an eloquent, informing & fascinating letter. Would you could find time to write oftener. Luckily one can feed a whole year on such an epistle.

With you I deplore the absence of opposition. Long ago I began to be horrified by the completeness of the turn over after elections. The first was after the Boer War in England. Since then the majorities for the winning side have been more & more smashing until finally in Russia first, then following closely in Italy & finally in Germany, these majorities took the plebiscitary unanimity.

The last great elections in England & in America gave such majorities to the winning side that its back benchers could get up again & again in the House of Commons, gnash their teeth & cry to the opposition, "Why waste yr. breath & our time. We can vote whatever we like."

An assured majority makes parliamentary government a farce & turns parliament into a mere debate. This tendency to unanimity is a sad symptom & is perhaps connected with the fact that we liberals seem void of argument, of appeal, or even of ammunition. It can't be that we have no men. Only they are without arms.

I know that in my field a line of progress & decline is very much like a vein in a gold mine. When a given art formula has been worked out nobody can do anything with it. And so it must be with politico-sociological formulae. The problem is

[1] A house half way from Consuma to Vallombrosa, formerly belonging to the Corsini family and since 1940 to Miss Nicky Mariano.

how to discover a new vein that yet will yield gold instead of slag, or at least gold in sufficient percentage to make it worth while.

By gold I mean the good AND beautiful life.

(In art by the way we are up against exactly the same problem.) . . .

Here it is out & out Arcadia, an ideal setting for *As You Like It* alternating with *Midsummer Nights Dream.* I am rash enough to hope that we shall be here next summer & that you & Frances will come to stay.

Mary is in England & I expect her back early in Oct. but without the baby great-grandson to amuse her. If she is well enough later on at the end of Nov. I may take her to Egypt.

I wonder how long it will take you to decipher this screed. You are so young & have so much leisure.

Love to you both

B.B.

To HENRY COSTER

Casa al Dono
Vallombrosa
(Prov. di Firenze)
September 1938

Dear Harry,

Thank you & Byba for your greetings. I have often & often thought of you & missed you. We need the comfort & counsel of friends like you.

Having spent a good many hours this summer writing in behalf of refugees I may end by becoming one myself. Truth to tell if Mary were well enough we would all come & camp on yr.

doorstep for a while & think of what to do next. As it is Mary is going to Geneva to consult still more specialists & we may join her there.

Do you remember meeting a rather heroic looking young German-Jew named Kristeller? He found refuge in Florence first & as a student of Quattrocento Florentine Platonism, was made welcome here & finally promoted to a position in the Normal School at Pisa. He published some hitherto little known texts of Marsilio Ficino with a thoughtful & informing Latin Preface. Now he is thrown out, is stunned & in despair writes to me.

Is there anything to be done? He has a distinguished & impressive mind & indeed appearance. He is a first rate philologer & could teach Latin, Greek & German as well as philosophy. He would be ready to take any decent job that would secure him bread & safety.

Do not take this too hard. I am simply casting my bread on the waters in the hope it may come back to Kristeller.

We are just finishing the first vol. of a remarkable work on the Papacy that I recommend to you. It is Johannes Haller's *Das Papstum*.

I wish you knew this place. No spot on earth more idyllic, more silent, more peaceful. If only.

Love to you both from Nicky as well as myself.

Yrs.

B.B.

To Henry Coster

I Tatti
Settignano
Florence
30 November 1938

Dear Harry,

Yr. letter of Oct. 22 reached me weeks ago. I read it more than once. I have seldom received a more interesting one or one breathing more sympathy, friendship & even affection. You can scarcely imagine how welcome it was & how much it touched & comforted me. It is no little to be assured of such society as you & Byba could offer us if we knocked at yr. door.

I should do it very soon if I could get away. I confess I should be strongly tempted to leave if I could take Mary with me. Physically it no doubt would be possible to transport her to New York. She might survive the voyage. And then? I should have to deposit her in a nursing home & for that I have not the heart.

Here she has at least all the comforts & luxuries that can be procured & the greatest of all, the presence of the familiar & companionable objects that one has lived with for forty years & have become extensions almost of one's own body.

So I remain although the tension is great. In the first place Mary's suffering is so acute that it depresses & grieves me almost to the breaking point. And the earthquake, better man-quake-weather outside, getting more & more ominous every day since last August. If I can pull thro it will be a miracle.

Friends do what they can. Umberto[1] has been here a good deal, Guglielmo[2] too, the Johnnie Walkers,[3] Reber of our em-

1 Count Umberto Morra, Italian man of letters who met B.B. in 1925 through Salvemini.
2 Count Guglielmo Alberti. He was a Piedmontese friend of Count Morra, through whom he met B.B. in 1925, and became a frequent guest at I Tatti and Vallombrosa.
3 John Walker, the director of the National Gallery in Washington, and his wife, Lady Margaret Walker.

bassy, Clotilde[1] — all these staying. The Serristori[2] twice a week, [Ugo] Ojetti once in a great while, [Luigi] Russo, [Pietro] Pancrazi, Croce, but almost no real Florentines.

The weather has been more serenely beautiful, all but summerlike, than I can recall at any other autumn. We sat out today lightly clad.

I read with pleasure as I easily forget myself in a book. Chiefly early Teutonic & Slav history & archeology. I sometimes think it is the names that fascinate me & liberate wisps of longing & a *Dahin*-ness that takes me far away from the worries & stresses & distresses of actuality.

I hope you will come more rather than less to Florence. For one thing I need you very much & for another Florence & even Italy does. I wish you would come soon. It would mean a great deal to us & we could talk over subjects you start in yr. letters that are too complicated to be written about satisfactorily.

The word "writing" reminds me to add that I write a little on my new book, The Decline & Recovery. That too is a refuge.

Nicky would join me in sending love to you both. She is in town. Her [nephew] Cecil [Anrep] has passed splendidly & is going into business.

Ever yrs.
B.B.

Best wishes for a Happy New Year & *decent* 1939.

In the winter of 1938-1939 Berenson naturally became more concerned than ever with the fate of his villa and collections, and consulted the American Embassy in Rome. Mr. William Phillips, the Ambassador, was momentarily

---

1 Clotilde Marghieri, a gifted Neapolitan writer.
2 Count Umberto Serristori and his wife. Countess Hortense Serristori (1871-1960) was Spanish and had known B.B. since the nineties.

in Washington at the time of the despatch of the following telegram. From this point on, a few official letters and notes are included to supplement Berenson's and to make the situation clear.

PARAPHRASE OF TELEGRAM

Rome
29 November 1938
Rec'd 9.02 A.M.

Secretary of State
Washington.
    350, November 29, noon.
    The following telegram is for Mr. Phillips.

Berenson is concerned with regard to the future of his establishment in Florence on account of the present laws restricting the ownership of property by Jews of Italian nationality and the possibility that provisions of a similar nature may be extended to foreigners of Jewish origin owning property in Italy. After discussing the matter with Berenson it was thought that you may wish to talk over with the authorities of Harvard University the suggestion that the Corporation might take over the property at the present time and permit Mr. Berenson to keep a life tenancy. Professor Paul Sachs has already presented this suggestion. It might be well to take the matter up with the Italian authorities at once before any possible further restrictive measures are approved if Harvard University consents to taking over the property at present rather than at such a time as it would be left to the University under provisions of Mr. Berenson's will.

Reed

To Philip Hofer

I Tatti
Settignano
Florence
16 December 1938

Dear Hofer,

. . .

You know that for years it has been my intention to leave my entire estate here & at home to Harvard. I hesitated to do it in my life-time because I wanted to make sure art teaching was not getting either too professional and too technical on the one hand, or too philological & Teutonic on the other. I have now received assurances on both these points & am thinking seriously of turning over I Tatti & all its contents as soon as Harvard is ready to take it & reserving life-tenancy for ourselves. As you know this place, put in a word for it if you get a chance.

Let me hear of your activities. I am old enough to be more interested in what younger people are doing than in my own last driblets.

Ever yours
B. Berenson

William Phillips to Count Ciano

Rome
2 January 1939

Dear Count Ciano,

In accordance with your request, I enclose a brief memorandum with regard to the suggested acquisition by Harvard University of Mr. Berenson's villa, library, and collections of art known as "I Tatti" in Florence. May I point out again that in presenting this inquiry I am not acting under any instructions whatsoever, either from Washington or from Harvard or from Mr. Berenson, but merely in my capacity as a Harvard graduate and a former officer of the University and one who is deeply interested in all Harvard matters. According to my information, in 1932 Count Paliano, then in charge of the American Division of the Foreign Office, had told a member of the Embassy staff that the Duce had approved the transfer of this property to Harvard. For various reasons, however, the transfer was not carried out at that time.

The question which I asked you was whether, in your opinion, any changes had occurred since 1932 which, from the Italian point of view, would make it undesirable for Harvard to acquire this property on the basis of a life tenancy for Mr. and Mrs. Berenson, both American citizens, and I should be very grateful for any information which you might be able to give me with regard to this matter.

I am, my dear Count Ciano,

Very sincerely yours,
William Phillips

Enclosure.

MEMORANDUM ENCLOSED IN LETTER
OF AMBASSADOR PHILLIPS TO COUNT CIANO

2 January 1939

In November 1932, Count Paliano, then in charge of the American Division of the Foreign Office, informed a member of the American Embassy that the Duce was aware and approved of the suggested transfer of Mr. Berenson's villa and contents, known as "I Tatti," in Florence, to Harvard University on the basis of a life tenancy for himself and Mrs. Berenson. It was intended to attract to Florence American students and Americans of independent means engaged in research. The intention was that it should become an institution for the study of Italian Art, of all that went toward making it, and of all that Italian Art did to form the art of the rest of Europe. It would also create not only a cultural center but a social one for the deeper understanding, on the part of Americans, of what Italy has contributed to the world's civilization.

Under date of October 30, 1933, the Corporation of Harvard University voted as follows:

> *It was understood that the Corporation is enthusiastically receptive to Mr. Bernard Berenson's proposal to bequeath his villa and collection to Harvard University provided that Harvard is committed to its maintenance only to the extent that income is available from the endowment funds furnished by his estate or specifically given for that purpose.*

For various reasons, principally because of uncertainty in Mr. Berenson's mind as to the intention and general plans of the Fine Arts Department of Harvard, the suggested transfer was not at that time effected. Since then, Mr. Berenson has been in touch with Harvard authorities and has no longer any doubt in his mind as to the disposition of his property to Harvard, and furthermore, as he and Mrs. Berenson are nearly seventy-four years of age, it is thought that he might be willing to effect the actual transfer now.

Meanwhile, "I Tatti" has been put under the "Protezione del Paesaggio." Its future endowment is provided for entirely from American securities.

To Edith de Gasparin[1] [Florence]
5 January 1939

Dear Friend,

I hasten to tell you how deeply I sympathize with your un-happiness over losing the habitation you have had the greater part of your lifetime. One makes all one's adjustments with it so that it becomes in almost physiological sense part of one's self. Another part, if you like, but so are arms and legs. To be separated is a terrible wrench and leaves wounds very hard to heal up. Luckily everything passes *col tempo*.

You ask about Goethe's Faust. My own conviction is that real poetry like music or all the other arts bears no verbal restate-ment or exhaustive explanation. It is left for each to get what we can out of the Second Faust, according to our aptitude, our preparation and our momentary mood. Other gifted people can tell you what they have got out of the poem, but if you are dull you will not follow them any more than the text itself. If you are capable of having reactions of your own and of analyz-ing them you will find nobody else's reactions satisfactory be-cause they are not your own. A work of art is a vital experience like love and nobody can give it to you but yourself.

Thinking of Goethe, and his great Commentator, your old friend [Houston Stewart] Chamberlain. I ask you *ohne Feind-schaft* what he would think of the events and *Einstellung* in the country of his heart during the last few years. I wish I had a witch of Endor to raise him from the dead and ask him myself. I have all my life had a dread of facile doctrines about races nations systems. I was always aware that they would inevitably lead to blood and tears. What is happening is worse even than my worst fears.

With renewed good wishes for 1939

[1] Edith de Gasparin was a friend of the Wagner family and of Houston Stewart Chamberlain. She was first brought to I Tatti by the Countess Blandine Gravina, a daughter of Hans von Bülow and Cosima von Bülow (who married Richard Wagner *en secondes noces*).

JOHN WALKER
TO PROFESSOR PAUL J. SACHS

American Academy in Rome
Porta S. Pancrazio
Rome, Italy
2 February 1939

Dear Paul,

I saw B.B. yesterday on my way to Rome. He was delighted that I had seen President Conant and very pleased by everything that I had to tell him about my visit to Cambridge. He quite understands that Harvard must be protected against any contingent liability, and he repeated that he is willing and anxious that you and the Treasurer of Harvard should get into touch with his cousin and go over all of his investments. He suggested that it might be helpful if his lawyer sent you his income tax returns, and he is instructing him to do so. This will give you at least a preliminary survey and perhaps all the information you need. I told him that I had recommended to you that Harvard make him some definite financial proposal. He would be willing to turn over to Harvard the greater part of his capital provided they would guarantee to him the same rate of income on that part of his property during his and Mary's life. I believe he would turn it all over if a small annuity could be provided for Nicky. Whether this would be feasible or not depends of course on the amount of his capital and the nature of his investments, but if both of the factors are satisfactory I believe from what President Conant said some such scheme could be worked out.

Our Embassy meanwhile has not yet received a reply to their inquiry, but that is to be expected.

I shall send you shortly a statement of the present operating expenses of the villa.

As ever
John

To Professor Paul J. Sachs

Florence

9 February 1939

Dear Paul:

. . . The enclosure is an itemized statement of the cost of running this place as a house, library and garden. As you will see, it comprises everything including salaries. Should Harvard take over the place in my lifetime, as I trust it will presently, I must count on spending $40,000 a year. This is almost wholly, if not entirely, covered by my investments.

. . . I understand from Johnnie [Walker] that Harvard would want to take over my investments if it took I Tatti. To this I should have no objection *provided* Harvard could see its way to letting me have for life the same income that I have now. I fear I could not do with less, and I no longer earn anything as I have ceased relations with Duveen. When both Mary and I are gone there should be enough income to pay for running the place on the basis of the enclosed statement, as well as for the payments of the annuities made in my will.

Of this you have a copy in your hands. I have made one or two codicils to this will, but not to affect the amount to be paid out in annuities.

There is no likelihood, therefore, that I Tatti would add to the financial burdens of Harvard. On the other hand I cannot any longer hope to leave enough to endow fellowships. The Director will, I trust, be a man of independent means as well as a scholar, and able to pay his own way, more or less as I do here at I Tatti.

The idea would be if an endowment fund could be collected to cover a number of fellowships as well as a salary that would enable the Director without private means to run the place more or less as I have, although more economically.

Johnnie came away delighted with President Conant. It

seems the President, while expressing sympathy with the idea of I Tatti, spoke of a certain reluctance to take up any responsibility in Italy. I stressed that if I Tatti becomes a Harvard institute it will outlast all sorts of upheavals and even wars, as century old Spanish, French and German [institutes] have. The last weathered the Great War. Nothing worse is likely to happen to us. . . .

Yours,

B.B.

Il Ministro degli Affari Esteri

209045/39

Roma, li 24 Mar. 1939 Anno XVII

Caro Ambasciatore,

Con riferimento alla Vostra[1] lettera del 2 gennaio scorso, sono lieto di informare Vostra Eccellenza che il Prefetto di Firenze ha ricevuto istruzioni di porsi in contatto col Signor Berenson per comunicargli che nulla osta al trapasso di proprietà della villa fiorentina "I Tatti" e che egli potrà consequentemente, nei limiti previsti dalla legge, dar corso alle pratiche necessarie a tale trasferimento.

Vogliate gradire, caro Ambasciatore, gli atti della mia alta considerazione.

Ciano.

A Sua Eccellenza
William Phillips
Ambasciatore degli S.U. d'America
Via Rossini 5
ROMA

---

[1] In the last years of the régime, the second person (used in the South) was obligatory in official correspondence and it is to be noticed that Count Ciano uses it here.

Translation of the above letter:

The Minister for Foreign Affairs
209045/39
Rome
24 March 1939

My dear Ambassador,

With reference to your letter of January 2, 1939, I am pleased to inform Your Excellency that the Prefect of Florence has been instructed to get in touch with Mr. Berenson to inform him that there is no objection to the transfer of ownership of the villa "I Tatti" in Florence and that he may therefore proceed, within the limitations prescribed by law, with the formalities necessary to such transfer.

Please accept, my dear Ambassador, the expression of my high consideration.

Ciano

His Excellency
William Phillips
American Ambassador
Via Rossini 5
    Rome

To LAWRENCE BERENSON

Rome
9 April 1939
Easter Day

My dear Lawrence:

I sit down to answer your affectionate, important, and valuable letter of March 27th after coming back from seeing the

Pope[1] bless the crowd in the Piazza of St. Peter. It was an inspiring occasion.

Thank you from my heart for the letter and the account enclosed. Thank you for all suggestions and proposals, as well as the offer of your services and of Grenville Clark.

By the way, is he not a friend of Ralph Perry's and was he not to come to see me at one time and inspect I Tatti? I think it must be. And it is splendid that you are so sure of his support.

By "support" I mean his support in inducing the Corporation to accept I Tatti for the purpose they know I have in mind, on terms following out your proposals and suggestions.

The one person at Harvard who really wants I Tatti is Paul Sachs. All the driving power that is in him — and he has a great deal — will be called upon to put our proposal through. I have every reason to expect that Sachs will further any legitimate demand of ours to which the Corporation can be induced to consent. So I beg you to get in touch with him and give him a copy of the detailed account you have sent me and copy of the proposals and suggestion you are making to me. By the way, Sachs or the Harvard Corporation have already a copy of my will, which you can ask to see. It was made out ten years ago.

As you will see it provides for a considerable number of annuities. These (while they have to be paid out) and the expense of running I Tatti will eat up the income of my estate. Fellowships will have to come from the outside and for these (assuming Harvard takes over I Tatti) Sachs will be invaluable. He, if anyone, can raise money for such a purpose. If he wills it, he can, he and Forbes.[2] I trust I am right in expecting Forbes to do almost as much as Sachs. I have already told Sachs that I shall require an annuity of $40,000 for my lifetime, extended to Mary should she survive me. This would, of course, include all running expenses of I Tatti as a house and a library,

---

1 Pius XI (Achille Ratti).

2 Edward Forbes, the then Director of the Fogg Museum in Cambridge (Massachusetts).

etc., etc., as well as her and my private expenses. How this is to be arranged I leave to you and Clark and the Corporation.

I wish you would see President Conant and tell him how much I regret that he has not been able to visit I Tatti, see what it is like, and hear what were my ideas and hopes. I do not mean it to be a workshop for the petty and parochial study of Italian Art. Far from it, I should wish it to be an institute where gifted young men could soak themselves in Mediterranean culture as centred in Italy and focused in Greco-Roman-Byzantine-Italian Art. I should wish these students to have the privilege of travelling half the year and living in loose community the other half, discussing with those met on their travels on the results of these experiences, sensations and ponderance. My ideal would be to turn out ripe humanists and not mere teachers of facts about Arts and retainers of anecdotic information.

Let me add that our Ambassador here has been an Archangel of strength and devotion in his effort to get the authorities here to consent.

With every kind of anticipated thanks and much love to you and yours,

Affectionately,

B.B.

WILLIAM PHILLIPS TO PROFESSOR PAUL J. SACHS

Embassy of the
United States of America
Rome
13 April 1939

Dear Paul,

I hope you understand that the long delay in securing anything definite from the Italian Government with regard to "I

Tatti" has not been through my negligence. Shortly after my return to Rome in December, I spent a weekend with B.B. in Florence and obtained his approval to a draft note, dated January 2nd, to Count Ciano, a copy of which I enclose herewith. The Foreign Office has no jurisdiction over such matters and my note, therefore, had to be transmitted to other interested departments of the Government. Weeks and even months passed. Inasmuch as I had presented the request as a purely personal one and not on behalf of the State Department, Harvard, or Berenson, I did not think it wise to press too vigorously for a response. Finally, however, on March 22nd I sent Mr. Reed, the Counselor of the Embassy, to call upon Don Renato Prunas, the head of American affairs of the Foreign Office. Mr. Reed pointed out that the long delay in replying to my written communication might, if continued, give the impression that there was some obstacle in the way of a definitive resolution of the matter. Mr. Prunas replied that the Prefect of Florence had already been instructed to get in touch with Berenson and to inform him that there was no objection to the transfer of his property to Harvard University, and to facilitate the said transfer. Two days later, on March 24th, I received a written reply from Ciano confirming the assurance conveyed by Mr. Prunas (copy and translation enclosed). However, this reply contained an ambiguous phrase, "within the limitations prescribed by law," which seemed to qualify the assurances in the letter itself, and I again sent the Counselor of the Embassy to inquire of Mr. Prunas the precise meaning of this reservation. Mr. Prunas said that there was absolutely nothing to worry about in that connection; that the legislation in question was Law No. 778 of June 11, 1922, and Royal Decree No. 363 of January 30, 1913. He stated that these laws related only to the preservation of real property having artistic or historic interest and to the protection of works of art in Italy. Naturally both Mr. Berenson and Harvard University would be required to observe the pertinent provisions of these laws during and subsequent to the consummation of the transfer of "I Tatti," in addition to conforming to the law and procedure normally applying to the assignment of real and moveable property in the Kingdom by deed of gift. We have looked up the law and decree mentioned by Mr. Prunas and have found them both to be as described by him.

Mr. Berenson is now in Rome and I have given him the whole story as outlined above. He seems entirely satisfied with the assurances given and on his return to Florence in a few days will consult the Prefect of Florence as suggested by Count Ciano in his letter to me of March 24th.

Perhaps in the circumstances it was unnecessary, but nevertheless on March 30th I addressed a further communication to Count Ciano in acknowledgment of his letter to me of the 24th instant, asking if he would be good enough to explain the precise meaning of the phrase in order to have in writing the assurances which Mr. Prunas has conveyed to us orally, but I have not yet received anything further from the Foreign Office in this connection. This, I think, tells you the whole story. As I say, B.B. himself seems perfectly happy about it. If there is anything else that I can do to be of assistance, please do not hesitate to let me know.

Sincerely yours,
William Phillips

Enclosures.

My kindest remembrances to you and Edward.

To PHILIP HOFER

Hotel de la Ville
Rome
15 April 1939

My dear Hofer,

. . .

I have been seeing Johnnie Walker of course. He is packing & preparing to take flight — has to report in Washington Aug. 1. I don't envy the prospect & I am old enough to be frank & to say that I shall miss him in every way.

Now I must "approach" you on the matter which is coming up for decision. It is the fate of I Tatti. Our ambassador has got the consent of the authorities here for the immediate transfer to Harvard — at least he & I hope there will be no hitches from that quarter.

I fear that Harvard is lukewarm & perhaps frightened. They may not like the responsibility in this historical horizon & they may not see much advantage. Of course I think differently. My library & my place could & should form an ideal centre for the mature & really intellectual study of the whole PAST of art. Not of Italian art in a narrow sense but of all art as it influenced Italy & all art influenced by Italy. It would be a school for that leisurely kind of study which the French & Germans have in their various institutions here, but which we Americans are without. Our Academy here offers almost no stipend for the study of Roman archeology, let alone later & more universal art.

My idea would to have fellowships & a communal life at I Tatti with the freedom to travel half the year.

I know you will understand & sympathize.

As for the political side of it, bear in mind that French, Spanish & German institutions have weathered wars & centuries. The German ones certainly suffered but temporary inconvenience in consequence of the last war when Italy was against them.

What I want is to engage you to use your influence in furthering my scheme. You may feel you can do little & that may be true. Yet every little counts & your little may by happy accident count a good deal.

I return to I Tatti today & shall scarcely move again till June. Then if all is quiet I may return to the Balkans or the Aegean for a few weeks. The summer I expect to spend as usual near Consuma.

Affectionate & nostalgic greetings to you both.

Yours
B.B.

To Reginald Nicholson
Casa al Dono Vallombrosa
21 August 1939

Dear Simon,

Thanks for Your letter and for Forster's little essay. I agree with every word of it and have expressed very similar notions, although nothing like so well worded, in a screed I work on when, on rare occasions, I still do work.

Of course *force* is an *ultima ratio* without which society may not be able to carry on. My way of seeing it is as something parallel to the gold reserve. This last is always lowest where prosperity order and freedom all rule together and biggest in poor despotically ruled badly administered lands. I believe that before 1914 England had the smallest gold reserve and Russia the largest. Likewise Russia had the largest police force and the greatest belief in violence, whereas England at that time had the very smallest recourse to pressure of any kind.

Unhappily England is now hoarding gold and magnifying Scotland Yard. Perhaps unavoidable but a pity nevertheless.

To Henry Coster

I Tatti
Settignano
Florence
14 September 1939

Dear Harry,

Thanks for a long, interesting & delightful letter. Events have answered much of it. They have marched forward at such a pace that the last twenty days seem more like twenty years — not because of their duration so much as for the abysses & Styxes — if I may say so — betw. one day & the next. And we here do not know what to think or hope. Saving Beppino Gherardesca & his flock at Doney's, I hear of nobody in any class or station who wants to join the Boches. But the 95% who do not may have to obey the 5% who do. It looks as if the Nazis do expect Engl. & France to make peace on their Nazi terms when these have had their will of Poland. How can one blame them after so much appeasement! The education in foreign affairs of provincial statesmen may cost not only their own countries dear, but the rest of the world as well. The Nazi idea would seem to be that they will have their way. If not then all their allies will be called in etc. etc. By the time you read this more may be known to you.

We are without coffee or tea & are not allowed to use automobiles. It is improbable that we shall have enough fuel for the winter.

Of course it is very quiet. Not a sound from the empty roads & few people. The very last foreigners are leaving. Washburn[1] says only 38 American residents are left.

A thin vol. fell into my hands recently called *Probleme der Spätantike* (Stuttgart, 1930). Articles by Laqueur & Wilhelm Weber attracted my attention. Of the first I can discover noth-

[1] Vice-consul in Florence until 1941.

ing further but by Wilhelm Weber I found two articles one on Hadrian & the other on the Antonines in vol. XI of the Cambridge *Ancient History*. At the same time the Journal of Rom. Studies reached me where I found a thorough drubbing of these very articles. I confess they fascinated me. Weber evidently has a creative sense of his personages rare in compilatory history of today. Of course he may be Nazifying but I am eager to get hold of more of him. The reviewer slaps a book of his on "Augustus." Perhaps you can find it in New York.

Mary is still at Friday's Hill, Haslemere. Alda & Bertie as usual. Olga Loeser[1] just back fr. Lausanne. Doro has sailed. This minute received such a dear letter fr. Byba. Please thank her for me & tell her I will write her by next boat.

Affectionate greetings to you both

Yours
B.B.

To JUDGE LEARNED HAND

I Tatti
Settignano
Florence
15 September 1939

My dear B.,

I hope you are safely back & at a safe distance from romantically adventurous & forced wanderings. I heard fr. Lady Colefax that you were in London, at which time it still could be hoped you might come on here. How fast all has changed. Twenty days are like twenty years & who knows what aeons have intervened between each that we communally & universally ignore!

1 Widow of the collector Carlo Loeser (d. 1928).

I came down here Sept. 3 when our cars were stopped. It is beautiful & silent & serene here but with the proverbial silence at the center of a typhoon. Luckily my Mary is in England & out of material danger. As for me I am all but indifferent, except for mere curiosity. I'd like to see what happens & if possible how this chapter closes. Of course I should be sorry if all I have been building up here should go to smash or fall into wrong hands. Yet as one or the other is bound to happen in the course of no very long time, why worry! I try to be resigned & half succeed.

Write if you can & take my affectionate greetings in which I include Frances of course.

Yours

B.B.

To Judge Learned Hand

I Tatti
Settignano
Florence
10 December 1939

My dear B.

This is to wish you & yours a Merry Xmas & a Happy New Year. I do this with good cheer & sincerely. . . .

You are better informed as to what is going on in Europe than we are here & my comments could be of small interest by the time they reached you.

Let me rather tell you that I had early in Oct. an encounter with Santayana. It was at the Hotel Danieli in Venice. He occupied two rooms over the entrance, probably as tumultuously noisy as any in Venice. That is his way of approaching life. He stayed in all day writing. He had to re-write all he had done last summer because a philosopher acquaintance occasionally disturbed the even tenor of his own thought. At table he read the newspaper. After dinner he went to the reading room & conned Nietzsche's *Gaia Scienza* in French translation. It was there I used to join him. He had enjoyed yr. visit & said you had scarcely changed since yr. student day[s]. I told him Hutch Hapgood [1] spoke so affectionately of him in his, Hutch's autobiography. He denied his acquaintance. I asked for news of his lifelong correspondent Mrs. Toy & with a snigger he told me she was too old to endure the Cambridge climate & had retired into the bosom of her Southern family where she was — a gurgle of sniggers — bored & unhappy.

As for myself, he asked what I was doing in Venice. I told him I was looking at the pictures. "Oh, I thought they had done all they could to advance you along the line of your ambitions." Not another word as to what I was living, writing, reading. I started the subject of Charles [Augustus] Strong[2] & he sort of belched back that they had fallen out over Franco, that himself was not really a fascist but that his patriotism as a Spaniard could not tolerate Strong's scepticism. Then he went to speak of his Spanish connections in the most disparaging terms, glad on the whole they were all dead or as good as.

I pumped him about his own work & its reception by the public. He was very self-complaisant, said he was just finishing the *Realm of Spirit,* the last of the series.

I was rather surprised that he went out of his way to praise such an impudent petty charlatan as Ezra Pound.

All in all after several talks he left on me the impression of a very self-satisfied, rather maliciously cynical, sniggering, sneering old man. "He has nor wife nor child," nor friend nor foe,

1 Hutchins Hapgood (1869-1944), American author.
2 A student of philosophy and an old friend of Santayana with whom he had lived and travelled in much earlier days. Owner of the Villa delle Balze at Fiesole, built by Cecil Pinsent about 1910.

no needs except the elementary ones & yet is happy, consciously happy. He was eloquent about the advantages of old age. His only remaining problem is where to live, now that the Bristol in Rome has been demolished.

My Mary joined me in Oct. & has been getting better ever since.

I spent a fortnight or so in Rome quite recently. The winds thence blow westward, slightly as yet, but unmistakably.

Affectionately
B.B.

GEORGE SANTAYANA TO MRS. C. H. TOY

Hotel Danieli
Venice
10 October 1939

Dear Mrs. Toy

. . .

The other day, awaking from absorption in the newspaper, whom should I see before me but Berenson! We had one good talk: but the second (and last) already flagged and made me feel how little sympathy there is at bottom between people who don't like each other but like the same "subjects" or have similar professions. These "subjects" become different objects to two minds that have grown old and have grown apart in considering them. Berenson surprised me by talking with juvenile enthusiasm about "art" (as if we were still in the 1890's). There is an exhibition of Paolo Veronese here, where he said he was spending day after day rapt in wonder, and always finding fresh beauties in the pictures. I haven't yet been to the exhibition (I mean to go tomorrow: I am not *deliberately* wicked) but it is impossible for me now to regard "art," any more than traditional religion, as a supreme interest in itself. It is an illustration to history, and a positive joy when it really reveals something beautiful in the material or in the spiritual world. But the social world, the world of convention, to which the criticism of art belongs, has come to seem to me rather a screen that keeps the material and the spiritual worlds out of sight. This is because my philosophy is not humanistic or psychological, like that of most people nowadays, but combines old materialism with old Platonism: *babylonisch über einander getürmten* systems, as Goethe said of the churches at Assisi. But this comes of trying to penetrate and not merely to "experience" this world, and to penetrate it in every possible direction. I may be wrong, but I find great comfort in Nietzsche. He is not explicit, he is romantic but he *implies* my world of two or more storeys, if he does not draw its plan and elevation, as my architectural propensities lead me to do — without, I admit, any technical accuracy; because I am really a self-indulgent impressionist, like Nietzsche himself, and wish to sketch my buildings in perspective.

In order to keep up the game with B.B., however, I mentioned the constant pleasure I find in the light in Venice and in the aspects of the sky. "Yes," said he, "*they* were wonderful at catching those effects, due to the reflected light of the lagoon in the atmosphere. Paolo Veronese was supreme in rendering them." I thought of Titian and Tiepolo, but said nothing, because I don't really know or care who *painted* or who *saw* those harmonies most perfectly. Each probably saw a different effect, and painted it according to his own convention. What I care about is the harmonies themselves, which can't be had at second hand; they are strictly momentary and incommunicable; if you can get them out of a book or a picture, very well: but it would be an illusion to suppose that the *same* harmony had been felt by the poet or the painter. He had merely worked in a material, that could offer such harmonies eventually to the properly prepared mind; and his own interests — think of Shakespeare! — were probably much more mixed and hurried than those of a devout modern reader or connoisseur. It is lucky for B.B., in one sense, that he keeps the old flame alive; but I can't help feeling that it was lighted and is kept going by forced draft, by social and intellectual ambition, and by professional pendantry. If he were a real poet, would he turn away from the evening sky to see, by electric light, how Veronese painted it? . . .

Yours sincerely

To R. C. TREVELYAN

I Tatti
15 October 1939

Dear Trevy,

Many thanks for the translations of the Prometheus and the Medea. I shall read them as soon as I can. It is hard to find leisure for anything except the present and its parallel in the history of the *Oecumene* 1500 years ago. Then as now the Teuton furiously rages, driven forward by the Sarmatian at his heel. I hope we can defend ourselves better this time.

If your ultra-paternal government, behaving in a most un-English way, does not prevent you there is no reason why you should not come here. My deepest conviction is that we here are not going to join the "Dance of Death." You would scarcely feel any privation, you who are so hardy, indifferent to cold, careless of cars and abstemious as to coffee and tea. For spoilt and naughty old babies like myself the fuel question may get serious.

. . . We had a bitter cold September and are repaid with a hot October but it is enchanting and while I have eyes and senses life is pleasant — and fascinating.

To Henry Coster

I Tatti
Settignano
Florence
13 December 1939

My dear Harry,

I send you my best wishes, I send both of you my loving wishes for a Happy New Year.

That gives me an excuse for writing. There is so very little to say that you are not far better situated to know than we are here. And a *sfogo* by letter would be pretty cold by the time the "belligerency" boat brought it to you.

Home news. Mary is better & better. You ask me why I cannot tell. Her doctor does not know. Perhaps it is because he is new & Mary likes him. She goes out, she comes down to meals when she expects to be amused & when we are alone she reads aloud. We have for instance been listening to Flexner's very entertaining *America's Old Masters.*

Our world is reduced. Scarcely a sign of the "Highlife." This I am told meets daily at Doney's to hear G. Gherardesca read out passages fr. divers books tending to prove that Jews are "sub-human" & must be wiped-out. We do see Morra of course who leaves in three days for Rome. Alberti who comes today for a week, Clothilde Marghieri who is expected, & fr.

Florence, Russo,[1] Pancrazi,[2] Loria,[3] Elisabetta Picolellis,[4] Olga Loeser, Alice Dick-Lauder[5] were here, the Serristoris likewise (but they are just leaving for Rome) & Placci of course (although he is still in Rome).

We were there ourselves for more than a fortnight, staying first with the Aldriches & then with Visconti over Nemi before settling in to the hotel. We saw the Phillipses of course, the French & English embassies & French people like Carcopino head of Pal. Farnese school & the Iberts[6] of the Villa Medici. Besides we were quite sociable & saw lots of ex-*jeunes femmes* & their momentary "gelmen friends." I enjoyed this bath of bubbling frivolity & heard a great deal of contradictory political gossip.

I have been reading chiefly about the Decline & Fall. Did I in my last mention Gaffkens [Johannes] *Ausgang des Griech. Röm. Heldentums?* Since then I have perused books about Julian Apostate. Bidez is a masterpiece. I read all I can lay hands on of Weber, Laqueur & Oertel. If only I had ten-fold houses I could make full use of them. The strange fact about my age is that time almost disappears leaving no leisure for concentrated work. Hence we oldsters produce little or nothing.

Do let me have yr. news inward as well as outward. Much love to you both

Affectionately
B.B.

1 Luigi Russo (1891-1952), Professor of Italian Literature at the University of Florence and from 1946 head of the Scuola Normale in Pisa.

2 Pietro Pancrazi (1895-1952), a man of letters and a friend of Count Morra through whom he met Berenson.

3 Arturo Loria, Berenson's translator and close friend.

4 Elisabetta Picolellis, wife of Lucien Henraux, Carlo Placci's nephew, to whom B.B. was devoted. After Henraux's death she remarried and later resumed her maiden name.

5 Lady Dick-Lauder, the widow of Sir George Dick-Lauder, owned at the time a charming villa in Via S. Leonardo and was frequently a guest at I Tatti.

6 Jacques Ibert (1890-1962), French composer and musicologist, was for a long time Director of the Villa Medici in Rome.

To Mrs. Alfred Barr[1]

> Casa al Dono
> Vallombrosa
> (Prov. di Firenze)
> 1 October 1940

Dear Margot,

I wrote you toward the middle of July & sent by Clipper, but have not heard from you since. What has become of you? Why so silent? Even if my letter failed to reach you, you might have had the charity to inquire. Answer this at least & by Clipper. Ordinary post takes anywhere between three & six weeks.

On my part I have little to recount. All three of us came here soon after I last wrote & have been here ever since, but now on the point of returning to I Tatti. I have in all my days never enjoyed such complete solitude. For various reasons grave & gay locals have kept away & others have grown very rare. The only visits have been of the Aldrichs & Kinkaids[2] fr. Rome & just now Brelio[3] wh. you may have met here or in N.Y. Even callers have been very few. For instance Romaine Brooks[4] & Nathalie Barney. Do their names mean anything to you & have you ever come across them?

A year or more ago a N.Y. youth named Stuart Preston came my way. I don't remember how. I rather took to him & encouraged him. . . . Be kind to him.

So the summer here has passed in reading a great deal, in writing a little & walking a great deal. Nicky & I have tramped

---

[1] Margaret Scolari Barr, wife of Alfred Barr, the director of the Museum of Modern Art, New York.

[2] Admiral Kinkaid, at that time American naval attaché in Rome.

[3] Marchese di Brelio. Berenson is using the second title of Enrico Visconti-Venosta, the son of the celebrated Minister of Foreign Affairs, the Marchese Emilio Visconti-Venosta (1829-1914).

[4] The painter Romaine Brooks and the poet Natalie Barney left their adopted country, France, in 1940 and occupied a villa in the Via San Leonardo till the end of the war.

the forest in every direction, exploring paths & trails. We enjoyed it divinely. In fact I can say that but for the horrors going on at an ever shorter distance I have never enjoyed nature & the beauty of sky light & color as I have this summer. Where were my eyes & senses previously!

Is there any news [that] drifts thro of people like Adolf Goldschmidt, of Max Friedlander & others who had taken refuge in Holland, Belgium & France? And what art-news is there on your side? Is it business as usual? Have the French dealers got away in time, the Wildensteins, the Seligmanns etc. etc. What has become of McComb & what of Janice Loeb?

Magazines, pamphlets & apparently all unbound publications come thro again. In fact I receive the *Art News* & the other mags that I subscribe to. I peruse them with avidity, but seldom without nausea or headaches. A hundred times in my life I have thought seriously that the only way to get at art, music & literature was to forbid any & all writing & teaching regarding them. "Away with art." "Away from art." That is their result. Stuffed with information as with chopped straw & too full to leave room for any art-enjoyment.

Remember me to friends & do you count me for one.

Yours
B.B.

To Judge Learned Hand

Casa al Dono
Vallombrosa
(Prov. di Firenze)
3 October 1940

My dear B.,

Your letter of Aug. 27 reached me yesterday & was worth waiting for. I seldom enjoyed one as much. What you say about Johnnie Walker went to my heart. I could not love him more if he were my son. He is as responsive, as stimulating, as affectionate as the best of women, & yet has very much of the maturing man about him. Part of his charm is the promise that he never will get over-ripe. . . .

Mary & Nicky & I have spent a wonderful summer together. Excepting two visits from the Aldriches & one from the Kinkaids we have had no "House-guests." Just Brelio.

Of course I will give messages to the darling Aldriches. I wish you knew K. our naval *attaché*. In looks he might be yr. brother or cousin at least. In the absence of William Phillips he is a great comfort. We enjoyed the cottage we now inhabit; quaint, homely & quite lost in the forest. Such a forest & we have had the leisure to get intimate with it. Mary would drive out & wait till we returned fr. walking. In the evening she read aloud, lately Creighton's *History of the Papacy,* a book in six vols. which she & I last read more than 40 years ago. This time I, who have perused so much on that subject in the intervening years, found it better than ever, taking as it does so much more account of human nature than Continental works on such a subject do.

I have read a number of American autobiographies, the last being Lincoln Steffens, which begins so well & ends by telling you that all his 50 & more years of political study . . . have lead him to conclude that the ideal state would be run by a

Ford. I wonder what L.S. would say this minute. And what does Tommy Lamont say, he was so ready to trade with the greater Naziland. Does he still rub his hands with expectation of all he can do with the "New Order" being established on the European Continent?

May this find you in fit condition for yr. job. Love to Frances as well as yourself.

Affectionately

B.B.

To John Walker

I Tatti

Settignano Florence

24 February 1941

Dear Johnnie:

I am entrusting this to the Kinkaids, not because I have anything to say that might excite even the fussiest of censors, but to make sure that it reaches you. I want you to be sure to arrange a meeting with them and Walter Lippmann. They will be able to tell him all about us for they stayed with us a few days ago. We are truly sorry to part with them as we got to feel more at home with them than with any American friends over here excepting of course the Aldriches. Now Chester is dead & Amy will leave soon for home & we shall be left lonely. Our non-American friends are dear and devoted, stimulating & companionable, but naturally they are they & we, despite all temptations, remain Americans.

When yr. letter proposing that Olga & Mathilda should combine to give you Carlo's Cézannes reached me, I passed on yr. message to her. But it is questionable whether my letter has reached her yet. I certainly have had no word fr. her about it. I believe she means to leave Lisbon in less than a month's time, and she no doubt will present herself before long. I wonder, though, whether you are wise to launch out on very recent art. People may overwhelm you with their "treasures" & pressure may be brought to bear making it difficult to refuse. I can see you regretting the first step — beautiful as that was. Wherefore, I beg you to reflect.

Besides, recent art cannot be taken in along with what is already ancient. They take different cooking so to speak, & the one or the other will be underdone or overdone, & give us an indigestion — if our stomach in this connection is of the mind & heart & not of asbestos & steel.

— Here it is almost spring. Daffodils & narcissus blossoming freely in the garden, violets of course, & mimosa just coming out.

I am deep in a book I have never had in my hands before. It is Hoernes' *Urgeschichte der Kunst*. Published in 1915. Wonderfully free from Teutonic bosh, murk, bluff & self-delusions. It is a real treat to read even though it has little to tell me that is new to me. — Have you read Berdiaev's *New Middle Ages?* The two last chapters dealing with Russia & the Revolution are first rate. Now I am reading a more interesting Russian, Soloviev by name — on Love. "Beautiful soup."

What would I not give for days spent with you. Love to Marghie & the Finleys.

Yours,
B.B.

To Mrs. Alfred Barr

I Tatti
Settignano
Florence
22 April 1941

Dear Margot,

I can never thank you enough for the gorgeous letter about the Gargantuan opening of the Brobdignagian N.G. [National Gallery] in Washington D.C. How you can write when you have *passion*. We have each & all read & reread yr. so evocative description of the stupendous affair. How close you bring it & how happy we are that we approach it thanks to your pen in ideated form only. The actuality would have killed me & confirms me in the belief that I am more likely to survive concentration camps than our social gatherings.

You mention *Miss Greene*.[1] This fair lady has so Freudishly if not deliberately forgotten my existence that she has not sent me the catalogue of a show of the "Animal Kingdom" as represented in the Morgan library. Could you to spite her & to help me, get hold of a catalogue & send it. (Almost everything in print can be sent if not bound & I dare say not too bulky.) A day or two ago I gave a note for you to Olga Loeser on the small chance that you have not met already. She will be able to tell you how life is lived here now. I suppose you know all about her, widow of Charles Loeser, my most fierce enemy-friend & would be competitor, as well as really fine collector. No doubt you have been to her house & seen her things. Don't be put off by her dreadful German accent. *Elle gagne à être connue* & is capable of being a very good friend — a friend in need. . . .

Remembrances to friends & gratefully affectionate greetings to yourself.

Yours
B.B.

1 Miss Belle Greene, J. P. Morgan's librarian.

TO MLLE EDITH DE GASPARIN

Casa al Dono

7 September 1941

. . . I am still in this enchanted spot in ideal weather for which however the crops are suffering as they sorely need rain. But as I am not responsible, as I have not set Rome on fire, I have no remorse in gathering all the roses on my path. I look toward an horizon bounded by the Carrara mountains and the highest Apennine peaks, and in between the lower Valdarno with its gleaming river and fold upon fold of hills. If I walk a couple of hundred meters up the ridge I have a wide view over the Casentino to Camaldoli, to La Verna to the mountains above Urbino.

. . . Remember me to Jacques Blanche and tell him I never cease regretting that he did not write ever so much more about 19th century painting. He could have been its Vasari.

. . . Nicky Mariano reads me to sleep with Sainte-Beuve's "Volupté." How slow and monotonous it is and yet one goes on because the book oozes a value. What I am really enjoying is Seek's *Untergang der Antiken Welt.* It happens to be a subject I know something about and I am amazed at Seek's readableness, as well as at his soundness of judgment and great horizon. The subject fascinates me beyond all others and I keep asking myself "Are we already where the Ancients were 1500 years ago or is there still a possibility of retaining our civilization?" The parallels are frightening.

TO EDITH DE GASPARIN

12 November 1941

Dear Friend, just a fortnight ago I received a delightful letter from you which had but one blemish. I beg you to remove it.

You address me as "illustre ami." *Ami* as much as you like but *illustre* not at all. You know that as an empty form it is silly. If the least bit genuine it is absurd. I am what I am but not one bit "illustre."

. . . I wish I could see Blanche's book on his English friends that appeared in England unfortunately I am entirely cut off from England and even from the U.S.A. almost no books pass except those of a purely archeological order.

I congratulate you on having read Renan's *Peuple d'Israel*. I would urge you to follow with the four or five volumes on the first two centuries of Christianity. They are fascinating. Pay no attention to micrographers and Catholicizers who finding nothing else to say against Renan accuse him of lacking scholarship. Of course this or that infinitesimal fact has been brought to light since he wrote. Rest assured that it does not change the pattern of the picture. The fact is that the truly great historians never fall out of date. How very little correction Gibbon requires after 150 years, or Michelet, or Ranke or Creighton or Sorel or Vandal. The point of view may veer from a more liberal to a more reactionary attitude. It does not alter the perspective or change the value of what great historians give. By a great historian I mean one who can render a period and its characters fascinatingly alive and in a way that no facts big or little can seriously alter. From such a standpoint Renan ranks with the best.

. . . But for the thought of what is going on in this hag-ridden world I should have little to complain of. I enjoy my hours of reading my bits of writing, the talk of the few friends and more numerous acquaintances who still come to see one. I confess I would enjoy French and anglo-saxon ones for a change. My German distresses me and even in Italian I stumble. I can express myself least unsatisfactorily in English, the language almost unknown to the people with whom it is worth while conversing.

Nicky Mariano to Professor Paul J. Sachs

18 Borgo San Jacopo[1]
Firenze
25 November 1941

Dear Paul:

After a long lapse of silence I am trying my luck again to send you and Meta most affectionate messages from all of us for the approaching holidays. I hope you and all your dear ones are well in health, even if one's spirit cannot help being oppressed by what is going on in the world. Will the new year bring us a Wiedersehen? I doubt it. We are still here as you see, B.B. and Mary having both decided that for people of their age the wisest thing is to stay at home. We still live our former kind of life with work in the library and walks on the hills between Settignano and Fiesole and friends dropping in to lunch or to tea. The evenings we spend very quietly, reading together and sometimes [listening] to a radio concert. B.B. has enjoyed his summer at Vallombrosa rapturously, is feeling very fit and optimistic and works regularly at the book he is planning to publish as soon as the war is over. Mary too is at work on a biography of her daughter Ray Strachey and it gives her great happiness to feel through it in close touch with one who is no more. Within the limits of her invalid condition she too is fairly well, joins us frequently at meals and for the evening and on fine days drives out with us. Thinking of what has happened to so many of our friends in the rest of Europe we consider ourselves indeed privileged to be allowed to go on enjoying such a peaceful existence.

Besides giving you news of us and sending you our greetings for the holidays B.B. is very anxious to have me consult

1 The house from which Miss Mariano writes was destroyed in the tragic first week of August, 1944 (at the same time as the Trinita Bridge). It was occupied by Baron and Baroness Anrep. Baroness Anrep (Miss Mariano's sister) was until recently Head Librarian at I Tatti.

you on the subject of his beloved friend Doro Levi.[1] It pre-
occupies him greatly that after three years of residence in the
States and in spite of all the efforts made on his behalf by B.B.
and other friends he should not have been given a position. In
B.B.'s opinion few of the emigrant professors who have been
able to settle down are Doro's equals for capacity, learning and
character. Is there any reason for it? Are perhaps some of his
most charming qualities, the fact that he is not a go-getter,
that he does not know how to advertise himself, that his appearance is so youthful, his manner so unprofessorial, against
him? When in the spring of 1940 a few friends accepted
B.B.'s proposition and helped him to finance a course of lectures to be given by Doro at Harvard, B.B.'s chief object was
to have something stable develop out of these lectures. And
yet it has not happened. That the lectures have been a success
is proved not only by what several people have written to B.B.
about them, but chiefly by the fact that Doro has been invited
to lecture again at Harvard next spring and, as far as we know,
without anybody's help.

A rumour has reached B.B. about a chair of archaeology to
be created in connection with Dumbarton Oaks, chiefly with
the object in view of training young archaeologists. B.B. cannot
think of anybody who could be more suitable for it than Doro,
combining as he does great learning with considerable experience as a field archaeologist in Greece as well as in Syria. If
this rumour corresponds to any facts B.B. hopes that you will
not fail to put in your authoritative voice in Doro's favour. He
hopes this not only for the sake of the great personal affection
he has for Doro, but for the sake of Harvard. B.B. is deeply
convinced that as a teacher in a Seminar, which such a pro-
fessorship would essentially require, you could not the world
over get a better man than Doro.

---

1 Doro Levi was Professor of Archaeology at the University of Cagliari but was
obliged to leave Italy in 1939. He is now Director of the Italian School of Archaeology in Athens.

Please forgive my very imperfect typing! I have learnt this useful art in theory, but with all the other things I have to do I never have enough leisure to practice it.

Ever so many messages from Mary, B.B. and also from my sister and brother-in-law. Do let us hear from you soon!

Very affectionately
yours
Nicky

To Lawrence Berenson

8 August 1942

Dear Lawrence:

I have just received yours of May 27th, of June 5th, of June 16th in the same envelope forwarded from Lisbon. The one of May 27th addressed to Geneva never reached me so I am glad you sent the copy. I cannot begin to tell you how happy I am to hear from you after such a long interval and how interesting all you say is. I have no comments to make that would avail, so I can only go on thanking you with all my heart for what you are doing for us and some of my gratitude flows over to those who are helping.

Sam is entirely mistaken about Mary; even if we were in Switzerland the attempt to take her home could only be fatal. She is fairly happy only while in bed, gets out of it at my urgent request for an hour or two but says that every step she takes hurts her. She herself has no idea how much we, that is to say Nicky does to provide her with every comfort and to keep worries and annoyances far from her. Sam seems unaware that the journey to Lisbon cannot be done by air, and that by rail it is enough to try normally healthy people. If he could see me, let alone Mary, he would understand why we must not under present conditions of travel and life attempt to move. I have mentioned my health but do not get alarmed; I am probably as well as a studious, bookish, never strong person can expect to be in his 78th year. I keep going only by avoiding the least fatigue especially of a physical, uncomfortable kind.

As for money, our authorities seem to ignore the fact that I am not asking any for ourselves. I want the least necessary for carrying on the institutional part of my establishment and for taxes. Not only would these have to be paid if I was not here but I have reason to believe that everything has gone thus far so smoothly because I am here in residence and that the civil authorities have a certain regard for my being on the spot.

I await with keen interest what further news there will be from Mrs. Shipley.

I beg you to do all you can for little Mary[1] and if you can't afford it perhaps friends of mine will help you out. By the way please tell Addie[2] that I have not heard from her for months, and miss her and think of her ever so much. Nor have I had word from Senda or Bessie[3] since I got the letters written by them in January. Assure them that they are seldom out of my thoughts and keep them informed of all you hear from or about me.

We have not gone up the hills but they have come down to us; we are having an ideal summer and as it is as silent as if we were in the heart of a wilderness; it is most restful. We see almost nobody as even Alda and Bertie have gone to the seashore. So I read and write and walk and the days go very fast and beautifully. Gladly should I see them go but that winter

---

1 Maria Rosselli, the widow of Nello Rosselli who together with his brother Carlo was killed at Bagnoles in 1937. As they were well-known anti-Fascists, it was no doubt a case of a political murder.

2 Mrs. Otto Kahn.

3 Sisters of Bernard Berenson.

will follow and I dread the cold and the probable difficulties of keeping warm.

Enough for the present. Yes one more thing. Can you not re-invest my funds? . . . If you can, do consult Kidder. They have advised me well and invest all but some ten thousand.

With love from all three of us to you.

B.B.

To Edith de Gasparin

24 March 1943

. . . How splendid is your description of your winter sea [at Varengeville, Normandy]. It called up recollections of my boyhood on the rock-bound New England coast where in the winter the Atlantic is a fascinating Leviathan whose waves are always coiling and tormenting. I used to enjoy rowing out to take the monster waves as they tossed under me. That is sixty years ago but your words brought back the memory as if it were but of yesterday.

. . . I do not like it at all when Aldous [Huxley], partly out of real soul-need but partly out of sheer tropism, turns towards the "grand peut-être." Real religion it seems to me is based on animal faith, what you French call *la foi du bûcheron.* When you have it you need no metaphysico-theological justification. You take it as an ultimate. When you have it not, all the wishful thinking in the world will not give it to you, and lead you back *au sein de l'Eglise,* to hide there from the hounds of doubt. Even there, having returned to mother's womb you will find not theological, dogmatical security, but only numbness, torpor, often voicing itself in eloquent quibbling. So I pity them that cannot believe as I pity those who cannot love. Both are incomplete, sterile animals and failures as human beings. Real religion is a gift like the quality of temperament or heart or mind. No amount of discussion or persuasion on the part of theologians or metaphysicians will give it. One has to be born with it. Then one can intellectualize it, refine it, perchance even communicate the joy of it as the great preachers have to those who are born with it.

Owing to the war, communications between Italy and the United States were naturally difficult. The immediately following letters will show that Berenson maintained a tenuous connexion via Lisbon and Berne.

M. JIRMOUNSKY[1] TO LAWRENCE BERENSON

Lisbon
13 July 1943

Dear Mr. Berenson,

I have just received a letter from your cousin Mr. Bernard Berenson (with the date of June 13, 1943), who begs me to write to you and to communicate you that the only letter he received from you is that of the January (I suppose and hope that he Mr. B.B. might receive another one, that I sent him, but which could reach him only after his letter was yet sent to me), the first since last August.

He is pleased to learn that you can still help out Mary[2] and

1 Myron Jirmounsky, a Russian émigré, an art historian attached to the Academia das Belas Artes in Lisbon. Berenson took a friendly interest in him and his publications, which were chiefly on Portuguese art.

2 Mary Rosselli.

her children. As for health, he will be 78 in a few days; and many not too pleasant symptoms appear, to make sure that he realizes how old he is. Mary is worse and worse as to her legs and bladder, but in no alarming way. The worst of her troubles is that she has lost all taste for life and it is difficult to rouse her. The only thing she seems still to enjoy is reading aloud and she has read to them Longfellow's, Holmes', Lowell's, Prescott's, Morley's Life & Letters. They have made him (Mr. Berenson) quite homesick for the places and persons of his youth, and Mary much the same. He is working all the time, as there are almost no interruptions as they see almost nobody and receive almost no letters. His walks too are curtailed, as it tires him to climb up the hills, and there are no other walks. He learns a very great deal each day and adds a line or two to his book on Decline and Recovery. If they go up the hills he will devote himself to giving finishing touches to his two completed books.

Mr. Bernard Berenson sends to you love and his best remembrances to Paul, Felix, Mack, Walter, Sam, Johnnie and other friends.

With best regards, dear Mr. Berenson

Sincerely yours,
M. Jirmounsky

To Mrs. Alfred Barr

c/o Prof. Jirmounsky
Academia das Belas Artes
Cale Biblioteca Publica
Lisbon
July 43

Dear Margot,

Take pen & paper & write all about yrself . . . & tell me all about common friends. I shall be so grateful! I am as well & as comfy & as busy as a man who has already had his 78th birthday can expect to be. I read prodigiously & do some writing. At present I am engaged on "Decline & Recovery in the Figure Arts." It is a book that will take at least thirty years to finish. So you can see how long I expect to remain not only living but alive. I have published nothing for years but when the floodgates are open I shall have two books to cast upon the waters. Here no end of books & publications keep appearing, marvellously illustrated & inexpensive. I doubt whether they are meant to be read. Indeed most of them have little text. Translations in quantity, particularly of our most advanced story-tellers & novelists; Faulkner, Caldwell & all Steinbeck except *The Moon Is Down.*

Is Kress still alive as I hope? What is happening to the Metropolit. Mus. & to the Fogg & to the Walters & the Washington National Gallery? I have heard from none of them for a very long time. I hope they are carrying on as usual. Are many serious art books appearing & Leonardos popping up like mushrooms from the ground, not to speak of Raphaels & Giorgiones. You see I confine myself to my own exiguous parish & do not ask about the masterpieces of other schools.

You see dear Margot how incurably frivolous I am. Age will not cure me.

Nicky joins me in most affectionate greetings

Ever yrs.
B.B.

To the Honorable Leland Harrison

Tuscany
6 December 1943

Dear Mr. Harrison:

The watchful and helpful Swiss authorities tell me that you want to know how we are getting on and propose that I answer with my own hand.

My health is excellent for my age. I get tired easily and am unable to concentrate more than an hour at a time, or to walk as long.

Unfortunately my wife is not so well. Her condition is pretty low although not alarming.

Thus far we have little to complain of, and I hope we shall remain safe and sound to the end.

Sincerely yours,
Bernard Berenson

To the Crown Prince of Sweden

[Le Fontenelle
Careggi]
March 1944

Sir,

Your Legation tells me that you have been inquiring about me. They invite me to write to you and offer to forward the letter by your bag. I am happy to take advantage of this opportunity to tell you about my life and — unberufen — absence of adventures in the last six months and more.

But first let me thank you for the interest you continue to take in me at a time when you must have so much to occupy and pre-occupy you. I hope that your health is not suffering under the strain and that You and Yours keep fit.

To return to myself — the moment the Germans and

revenant Fascists began to occupy Florence, responsible people told me that my home was not a safe residence for me. A day or two later friends spirited me away to the estate where I have been ever since. It is a beautiful place with a good climate, a house with every comfort and a park that furnishes pleasantly varied walking for an hour. I am materially well off and physically I keep as well as a man of my constitution can expect to be at my age. I shall be 79 in three months. If things get no worse before they get better I shall count this period of reclusion as one of the most pleasant and peaceful ever enjoyed by me.

At my age I do not seem to need change of scene and a variety of company so I feel no hanker to stray out beyond the park-railings nor a keen desire for miscellaneous society.

I was able to bring along enough books of my own treating of subjects connected with my work and the house has an abundance of general literature. So I am not hard up for reading and the days rush by with astonishing velocity. "Nicky" — who is with me — reads aloud subjects connected with my work and other friends here lighter literature, French and Italian.

I am writing, or rather I have barely commenced a book that is to be called "Decline and Recovery in the Figure Arts", and may take several volumes. I can scarcely hope to complete it but may do enough to show where and how I am going. If only I am not overwhelmed by too many calls on my diminished energies.

You will want to know about my library and works of art. Nearly everything has been put in places where they have a good chance of remaining unharmed.

My wife was too bedridden to be taken away from her house and her habitual attendance. She has been at death's door since I left but is happily better and I hope to see her again before the final separation. She was 80 last month.

Let me end this too long epistle by telling you that the last six months have offered abundant proof of the depths of human iniquity; but, what is wonderful, also demonstrations of angelic kindness, of eager friendliness of affectionate care and attention that I not only never expected but could not imagine as coming from people I had scarcely known previously. That has been, as my countrymen say, a "liberal education."

I cannot tell you how much I wish to see your beautiful uncrowded, so humanized country again. I dream of coming as soon as travelling is safe and to see your museums again but with deeper understanding than I had on my last visit. By the way, if anything of interest on Chinese or other ancient arts has appeared in Sweden will you be so kind as to ask a bookseller to reserve copies for me and to send them with the bill when communications are open again.

The following extract from a letter of Captain Robert Berenson,[1] dated 6 September 1944, and Miss Mariano's undated letter to Mr. Lawrence Berenson following upon, and supplementing Berenson's own letter of 13 December will illustrate the train de vie *at I Tatti in the difficult closing months of 1944.*

FROM CAPTAIN ROBERT BERENSON

I have just come back from Florence where I have been several times before in the last month or so looking for B.B. I finally found him safe and well and absolutely beside himself with joy seeing me. I actually got to him several days after the Germans left the area where he was hiding. I am happy to say

1 A cousin of Berenson.

that B.B. is wonderfully well considering everything. He has been hiding in a friend's house[1] for a full year, not able to move outside for one minute. Imagine what he has been through. He is really remarkable. Rather than worrying about himself, he locked himself up with his books, studying and writing. He came out having written two books and a bunch of short stories. Mary who is just about alive is living at I Tatti. She is very old and weak and doesn't make much sense, but is still just as sweet and lovely looking in her tired old age. B.B. had to get out of this house and hide but there was nothing Mary could do or anybody could do to her, so she stayed at I Tatti with the servants. Nobody bothered her at all. The Germans came to the house several times to drill her on where B.B. was, but she evaded them every time. The most remarkable thing was the way he had his books and collections. They are all safe, with few exceptions.

To Lawrence Berenson

Fontanelle
Careggi
Florence
13 September 1944

Dear Lawrence,

Thanks to our charming and dear Robert I am able to write directly and at length. Within a few days of our being liberated from the Nazi-Fascist terror he appeared, having previously sent others to find out how I was. He is with his general and not often free to come, but I hope to see him again and again. He is

---

[1] The house of the Marchese Serlupi, the Minister of the Republic of San Marino to the Holy See.

full of affectionate helpfulness and will do his best to alleviate our no small material difficulties.

In the main the Tatti has suffered no damage from German occupation and our own bombardment that dollars five thousand would not repair. The great difficulty is finding the materials. No tiles, no brick, no cement seems to be available and above all no glass for the windows, not one of which has remained undamaged.

Then the Nazis destroyed the electric plant and we are without light, without current for the kitchen, the frigidaire and larder or for the stoves. There is no coal, no other combustible. We are reduced to sitting in the dark or trying to read by miserable pseudo-candles. Even oil is very scarce and gives a faint light anyway.

Then there is the hard food situation. My staff between secretaries, librarians, two trained nurses for Mary, and indoor servants comprises at least 12 persons and there is almost nothing to feed on. Wherefore I appeal to you to send if possible the following:

1. Hams or any other preserved meat or fish
2. Semolino flour
3. Cereals and crackers
4. Butter and condensed milk
5. Sugar
6. Coffee, tea and chocolate
7. Soap, both toilet and washing
8. Stearine candles

I may be crying for the moon but please hand on my cry to Addie and other friends disposed to help us out.

But for that criminal of a Gherardesca, who did locally all he could to rouse hatred against me and to restrict our lives, I felt tolerably safe under the protection of the Central government.

As long as Ciano was in power he kept the word he had given to William Phillips and except for local intrigues I was left unmolested. When the Nazis and ghoul-Fascists came, both German and Italian friends urged me to lose no time in disappearing from view. My absence for a time was not remarked and when it was, the assistant chief of police made public that I had escaped and was in Portugal. I cannot tell you how much I owe to the police here, to officials who scarcely knew me personally, to friends both Italian and German. They not only helped to save my life but my art treasures and great library as well. First and foremost among them the man who happened to be my sequestrator and scarcely yet a friend. A year ago he came and took Nicky and me to his place where I have remained without stirring till this day. Twice in the dark winter hours I went to the dentist and directly after the retreat of the Germans I went in an armoured car to see Mary. She had remained there all the time and the Anreps, Nicky's relations, came at once to stay in the house and take care of her, and of the whole property. When the house was occupied by the Germans, their tactful way of dealing with them prevented its being sacked as most other villas have been. I found Mary very feeble and rather wandering. She has two trained nurses and her own maid. All complain that she is a difficult patient.

The place where I have been in hiding for exactly one whole year happens to be a paradise for climate, for view and for beauty of surroundings, but two miles as the crow flies from I Tatti with which we remained in almost daily contact. Here I have been treated as a favourite grandfather, enjoyed the most affectionate company and every comfort and luxury possible in wartime, far beyond what I could have had at my own home. This angelic family are the Serlupi-Crescenzis. The Marquess is Minister of San Marino to the Holy See and therefore had all diplomatic immunities and privileges.

Enough for today. Please communicate the gist of this to

my sisters, to Paul, to Johnnie, to Walter, to Felix, to Mack, to Byba, etc. etc. When you can, write about yourselves, including the girls.

I fervently hope that my finances are in tolerable state and that my income will permit me to carry on at I Tatti.

Most affectionately

B.B.

Nicky Mariano to Lawrence Berenson

I Tatti

Settignano

Florence

[n.d. but undoubtedly end of November

or beginning of December 1944]

Dear Lawrence,

You cannot imagine what an event your letter has been for this household! It was the first sent off after the liberation that reached us, and except for the unsatisfactory account of poor Ralph's[1] health full of good news. Unfortunately the improvement in his condition you speak of must have been followed by another setback for Bob[2] when he was here the other day had had recent news through his mother of Ralph's being worse again and of Senda and Bessie having come over to be near him. That sounds very disquieting and we feel very anxious about him.

Meanwhile the long and detailed account B.B. sent you through Bob in September must have reached you. About the

1 Ralph Barton Perry.
2 Captain Robert Berenson.

end of September the house here had been, in spite of all the incredible difficulties about getting glass, bricks and other building materials, put into shape again and we were able to return to it followed by the pictures that had been in hiding with us and gradually also by all the books that had been stored away in different places. Bob has been most helpful about the means of transport and in many other ways. Unfortunately he is terribly busy and we see him but rarely. Here we found Mary turned into a complete invalid, physically quite helpless and frequently in great pain. Mentally she is all there and we take turns in going to see her whenever she feels up to it. I do not think she realizes any more what has happened with the world and I don't wonder. It is hard enough for any of us who move about and are more or less in touch with events and people. My people are still here living with us. They plan to settle down in the San Martino villa here on B.B.'s estate, but fuel is so frightfully difficult to procure that it is by far the most practical thing to enjoy whatever we can get together. Of course the libraries cannot be heated, but the small furnace in the front part of the house has been started and we hope to go on getting the fuel for it. For B.B. the most serious privation is the electric light, which has returned to the town of Florence but not yet to the outlying districts, and to do his reading with wretched little kerosene lamps is bad for his eyes. In the evening he manages by letting me read to him, but in the early morning hours I am not available and he has to manage as best he can. The food question is difficult, but we have managed so far and hope that in the future some parcels from the States will help us out. If we had only to think of ourselves it would be relatively simple, but what with the servants and the guests coming and going it is sometimes quite a problem. For we are now leading, in contrast to what it has been, an extremely social life, with friends in uniform turning up all the time, sent or brought by friends or just curious to look up B.B. and talk to him or to see the house and the collection. They arrive at the most unexpected hours and sometimes we get a little tired, not being accustomed any more to so much social life, but it is a great pleasure all the same and B.B. enjoys being hospitable to them and making them feel at home. Besides it interests him immensely to come in touch through them with so many things and events and currents of thought and opinion in the States and in England. Hardly a day goes by without one or two of them being here to lunch or to tea. So I come back to the subject of the parcels and of how grateful we would be for a little help. It seems that they cannot be sent to Florence yet, but perhaps you could use the same address as for letters in Rome and have them sent also to me and to Alda in the same way. Besides B.B. would like very much to do a kindness to the people who have been particularly good and helpful to him during this last difficult year and wonders whether you could arrange to have parcels sent to them at his expense whenever it is allowed to send them to Florence. I therefore enclose a list of names of which the three first ones, he would like to be particularly considered perhaps with more than one parcel as they are the people in whose house we lived, who took in our books and who helped in the storing away of the pictures. Sugar, coffee, tea, chocolate, candies, jam and soap (for ourselves also any kind of fats or cereals or biscuits would be lovely, and sewing thread) would be I think the most welcome things.

We are gradually turning into sturdy beggars! Please communicate this sad fact to all our friends and let them act in accordance with it!

I have not had a line from Byba[1] yet and I do not know whether the different messages I sent her have ever reached her. I hear from her nephew who has been to see us that she is very busy as president of an Italian relief committee. Please

1 Byba Giuliano (Mrs. Henry Coster).

communicate to her some of our news and all our love. And of course you will send this letter on to Senda and Bessie, for it is meant for them as much as for you. . . .

With ever so many loving messages for every one around you and to all friends you may happen to see

Very affectionately yours
Nicky

To Lawrence Berenson

Settignano
1 December 1944

Dear Lawrence,

Yours of Oct. 10 reached me but a few days ago and we have read it over and over again. First let me thank you for family news. I am delighted to learn that Louise is happily married to a naval officer and that Marion, Elsie and you are well. My love to all of you and best wishes for 1945. Please hand on same to Ruth with congratulations. I was distressed to hear of Ralph's[1] serious illness but your account made me hope he was out of the woods.

I am deeply touched by all you tell me about the various inquiries you were receiving regarding our safety. I tried all I could to pierce the fog and get through. It was made impenetrable by censorship all round. Only once could I send a long letter to Berne to that angelical minister Harrison. You surely received a detailed letter Robert undertook to send you, in which I gave you a succinct and comprehensive account of our adventures. Except for the month of August when we were in

---

[1] Ralph Barton Perry.

the hands of the Nazis and being bombarded by our own artillery, we were ever so much better off than since our "liberation." Then we lacked for nothing. Now we lack a great deal. The greatest privation is electric energy. It leaves us without many domestic necessities, but for me the absence of light is an affliction. The days are short, the skies cloudy. And for eight or ten hours a day I work by the light of smoky, smelly, flickering little lamps. It is hard on the eyes. For this there is no remedy, seeing I cannot expect the Allies to let me have a generator all to myself. Heating precarious. Food uncertain, and not abundant. No buses, no taxis, no cabs. So Italian friends cannot come to see us and although we have a miserable vehicle we dare not use it much for fear of using up the irreplaceable rubber tires and the skimpy allowance of gasoline. Walks are dangerous because the Nazis before leaving ruined the hillsides and all paths.

Nicky is sending a list of what we most need by way of food. By the way we never received the box of food Byba's nephew was to bring over. He said Sam Reber would not let him. Clothing I need none just yet, unless it be an uptodate tie or two. Nicky and Alda may want some and Nicky will let you know.

Please thank friends for their affectionate interest and tell them I shall write to each of them soon. Communicate with Mrs. Humphrey Roberts and assure her that her friendship means a great deal to me and that I look forward to seeing her again. I am deeply sorry to learn that Mack is no more. What of his Ruth? I have several books blocked out but they need considerable revision. I am not yet in condition to work hard on them, and besides uniformed visitors take up time and even more reading of periodicals and books that give some idea of what has been going on in our worlds while I was cut off from them.

One of the books, the most important, is to be called "Aesthetics and History." Another is vaguely autobiographical. A third is a diary. A fourth a short book which might be entitled "A Letter to the American Jews." But I have cold feet about publishing any of them.

What of Edward Forbes? [1] If he still is in N.Y. remember me to him and tell him I would like to hear from him.

All good wishes to you and yours, dear Lawrence. I appreciate anything you have done and are doing for me.

Yours
B.B.

To Mrs. Alfred Barr

I Tatti
5 December 1944

Dear Margot,

Let me wish that 1945 may be kind to you & that among other good things it may produce our meeting again. It will have to be over here, as under present conditions I do not see myself going over to the other side. And yet I am dying to do so, to see friends & to revisit the museums & find out how they look & how they have grown.

Meanwhile I count on you to send me [word] regarding all & sundry. Remember I have heard nothing for nearly five years. You need not fear my crying *connu*. Everything you vouchsafe to tell me about the art world will be news to me.

About myself you know already the very simple story of my having remained at I Tatti till Sept. 10, '43, when on the arrival of Nazi-cum-spook Fascists I went into hiding & remained there an entire year. It proved comfortable enough but for

1 At the time, Director of the Fogg Museum.

August when indeed we lived dangerously in the thick of the fight, in the midst of German troops being bombarded by our own.

I am home again, a home rather worse for Nazi occupation & our own shelling, without light, precarious heat, food ditto & other returns to cave dwelling. But we make the best of it & I waste spare time in reading up what happened in America & England when I was cut off from both & in seeing the uniformed youngsters who come to inspect me as a monument.

Affectionate greetings from Nicky as well as myself.

Ever yrs.

B.B.

To JUDGE LEARNED HAND

Settignano

5 January 1944 [*sic*, inadvertently, for 1945]

Dear B.,

Our best wishes to you & Frances for the year now beginning & all future years.

Where shall I begin after four years of interrupted correspondence! Rumours have reached you no doubt of my hiding during the Nazi-Fascist occupation. Only a few days ago I learned that at home evil tongues have been accusing me of having thought of my own safety only, leaving my wife at home to the tender mercies of the enemy. The facts are that Mary as a pure Aryan & immobilized invalid had nothing to fear, particularly as I left her not only in the care of three trained nurses but of Alda,[1] Bertie[2] & Cecil Anrep.[3] They sheltered her from

1 Baroness Anrep.
2 Baron Anrep.
3 Their son.

every annoyance when I Tatti was occupied by the Germans & did all that under the circumstances could be done for her comfort. Serious trouble came when our own troops were bombarding I Tatti as well as the place where I was hiding.

That was only as the crow flies, two miles away & thanks to the connivance of the German consul & the Italian police (who urged me to disappear) I remained safe & sound not only during the occupation but during the siege & terror of August. Nicky was with me all the time & during the siege we were entirely in the hands of Nazi *parachutists* & if Nicky had not been there to smooth them down with her intimate knowledge of the German language & German ways, it might have gone hard with us.

This is ancient history. I have been home 3 months feeling a collapse from the strain of the previous 12 months. Then I am on the shady side of 80 & tire easily & am apt to doze in the evening as old men will do. Moreover I am overwhelmed by uniformed callers at all times of the day & much time goes in reading periodicals, back numbers for years past, eager as I am to find out what Anglo-Saxon & French have been thinking these years. Yet I am eager to write, or rather to revise & prepare for print what I have written. As it is not about art I have a certain fear of what I may incur if I publish. . . .

Ever affectionately
B.B.

To Professor Paul J. Sachs

I Tatti
Settignano
Florence
29 January 1945

My dear Paul,

As I have not heard fr. you since Sept. when I wrote at length first to you & then to Edward & as I have learned that other letters written at that time never reached their destination I have been wondering whether you received mine. If you have not, please believe it is no negligence of mine, any more than your failure to receive a long letter I wrote on receipt of yr. catalogue of the Fogg drawings.

I need scarcely repeat that I was truly distressed that you & Edward so much my juniors should be falling out, he altogether & you for connection with the museum. It made me feel immeasurably ancient, but at the same time, left me wondering & rather anxious about yr. successors. Please let me know.

Here it will be a long time before we have "normalcy." Meanwhile the sands of life are running & it does not look as if I shall live to see better days. Damage to house is being repaired & pictures that were buried under the ruins of Borgo S. Jacopo are being restored. The library is already itself again — with the absence of all periodicals & books published in England or America during the last five years. I fear it will not be easy to procure them, & a gash will remain in the continuity of art publications of every kind.

I have little leisure for work as I am taken up with seeing people, trying to help them out of fixes, trying to explain, to smooth over misunderstandings & other unavoidable, but probably futile efforts to do good.

My own health is fair but my poor Mary is in almost unceasing, unrelenting pain & seldom well enough to see me for more than a few moments a day.

Affectionate greetings to you both & to Edward.

Ever yours

B.B.

To Mrs. Alfred Barr

I Tatti
Settignano
Florence
3 March 1945

Dearest Margot,

I cannot understand by what miracle yours of Febr. 11 flew into my bedroom yesterday when I was getting over, at least I hope so, an attack of pneumonia. It was carried in an envelope wh. had on its back the printed words: *Consiglio Provinciale di Terra di Lavoro Il Presidente.* The only address in very stylized handwriting was "Mr. Bernard Berenson." Blessed be the ways & means by wh. this word of yours has reached me & the first so swiftly, under 20 days.

You must realize that we civilians are only an unavoidable nuisance & are treated accordingly. For instance, the ordinary post brought me yesterday a letter posted in Rome Febr. 12. Sometimes it takes weeks for a p.c. to travel fr. Florence to the Settignano p.o.

Well darling Margot, this letter of Febr. 11 is the first word of yours to reach me. Let me hope the two others you say you have written will follow for I am insatiable for news of all of you. Meanwhile I am truly distressed to learn that yr. mother in

Rome has been starving, but happy to hear how much you enjoy the company of yr. little girl. We at I Tatti have greatly enjoyed for the last three or four years the presence of Igor Markevitch's small boy, a most gifted child, not a bit precocious but fascinating in every way that a small boy can be. Nicky of course has entirely lost her heart to him & he has been, after me, her chief occupation & pre-occupation. She is recovering from the breakdown she had at the end of the German occupation & is more "helpful & good" [1] than ever. Next to God Almighty I owe her everything. . . .

If you read the charter of the Metrop. Mus. you will find that it was started as an association of collectors who wanted each others advice & a place for the safe keeping of their treasures. As late as J. P. Morgan Senior the Metrop. was only that. The Boston Mus. of F. A. has never been anything else. In short Art Matters are again where I found them 60 years ago. In those 60 yrs. I did what I could for collectors & collecting. All in vain. Charlatanism *cum* pedantry reign more absolutely than ever. On "what there remains of this Psalm" one might expatiate at length & produce a best-seller. *Absit omen!*

To come down to family news, my wife is a distressed & distressing invalid & just now so low that the worst may be feared. I cannot understand why I am so bent on her living on, seeing life is only a hell for her. Of Nick I have spoken already. Her sister, sister's husband & son, having lost everything in their bombed out [2] house [in] Borgo S. Jacopo, are living with us, keeping house & helping to keep going under conditions all but impossible. Fuel, food precarious; no transport, as there

---

1 Cf. Goethe:
Edel sei der Mensch
Hilfreich und gut . . .
Berenson was an admirer of Goethe and must have been thinking of the poem since he has put this phrase in quotation marks.

2 More precisely, dynamited.

are no buses, no taxis, no cabs, practically no way of getting in & out of town except on foot. We have autos, but no tires & even a license to circulate is reserved for the especially privileged & as you know I am not one.

My books: I have kept an intermittent diary, particularly of the year I was in *Macchia*. As I read it over I get my doubts. It is so sober, so wanting in the pep contemporaries are accustomed to, so reflective & so free from "warm, revealing personality" that it may be judged unpublishable. The other book will require no little licking into shape for some four or five years ago I left it as a torso & have not looked at it since. It is to be my last word on art criticism. I have other work on hand, but of that "in my next." Do write all you have time for & yr. reward will be that I shall clamour for more & more.

Ever affectionately
B.B.

To Robert C. Trevelyan

I Tatti
31 March 1945

My dear Trevy,

This is only to tell you that Mary died eight days ago. The end was peaceful.

When I left her September 1943 she suffered a great deal and acutely but she still had enough strength to join us in the little drawing-room on the library floor or on the terrace to read aloud after meals. That she enjoyed and did well. But after my return she never left her room and was seldom well enough to talk for more than a few minutes. One felt that nothing interested her any more. So she gradually faded away. Nicky remains with me and you know what that means. There are other good friends but I long for my English and American companions who like you dear Trevy must go on living a good bit for my sake. Younger friends have not shared the years with one. You cannot ask them "do you remember" what happened to you and them forty and more years ago.

To Professor Paul J. Sachs

I Tatti
Settignano
Florence
11 May 1945

Dear Paul,

Two days ago I received by ordinary post yours of March 26. This will go to you, thanks to the kindness of our Ambassador who is forwarding it by the embassy pouch. Perhaps you can wangle fr. Bob Bliss to address me in the same way.

I received what you sent in 1940. After that but one letter reached me last autumn & of before that, nothing you sent in '41, '42, '43 & '44 reached me, whether letter, photo or printed matter. No doubt you addressed them c/o Jirmounsky at Lisbon, but either he disappeared or was not allowed to forward or even write, for I have not heard from him for 30 months & more. It is a great loss for the library if the bulletins, Fogg & Alumni cannot be replaced & photos of course. At present you cannot send printed matter or photos by post to me, a mere civilian. It can however be done through the embassy pouch if the gods consent.

As the head of the Fogg is the invididual to direct & control the institution which I hope I Tatti is to become, I am interested in his character & preparation for the task. It would be a disaster if he was on the one side a mere museum hand, or philologer; or on the other hand, a person absorbed in questions of pictorial technique. I should wish him to be well planted with his feet in Europe but able & eager to sway backward & forward over the rest of the entire earth. In short I want him to have had a Greco-Roman-Renaissance-Franco-German-English training & "zum Schauen geboren," & generously interested in present as well as past.

Where to find such a man? And you have found him — I hope.

With affectionate greetings

Ever yours
Bernard Berenson

To Mrs. Alfred Barr

Settignano
Florence
16 June 1945

Dear Margot,

Some ten or fifteen days ago an envelope was left here anonymously. It contained a letter dated Apr. 5 enclosing one of Febr. 11 & another of Jan. 14 all from you, you Great Dear. I should have written at once but for the fact that what drops of energy I could squeeze out of myself had to be devoted to a preface I was writing for an exhibition of French pictures to be opened the 27th of this month at the Pitti Palace. If only you were here, what fun to look & comment in those stately halls opening on the Boboli & a view of roofs, bell towers & distances that have not [been] changed in my all but 60 years of acquaintance with them, not even by German dynamite. By the way the ruins are a fascinating sight, nay spectacular, more picturesque than in any Guardi or, no Piranesi is another matter. When I go to Florence as I rarely do I spend my time staring at them with open-mouthed delight. Very interesting case wh. I could develop if you were here. The only good pictures (to return to them) have been carried off by the Nazis & have not yet [been] returned. Still, I could lean on yr. arm as we enjoyed or poked fun. My preface was written in a hurry for it had to be done in time to permit its translation into Italian & French. Like everything else I now write I feel as sure as sure that people will say "what can you expect fr. a senile dotard?" However if it can be mailed I shall submit a copy to yr. judgment.

You ask about Nicky. She is still busy sitting up nights revising proofs in three languages of aforesaid preface as well as catalogue. She types my MSS., she discusses my prose, she keeps house, runs affairs & charities, smooths down malcontents, receives troops of callers, arranges all social matters, walks with me, etc. etc. etc. At times she looks worried & bedraggled & I beg her to let up. I ask her whether there is not somewhere in her makeup some secret closet no matter how tiny & how remote where she thinks, feels & lives for herself. No, all dedicated to my all-absorbingness. I ask her what she will do when I am gone & she answers that she will write about me. I trust that life will see to it that she soon finds more cheery occupations.

If anybody divides Nicky's worship with me it is a boy of 8, the son of the Russian composer & orchestra director Igor Markevitch. About this brilliant, lordly, highly gifted young devil whom I have sheltered in my villino & done much for, I could write a volume. This small boy, grandson of Nijinsky, is a fascinating creature whom Mary worshipped, Nicky idolizes & mothers & I grandfather. If yr. little girl were here what a pair they would make.

There is a limit to what one can write in a letter. So what of the thousand things I want to write about shall I say. Oh yes, my growing distress & indignation over the fact that the newest recruit in uniform can receive all the mail he wants, air mail letters, printed matter of any & every kind, dailies, weeklies, monthlies, quarterlies & books — & what mountains of rubbish they wallow on or in! — & I none. Since my liberation I have received directly but two books, the coloured reproduction of the National Gallery & the book by Frankfurter on the Kress pictures. Everything else has been handed me by our "boys" or their British cousins. Now that these are gone I shall not see a publication of any sort in the Engl. language for God knows how long. Nothing fr. France & of course nothing fr. Germany, so that one is even more cut off fr. the rest of the world than in war time.

I have had but three glimpses of Dewald. He is very busy running about all over the place & in his three brief visits here had no leisure of spirit for talk. I see Fred Hartt[1] once a week on the average & he gives me on every visit a full report of his activities. He works devotedly & intelligently. It is no easy task fighting e.g. Tuscan inertia, Italian *confusione* & army-engineer Philistinism. He could do more if red-tape & the deadly machine did not keep him down to a lieutenancy & the small authority that rank carries. I understand that 98% of what the Nazis carried off has already been found again. I fear the 2% lacking includes the little Pollajuolo — the Hercules — & the Watteau & like jewels.

I dare say when you read this you will know who the new [director of the] Fogg is to be. I dare say he will have been chosen either among men with independent means or someone with a blinding interest in "technique." And O the difference to me! For said Fogg will presumably rule over my place when I leave it. Luckily I am still able to kick if I must.

[1] American art historian at the head of the Fine Arts Commission for Tuscany from 1944 to 1954.

I shall be grateful for the novel on Boston society that you speak of sending. . . .

Write as often & as much as you can find time for. It will be a charity as well as an act of friendship.

Love
B.B.

To Robert C. Trevelyan

I Tatti
10 July 1945

My dear Trevy,

We have just finished reading your Windfalls which we sipped like a liqueur. Every bit went straight to my heart and understanding. All so sincere and so thoughtful, so un-rhetorical, un-gesticulating. Each page as I read it or rather heard Nicky read it seemed like the one I must thank you for especially. I could but enumerate each and if I tried to praise them epithets would fail me. I liked the verses about the modern versifiers more than words can say, for they say what I think about them only you say it far more gently than is my vehement want. I look forward to the Chinese Anthology and your Georgics and the Christmas poems. Your brother George's Social history we have already and are reading it with keen interest.

I have spent most of the last ten months gobbling up information about events and now I feel I must wrench myself away and return to my studies and to revising what I have written during the years of occultation.

To Judge Learned Hand

I Tatti
Settignano
15 July 1945

Dear B.,

. . .

My Mary's youth was all an animal could enjoy & all a human heyday could desire. When I, a junior, had my first glimpse of her in the Harvard Yard she was a vision of "cypress-slender" beauty. Later as my wife no German in the Fatherland would take her for less than a duchess & so late as 1922 in Egypt the natives took her for an Emira, i.e. the consort of a great feudatory. By the time you knew her she was no longer her physical self & she had got indolent mentally. In death she looked heroically beautiful, like the grandest tomb statues of the French 12th century. . . .

Ever affectionately
B.B.

To Mrs. Alfred Barr

Casa al Dono
Vallombrosa
(Prov. di Firenze)
26 August 1945

Dear Margot,

Yrs. of July 2 reached me some days ago but had to wait till urgent beastlinesses had been attended to. How I wish you could come over & include a visit to I Tatti in yr. stay. Perhaps Johnnie Walker could help you if you are, as I hope, on the best terms with him. You know he spent five days here a little while ago. When he left I entrusted to him for you the catalogue of a French exhibition held here. To this in 9 days I composed a preface. I submit it to yr. indulgent judgment.

I am writing in the room you may remember. What walks we took together! They are much curtailed now. Not only that I am so much older, but that we have no car to take us afield & bring us back after long jaunts. Luckily those close by are fairy-like in their woodsiness.

Thanks for books received through Fred Hartt. Such a meritorious creature! He really did *il grosso del lavoro* in saving buildings & works of art in Central Italy as well as bringing back those the Nazis had carried off. Now he too has left — the last of our Anglo-Saxons with whom I had truly affectionate contact.

Morey I have seen but once & in haste. Dewald whom I liked more & more left before we came here.

I worry over the Fogg & who will direct it. I wish you would tell me in *confidence* what you think of Pope, for it looks as if they meant to keep him on from year to year indefinitely.

Am revising my diary & feeling dubious as to its readableness & interest for any but friends. Then I shall see whether a sort of *auto-ritratto* I scribbled off as it came five years ago & have scarcely looked at since, is printable. That discarded or revised I shall deal with "Aesthetics & History," i.e. my last will & testament regarding art theory.

Of returning to America no possibility just now. I must wait till passage there & back is comfy, till hotels at home are accessible, most of all till war-fear, patriotism & magniloquence are calmed down. Stupidity poisons me & what so stupid as a society that flatters itself to have been victorious. I must stop for there is too much to rile me in that mood.

Ever affectionately
B.B.

To Henry Coster

Casa al Dono
Vallombrosa
(Prov. di Firenze)
27 September 1945

Dear Harry,

In Byba's last came the news that you were back home.[1] I am delighted not only for yourself but that now I can write to you & hope to hear from you. Please send by post & do not trust private carriers. Uncertain as posts still are they are much more reliable than private persons.

Again & again Byba has spoken of yr. letters to her & how interesting they were. It is easy enough to believe this, seeing how well I remember what letters you wrote from Cyrenaica. Perhaps you will allow Byba to extract passages from yr. letters of the last five years & let us read them. Meanwhile do take the trouble to give me a chronology of yr. wanderings & some notion of yr. occupations & "contacts."

Byba & others will have told you about our stationary experiences. If my diary gets published, as soon it may, you will receive a copy & read about our daily life. The great difference is Mary's departure which [leaves] a void.

When I had to leave I Tatti I was engaged in research & writing concerned with our 4th to 7th centuries. It obliged me to read all I could lay hands on of the history & thought & literature of those centuries. I want to return to these studies as soon as I have sent off my "Aesthetics and History." I ask you to help me with publications. I want all of *Byzantion* & *Speculum* since 1940. I trust "second class mail" will soon be available. At present they might be addressed to Cultural Attaché, Prof. Morey, U.S.A. Embassy, Rome with a note to say they were for me. Of course if you have published anything yourself — I

1 Harry Coster served in the American Field Service from 1940-1945.

rather think you have — not included in those reviews, you will send it.

We have had a relatively restful summer here & it is already quite November-like. Yet I want to stick it through for another fortnight. We then may go to Venice for a few days before settling down for the winter at I Tatti.

I, we, all yr. friends, long to see you both. Love to Byba.

Ever affectionately
B.B.

To Henry Coster

I Tatti
Settignano
Florence
18 November 1945

Dear Harry,

I had barely posted a letter I addressed to you early last month when yrs. of August 18 reached me. It told me much I wanted to know, but only whetted my appetite for more. I repeat my wish that you would let Byba copy salient passages from what you wrote to her in those dolorous years & let us read them. Or indeed why not publish extracts; they surely would interest many people like myself.

Do not think me indiscreet if I venture to urge you to return to historical work, which you could & should supplement with more specifically literary work. You possess the historical method as well as anybody; you have given samples of pioneer work both in research & interpretation; you have the gift of the pen. I am convinced that as a scholar & author you will be happiest in yourself & most useful to the community at large. We need you too as an essayist. I cannot think of a single survivor of the many we used to have, of whom Paul Elmer More was the last. Not that I would have you think I rank him highly but he was still an essayist & not a "columnist."

I have not had the *Byzantion* that appeared in America. I should be deeply grateful if you could procure me copies. And Grégoire, has he returned to Belgium? Has *Speculum* been appearing through all these years? That I expect will be easier to procure.

I am so overwhelmed by visitors, callers, people who come for help & advice & I am at the same time so greedy for reading that I literally find no time for work. I miss it & feel debauched.

I do not touch on politics & try *non veder non sentir*. It would seem as if in Germany we left no folly untried.

Love to Byba & beg her not to be cross with me. I know what can be done here & what I in my 81st year can contribute.

Affectionately
B.B.

To Arthur McComb

I Tatti
Settignano
Florence
3 February 1946

Dear McComb,

Yours of Nov. 24 last reached me in good time. It has remained unanswered until now because I am without secretaries (for Nicky has a 1000 occupations that leave no leisure for helping me with my overwhelming correspondence.) There are no Anglo-Saxon women left here capable of helping one out.

I am glad that you can spend so much of yr. time in Boston[1] & I hope you employ some of it in writing. There is so much you could do, even in this CHAOTIC WELTER that has overtaken the so-called arts in the U.S.A. In fact nobody understood how to go to work at our job better than you did. Hence yr. reward.[2] Art museums, art teaching are now a matter of "selling art," & art dealing is a far more creative occupation. After all it ends by adding to our *patrimonio artistico* & I'd like to know to what art teaching leads — except to museum posts. I have come to the conclusion that genuine culture would be advanced if the teaching of art literature & kindred subjects were severely forbidden & as for artists none should be allowed to practice who did not have a good income, unless he was such an obvious born genius that he was universally acclaimed as one.

You mention having been instrumental in the purchase of Ruth Berenson's "Giotto." I should like to know what has become of it, for I try to know the whereabouts of all Italian pictures on their migrations. By the way Mr. Jenny came a couple of days ago with a picture. Let me tell you that except for Duveen & Wildenstein & that stopped 8 years ago, I never for forty years have consented to look at a picture for sale. I have done it for you & you alone. The picture in question is not in too satisfactory a condition but an undoubted & interesting Ercole Roberti.

Olga Loeser's son-in-law is recovering the Loeser works of art. Most of them are safe. The Cézannes were shown here in an exhibition of French painting held in Pitti Palace last autumn. Nicky & the Anreps send greetings.

Sincerely yrs.

B. Berenson

1 Berenson had always a sentimental attachment to Boston and guessed how much I preferred it to other American cities.

2 This reference is sarcastically intended and relates to the non-renewal of an appointment at the University.

To Professor Paul J. Sachs

I Tatti
Settignano
Florence
24 February 1946

Dear Paul,

Yours of Nov. 16 reached me after three months & one week.

I am glad to learn that yr. meeting with Lawrence was so satisfactory. Also that yr. catalogue of Fogg Drawings is coming out in a doubled edition. How I wish the long detailed letter I wrote on receiving this catalogue had reached you! By the way let me thank you for the Fragonard "Ariosto" as well as for many photos & pamphlets. The report of the Harvard Committee on "General Education in a Free Society" has not reached me, nor Schlesinger's *Age of Jackson* a book that would interest me greatly. I read American history with avidity.

I have not received Whittemore's photos of his restorations.[1] And may I beg you fervidly for photographs of *all* the Dumbarton Oaks exhibits that you are now holding at the Fogg. My very special interest of the moment comprises every European artifact done between 300 and 1300 A.D. I am engaged on a huge work to be called Decline and Recovery in the Figure Arts.

The appeal of the Director of the Italian Red Cross appeared in a December number of the *Art News*. I shall be deeply grateful for any contributions you can induce your friends to make.

I have mentioned Dumbarton Oaks & it reminds me to ask you to let me know what is going on there . . . & what provision has been made for [Barbara Sessions]. I have reason to believe that she started the library & photo collection on lines which she had learned to follow while working for me.

1 That is, those of the mosaics in S. Sophia in Constantinople.

I confess to no little alarm if Dumbarton Oaks instead of remaining a Harvard Institution is to become a Princeton one & instead of pursuing art studies is losing itself in the dismal desert of Byzantine theology. I must then make provision in my will that nothing similar happens here. *Ohne Feindschaft* but with much concern.

My best to you & Meta for this & many future years

Affectionately
B.B.

To Professor Paul J. Sachs

I Tatti
Settignano
Florence
14 March 1946

Dear Paul,

Thanks for Schlesinger's *Jackson* & the Harvard book on education.

The other day I had a letter fr. Robert Bliss in wh. he made a statement that surprised me. It was that Dumbarton Oaks was going "on its own steam" no more Princeton than Harvard. Have I then been mistaken all along in believing it to be as much a Harvard institution as I mean I Tatti to be?

Of course if it is an autonomous affair I must apologize for writing as I did in my last on the assumption that Harvard was responsible for what went on at Dumbarton Oaks. . . .

I feel too troubled to put in black & white all my anxieties about the future of I Tatti. I'd rather leave it to the Italians than have it become an annex to Princeton index, statistic &

iconography. I should wish all students welcome but only Harvard men, Harvard professors or fellows to run the place.

Yours
B.B.

P.S. Do not think I have anything personal against this or that Princeton man. I think the world of Morey[1] & like Dewald[2] immensely.

To Henry Coster

Settignano
29 March 1946

Dear Harry,

Yr. letter of Jan. 17 reached me Febr. 11 & is still unanswered. Finally I waited for Byba's return to get the last about you before writing. She has now been here for two & three days at a time & I have enjoyed hearing about you in the first place & then about her life in N.Y. She talks about it vividly & entertainingly & we enjoy it & get friends to listen as well as to talk to her. She has re-inserted herself quickly, almost instantaneously & is happy to be here. I do not wonder. Every day I feel more & more grateful for living here rather than elsewhere — not only for the landscape, for a nature so *à la mesure de l'homme* but for the people. With all their faults & I am neither blind to them nor is it easy to condone them, I feel more & more how human they are instinctively, how full of understanding, how kindly & when not ruined by rhetoric & Crocian *ideal-*

1 Charles Rufus Morey.
2 Ernest Dewald.

ismo — how full of good sense. They are not Simon pure but Sam. Butler observed when I was still a young man that a dose of naughtiness makes people gentle. Partly owing to general circumstances & partly no doubt to Nicky's now being the head of the household, I see more Italians than I used to & with my reduced expectations from people generally, I confess to finding them at least as satisfactory. Of course a certain intimacy is possible only with those of one's own language group. Yet that too is a matter of having common recollections. At my time of life few are the survivors to whom I can say "can you remember?"

To come to your own case which I have very much on my mind. I know that you have proved your ability to be an historian. No matter what subject you choose you could treat it thoroughly, illuminatingly, creatively even. Why not go on from where you left off with your first effort. To many of us the latest centuries of Antiquity are as fascinating as any. Much as has been written about them, the bias of the writer has always been for or against the church. If not it has been as is the case with Hodgkin too innocent in interpretation. Take yr. own subject if I may judge by myself — & I am a fair barometer — few subjects are so important as the continuation of an institution like the senatorial class from the 6th into later centuries until it is absorbed by the feudal aristocracy. Bear in mind that even intelligent students of these centuries have been satisfied hitherto to leave it in the vague belief that somehow the upper Roman classes disappeared & that that was the end of it. I would like you to pursue the subject till you reach definite results. It is more than a matter of disinterested curiosity. The answer to the question may throw light on our path & tell what may become of us.

I have not yet received any number of the American series of Byzantion. I hope you will be able to procure them. When you do, send them (each separately) by registered book post. I need not tell you how you would oblige me. I am doing my best to procure books & periodicals that have appeared in England, France & the U.S.A. during the war years. I want to leave my library in such shape that it will be easy to continue.

I have to write so many letters & to waste so much time resting that I have little leisure for writing books. Yet I do off & on.

I need not tell you how happy I should be if again you began to spend a considerable part of the year here.

Affectionately
B.B.

To Professor Paul J. Sachs

I Tatti
Settignano
Florence
9 May 1946

Dear Paul,

Your epistle dated April 22nd reached me two days ago. I have studied it and am glad that my snarling growl has called forth a clear statement of what "Dumbarton Oaks" is up to. I am deeply grateful to you for having taken such trouble and patience and time to compose it.

Yes, I have received the books you kindly sent, but not the Whittemore photos. By the way the one thing Dumbarton Oaks could do to the sister institution at the Tatti would be to send all its publications and photos of all its works of art. Thus far I have only photos of the fourth century pyxis.

I am truly sorry to learn that none of you have been well for months past and that Meta has been seriously ill. I fervently hope she at last is on the way to complete recovery. . . .

Forgive me for making you the scape-goat, the *souffre-douleur* of my feeling about the way art-studies are going at home!

With affectionate greetings to all of you

Devotedly

B.B.

NICKY MARIANO TO PROFESSOR PAUL J. SACHS

I Tatti
Settignano
Florence
1 June 1946

Dear Paul,

Will you forgive me if I venture to ask for your advice in a matter regarding B.B. that troubles me somewhat and about which I do not want to alarm him unnecessarily?

You may perhaps have heard about the queer not to say nasty way in which Mr. and Mrs. Myron Taylor behaved to B.B. last year. He never even acknowledged receipt of a very charming and friendly letter B.B. sent him after the "liberation," never came near us during all his repeated visits to Florence, and finally called on B.B. for exactly five minutes, shortly before leaving Italy. She filled the whole of Rome with most absurd stories about B.B.'s "shameful" behaviour in having put himself into safety and left his poor wife in solitude and desolation and even asserted that Mary has died in misery while B.B. was in hiding. Nothing that friends of B.B.'s who heard her say these things could tell her about the real facts seemed to have the slightest effect on her. Of course everybody knows that he (at least in matters of social intercourse) is completely under her influence, but the fact remains that when they left Italy in

1940, B.B. was on very friendly terms with them, and that when they came over in the summer of 1941 to hand over their villa to the Vatican, they sent him most affectionate messages to Vallombrosa.

Also Mr. Kirk[1] did not behave in the way his former friendly relations with B.B. would have led one to expect. When B.B. after the liberation asked him whether it was within his power to help him about procuring food and fuel for himself and his household, Kirk replied very curtly that nothing could be done to help him and that B.B. had *no business to be where he was.*

Now the Myron Taylors are in Florence again and through a friend who has met them, and whose truthfulness I know I can trust, I have heard (B.B. does not know this) that they go on speaking in the nastiest way about him, saying that he has played a "double game" during the war. This same friend assures me that both Mr. Taylor's and Mr. Kirk's attitude goes back to the "mauvaise presse" that B.B. is enjoying at the State Department, on account of his having chosen to stay in Italy during the war. Apparently the objection that valuable American property was saved through his staying here (our sequestrator told me again and again that only thanks to his personal presence and prestige were collection and library left in their place by the Fascists) is met with the assertion that it was not his business to think of that, but that he should have returned home when ordered to do so, and left it to his government to recuperate or restore works of art carried away or destroyed by Fascists or Nazists.

When in June 1941 I went to Rome to say good-bye to Mrs. Phillips and to Miss Aldrich who were leaving Italy, I had a long talk with Mr. William Phillips about B.B.'s difficulties, Mary's invalid condition, my not having in spite of every effort

[1] Mr. Alexander Kirk at the time referred to was U.S. representative (with the rank of Ambassador) on the Advisory Council for Italy. He had been appointed 31 March 1944.

obtained the permission to leave Italy with them, the impossibility of sending them off alone etc. He thought it over and said: "On the whole I believe he should try to stay for he has very valuable property to look after." When Mr. Phillips himself left in September 1941, he recommended B.B. and Mary to the Italian Foreign Office, particularly to Ciano, and it was, I believe, in consequence of this recommendation that on the day after the declaration of war on the United States the Florence Police got orders from the Home Office in Rome to leave B.B. and Mary completely unmolested. A few hours later a group of fanaticized Fascists appeared before the questore (the "préfet de police") and taxed him with not having yet arrested B.B. On being shown the telegram from Rome they went off in a rage saying that Ciano would have to pay them for this.

On one of the first days following the war declaration, December 11th or 12th, Carla Garabelli Orlando, the ex-Prime Minister's daughter and one of our intimate friends, managed with great difficulty to have an interview with the American chargé d'affaires who had remained in Rome when Mr. Phillips left [and] whom B.B. had never met and who counted as being on very good terms with the smartest set in Rome. Carla, not knowing about the step already taken by Mr. Phillips, wanted this individual to say a word in B.B.'s and Mary's favour to the Italian Foreign Office people during his negotiations with them. To her indignation he advised her *to keep her hands off B.B.* He assured her that B.B. was, through his being a Jew, in such a horrible and hopeless position that nobody could do anything for him and that she would only get herself into trouble by bothering about him. She then addressed herself to Vittorio Cini and to other influential people on the Italian side whom she knew she could trust, and it was chiefly through her help that B.B. got a special sequestrator (the same Marchese Serlupi who afterwards sheltered him in his house) and escaped having his property included into the general and very tiresome sequestration system.

In June 1942, when the Chargé and the other United States diplomatists left Rome, B.B. got a telegram from the Embassy proposing that Mary and he should join them. That would have been out of the question for the usual reason that both of them were not fit to travel alone and that nobody, neither I nor one of Mary's nurses, could have got the permission to accompany them. B.B. wired back stating the chief reason for his decision to stay here, namely age and bad health, and added that he had nothing to complain of the way the Italian authorities were treating him. It was in his interest to mention this in a telegram subject to censorship as it was likely to flatter and please the Italian authorities and to keep them up to their best behaviour.

It seems to me not unlikely that B.B.'s so-called "mauvaise presse" at the State Department has been created by this same Embassy official who, not knowing B.B. personally and being possibly prejudiced against him either through antisemitic poison or through other anti-B.B. rumours current in smart Italian society, may have handed in a very unfavourable report, representing B.B. as a kind of "collaborationist" who would let himself be protected by a band of sheer brigands. For I imagine that in the mood prevailing in the States after Pearl Harbour Italy's inhabitants must have been considered as little better than wild beasts?

Now you may say: "What of it? Let Mr. Taylor and others say and think whatever they like. B.B. does not need them and the essence of his life and work is not touched by their opinion of him. Unfortunately all this may have considerable influence on his status as an American citizen. You will have heard about the new law according to which the passports of alien-born Americans living abroad who do not return home before October will not be renewed. The American Consul who has been very friendly and helpful to B.B. seemed to me very gloomy about B.B.'s chances of being discriminated, when I went to talk to him about it a few days ago, but begged me not to alarm B.B. and said he would try sending in another favourable report and a medical certificate about B.B.'s fragile condition of health. When I tried talking to B.B. (who of course knows about the law and thinks there were good reasons for making it, but counts on a discrimination regarding his person and other people in his category) about the possibility of going to the States in September, he seemed curiously panicky on the subject and I don't like taking the responsibility of persuading him on me. As a matter of fact he would like very much going home and seeing his friends again and the art collections old and new, but would prefer waiting till next year when general conditions of travelling and finding lodgings should be a great deal easier.

To me it seems simply monstrous that a man almost 81, who has certainly not brought any dishonour on the country that took him and his parents in and who is showing his gratitude for whatever this country has done for him by leaving all he owns to one of its cultural institutions should be treated in this pedagogico-tyrannical way, instead of getting an honorary passport for the rest of his days. But I dare say I do not know enough about the evils that have called forth this new law.

Dear Paul, I would be ever so grateful if you could let me know your opinion on the whole case and whether you think there might be a way of fighting this unfavourable current in the State Department. B.B. does not know about my writing to you so you can express yourself quite freely.

With love to Meta and yourself and hoping this will find her completely recovered, very affectionately

Yours
Nicky

LAWRENCE BERENSON TO ELISABETTA MARIANO

8 July 1946

ELISABETTA MARIANO
I TATTI
SETTIGNANO
FLORENCE, ITALY VIA W.U.

RECEIVED COPY LETTER JUNE FIRST SHIPLEY INFORMED ME BB
CITIZENSHIP WILL NOT BE AFFECTED IN NOT RETURNING TO UNITED
STATES BEFORE OCTOBER SINCE HIS AGE AND HEALTH WILL NOT
PERMIT HIM PRESENT LAW AND PROPOSED LAW PROVIDE EXCEP-
TION AGAINST EXPATRIATION IF HEALTH DOES NOT PERMIT RETURN
THEREFORE BB SAFE UNDER PRESENT LAW OR NEW ONE IF NEW
LAW ADOPTED WHICH IS QUITE LIKELY BB WILL GET AUTOMATIC
EXTENSION ONE YEAR REGARDLESS OF HEALTH SHIPLEY NOT
SLIGHTEST AFFECTED BY ANY ALLEGED RUMORS KNOWS BB CASE
THOROUGHLY   PLEASE STOP WORRYING LOVE

LAWRENCE

LAWRENCE BERENSON TO PROFESSOR PAUL J. SACHS

8 July 1946

Dear Mr. Sachs:

I have just received copy of Nicky's letter to you dated June
1st. Enclosed copy of cable I sent today.

Nicky is extremely sensitive about the talk Taylor has been
handing out and apparently others as well. Mrs. Shipley, Chief
of the Passport Division in Washington is thoroughly familiar
with BB's case. I see her rather frequently and discuss B.B.
with her from time to time.

The best evidence of Mrs. Shipley's attitude toward B.B. was that she directed the Consul General at Florence to issue a passport to B.B. to visit France and the Mediterranean countries without even waiting for a report from him. This was done a few weeks ago.

On the question of expatriation, under the present law a naturalized citizen is automatically expatriated if he fails to return before expiration of the law. The law, however, contains an exception, — that a naturalized citizen, if too ill to travel, is not expatriated and his citizenship continues. During the war a new law was enacted and there is now pending before the Congress a Bill to extend the law another year.

If the proposed law is passed, and I am confident it will be, B.B.'s citizenship will be automatically extended another year regardless of his health. If it does not pass, B.B.'s citizenship will continue under the exception because of his health. Mrs. Shipley informed me not to worry on that score; that she would protect B.B. just as she has always done in the past.

I am sure she is not in the slightest interested in what Taylor or anybody else may say. She is a strong woman and makes up her own mind, and judging from her present and past actions on B.B., I am sure she believes in B.B. implicitly and believes what I have told her about B.B.

I know Mrs. Shipley gets thousands upon thousands of rumors about the thousands upon thousands of American citizens seeking passports to go abroad or about American citizens residing abroad. She cannot pay attention to these rumors and does not. She acts adversely only when there is real evidence of anti-American activities. In B.B.'s case, she knows that B.B. had never been guilty of such activities and that quite to the contrary his influence has always been for the good so far as the United States is concerned. . . . It is only a matter of time that he [Taylor] will be out of his job due to the pressure of the Federation of Christian Churches. W. is a subordinate and I am sure not a great influence. Bill Phillips' views about B.B.

which Mrs. Shipley knows about, also Sumner Welles' views on B.B. (and Mrs. Shipley respects his views tremendously) mean a great deal to her. I do not know that Mr. Kirk has hurt B.B. I know that he has not helped him but so far as I know he has not hurt him. Mrs. Shipley would have had to pay attention to Kirk's views but the fact that she cabled instructions to issue the passport to B.B. would indicate to me that Kirk has not injured B.B.

> With most cordial greetings,
> Sincerely yours,
> Lawrence Berenson

TO HAROLD ACTON

I Tatti
8 July 1946

Dear Harold,

Returning yesterday after a sojourn of eight days at Siena I discovered in the haystack of correspondence the precious jewel of a letter of yours from Paris. I could envy you what you are seeing, whom you are "contacting" and whom enjoying, if my flesh were not too weak to enjoy anybody or anything. Besides who can enjoy what I do enjoy more than I enjoy. Siena was sheer ecstasy, every brick, every stone, every stain on a wall, and the sculpture and the paintings and *les chemins qui cheminent.* The Palio — a mass of 60 or 70 thousand bipeds of the human species turned into a garden of blue and mauve hortensias.

I greatly enjoyed Waley's translation entitled "Monkey." What *Opéra bouffe* and how Aristophanesque a figure is Monkey!

By happy accident I am re-reading Lytton Strachey's *Essays in Miniature* and am delighted to discover how fine they are. Far the best he has left us. Perhaps their length was the measure of his best. We all are stewing pans that can cook only what they can hold — some more than others.

Casa al Dono Vallombrosa in a week or so. I wish I could look forward to a visit there from you.

To HENRY COSTER

Casa al Dono
Vallombrosa
(Firenze)
29 July 1946

My dear Harry,

I feel like a brand snatched from the burning: for at I Tatti it was already furnace-like & despite inertia & the pleasure of being able to browse in my own library & of being able to visit galleries & churches it was high time to leave. I should have done so even earlier but for the visit of Johnnie Walker who could not come earlier. We had eight delightful days together, sight-seeing, conversing, planning. What would I not give to have eight days of you at I Tatti! After these many years that each has been going his own way, you so much faster, there would be quite a bit we could tell each other. I would do my best. I would do no more than tell you what I am sure of. I would urge you to return to the question of the Senatorial Order in late Antiquity. What you say in yr. letter shows that you possess the facts & know how to marshal them. Why then not give us a book as scholarly & unpedantic as you almost alone can do it about this Order from say Severus down to the 9th century in the West & down to the 12th in the East — if indeed vestiges remain in either region as late. It would be a book of actuality; for our order is being threatened with the fate that overtook the "Roman" Senators, only that it will happen to us *per espresso*. Perhaps you could write this book easier here than at Warwick. In any event a change of moral & intellectual atmosphere may prove stimulating. And so may my interest in the problem.

I shall not attempt to politicize. Yr. papers bring you all the news & I fancy you know my reflexions. I fear the Russians will control Eurasia from the Oder & Adriatic to the Pacific & perhaps even the Indian Ocean. Perhaps too we can stop it only by war. No doubt we could beat the Soviets & smash their régime. And then? Considering how small is our success in running a bit of Germany, how could we hope to administer over 200,-000,000 bipeds speaking a couple of hundred different languages & knowing no "lornorder" except through *knout* & *nagaika*.[1] Yet we must resist or the Stalinites will soon be on the Atlantic. I confess I prefer the Nazis — despite everything.

Byba will have had much to tell you about Italy. On top, storm & earthquake & volcanic eruptions but realities are not half bad. Splendid harvests, people working, ever so much reconstruction being done, even in the field of art & without U.S.A. intervention. So far as I can see on the real plain *Italia fà da se* & better than one who reads the speeches & newspaper comments can imagine.

With affectionate greetings from Nicky & myself to both of you.

Ever yrs.

B.B.

---

[1] These belong to the old régime. The new had invented more effective methods.

To Mrs. Alfred Barr

Vallombrosa
20 August 1946

Dearest Margot,

Thanks for the articles about USSR. All we read about that vast desert is equally alarming & depressing. Eight centuries of Western advance into Asia — not civilized but barbarous Asia — have been pushed back in the last few years & nobody seems to have noted. Was it not done by Germans? Indeed it was & more honour & glory to them.

I wrote a few days ago so you know that we are at Casa al Dono which is always expecting you. How I recall yr. presence!

You ask whether I am interested in Cyril Connolly. Indeed, for he was a protégé of my brother-in-law, Logan Pearsall Smith, & indirectly my own. So I receive all he prints nearly every month in *Horizon* wh. he edits. I expect his visit with a brand new wife. . . .

Is there anything I can send you from here? Gladly should I do so. . . .

Ever affectionately
B.B.

To Henry Coster

Vallombrosa
27 September 1946

Dear Harry,

I fear I have not thanked you for the precious gift of *Byzantion* for 1940-1943. The fact is they reached me but a few weeks ago & only a few days ago did I find the leisure to peruse them.

I have enjoyed your article on Synesius. You exploit his text with fascinating acumen in order to pick out, as it were, your needles from the haystack. I can always read about Synesius. He has been a pet of mine ever since I made his acquaintance 65 years ago in the pages of Kingsley's *Hypatia*. Historical novels I read as a lad have served as springboards for plunging into more seriously meant "history."

Yr. article is so readable besides being so valuable that again I venture to urge you to take up writing once more, continuous writing.

If *Byzantion* is or is to be continued after 1943 put down my name as subscriber & let me know what I have to pay. My home account is now unblocked.

We are still in the midst of summer but everybody is gone. The whole *massif* is our private park. If only you were here, what talks & walks!

Love to you both from Nicky &

B.B.

To Peter Viereck[1]

Settignano
7 November 1946

Du liebster aller wilden Männer,

Thanks for both letters, e.g. Sept. 29 & Oct. 3, for inclosures, for photo of *my* godson & for yr. "Jews French, Germans" &

---

[1] American poet-historian who was in Florence as member of the P.W.B. (Psychological Warfare Branch) and was sent to I Tatti by the Italian Professor of English Literature Mario Praz. B.B. became very fond of him and of his Russian wife. He jokingly called him "Der wilde Mann." The "wild man" is a frequent figure in German literature. Professor Viereck teaches history at Mount Holyoke College.

Wilson's Santayana, as well as for a parcel of *New Yorkers* including one on Hiroshima. The photo of Anya & baby is too charming. Kiss them both most smackingly for me. As to Salvemini. I have written & sent the Placci portrait but addressed them to Lowell House G.24. Please warn him to retrieve both. Have not yet received Sept. issue of *Poetry*.

I do not envy yr. gadgets. I'd be ready to forego them all including telephones, electricity, autos if only I could recapture *la douceur de vivre* of the years before 1914. At the present rate of mechanization we soon shall be entirely dependent on machines. There will be no soul to save & TOTALITARIANISM will have reduced us to atoms in a cosmic gadget. Perhaps "the youngs" will not mind, nay enjoy it even, & serve them right.

What can I tell you about myself! I read too much & write too little. I peruse too many dailies, weeklies, monthlies, quarterlies, semi & whole annuals & get less & less expressive. I say with the skunk who first smelled a motor-car, "What's the use!"

Vallombrosa was Arcadian & we did not leave it till Oct. 5 when we trundled along in our battered tin-kettle to Siena & Pisa. Seeing beautiful things now goes to my head. Later we went to Venice whence I returned with a bad cold from which I have not quite recovered.

I am now giving "positively last" revision to my "Aesthetics & History." If it gets printed, or my "Rumour & Reflexion," copies will go to you. I am reading Charles Du Bos's *Journal 1921-1923*. Have you ever heard of him? He was a great friend & quasi disciple till he fainted into the panglossic bosom of hollow church. But how keen in this journal he is about happy & alas! far off discussions & delicious spiritual combats!

Much love to all three of you

B.B.

To Henry Coster

Settignano
16 November 1946

Dear Harry,

So glad to learn that you are half in harness & with Mommsen[1] to whom my remembrances. It will do you a deal of good to have to coagulate your ideas instead of letting them rise & unshape like scurrying mists. I never think so clearly as when attempting to write. And I am delighted to hear that you are coming in Febr. We shall have good talks & I shall try to cross the waste land that stretches between all rational beings when they get so self-aware as we have. I have heard on every hand how much Byba is doing & how successfully. I congratulate & rejoice.

As for the "Latin profile"[2] it was written without malice, with no thought in my head but to jot down what Placci had been to me. It was printed all but accidentally & I am surprised to discover how much it is admired & how much reproved. I wonder what will be said of the diary that is to appear simultaneously in England & here. No American publisher would take it. *Lässt das tief blicken?*

I shall not attempt to say anything about current events. The USSR is behaving here as in France with remorseless consistency. Yet I doubt whether here they will achieve their purpose. I know no European people so unlikely to yield to serious totalitarianism as the Italians. Even Stalin's most highly organized effort would break against their anarchy.

If you can find it or procure it, glance at Ch. Du Bos's *Journal 1921-1923* (Editions Correa, Paris). I find it fascinating.

Ever affectionately
B.B.

[1] Theodor Mommsen, grandson of the famous historian, was at that time teaching in Princeton and had persuaded Henry Coster to give a course of lectures there.
[2] Published in *Horizon*.

To Professor Paul J. Sachs

Settignano
22 November 1946

My dear Paul,

Far too long a time has passed without my hearing fr. you. My last letter never was answered. If it was severe, even harsh, it was not against you personally, but you as my point of contact with the people concerned *in the treatment of Barbara Sessions.* As for Dumbarton Oaks, yr. account of it was of an East Xian "Talmudshul," a *Yeshiba* — with no faintest connection with Western Humanities! I confess it frightened, it terrified me lest I Tatti should be thus transmuted.

All this is long ago — so long ago that I have lost touch with you, with Edward, with Agnes,[1] with the Fogg, with Harvard. It is high time to re-establish contact & in the first place I want to hear about your health. A vague rumour reaches me that it is not satisfactory & distresses me. *If you become incapable of keeping in touch with me I don't know who would* & besides I genuinely wish you a satisfactory old age, apart fr. any utilitarian considerations of my own.

I am ageing rapidly & am feeling it in many ways, not only by way of aches, pains, discomforts of every kind, but of an increasing tendency to fear, to anxiety, to melancholia. Thus far I get the better of all blue devils, but how much longer? Then capacity for work has greatly diminished while calls upon my time are on the increase. And I am an intemperate reader! *Nicky is a staff & shield & buckler.* If it were not going to complicate matters with regard to Harvard & if it were not ridiculous for a man of 81 plus 5 months to marry or if she preferred it I

---

[1] Agnes Mongan, the Curator of Drawings at the Fogg Museum and at present date (1963) Assistant Director of the Museum.

should make her my wife. If I do not write again take my best for yourself & yours for a Happy New Year & a satisfactory 1947

Affectionately

B.B.

To Philip Hofer

Settignano

23 January 1947

Dear Philip,

I mean to keep sending you duplicates that possibly the Harvard Library lacks — things of small importance, but still — I was glad to get yr. "Who's Who" at Providence, R.I. It reminds me of Miss Howe's "We Happy Few" we are reading. What you say about Sawyer interests me of course. Alfred Barr I do not know. Surely he can have no aesthetic convictions or he would not have written encyclopedically about "Abstract Art" & directed an *Institoosh'n* whose activity is so effectively anti-humanistic.[1] Windt I know not at all. What does he stand for, what has he published? . . .

It is pretty wintry today. I wonder what it is like at Cambridge, Mass. Love to you, to "Bunnie" & to Agnes.

Yours

B.B.

[1] Alfred Barr was at the time Director of the Museum of Modern Art in New York. Berenson's feeling about the deplorable influence of the Museum was shared by many who were not insensitive to the charm and erudition of its Director.

To PETER VIERECK

Settignano
16 February 1947

Dear Peter,

Thanks for a letter at last of a substance worthy of sender & receiver. First & foremost let me tell you that I like yr. "Justina" (For Two Girls Setting Out in Life) enormously. If you have not already sold it, do send it to Cyril Connolly, *Horizon*, 6 Selwyn House, Lansdowne Terrace, London W.C. 1. I am writing to him to say that if he receives it, it is because I urged you to send it to him.

I liked the other poem, the "Planted Poet," although not quite so much. You have passed the *pons asinorum* & now you are an unquestionable poet (in the two you have sent): an up-to-date Browning. You must try to send me every poem you write, even if "unpublishable" on yr. side of [the] Atlantic.

Which brings me to yr. kind words about me to Mr. Weeks.[1] I have received a note in which he speaks nicely of you & invites me to contribute anything "in reminiscent mood." I answered politely. To you I want to say that I am not, like you, a born writer. If I have a gift it is as a talker. Furthermore, I have no time for reminiscing. What I did in my diary was done because I was all but a prisoner & with consequent leisure. Now I am busy with work in my own field, the which seems to interest neither beast nor man. The fact is I was born to be the ever un-contemporary. For years I was ahead of my time although I may have helped to shape it. And now I am hopelessly behind.

My diary is something everybody wants to see but nobody in America wants to publish. I doubt whether the Atlantic would find there anything for its Münchhausen's horse of a public. I received a letter fr. Greenslet who wants to see it for Houghton Mifflin. By the way my brother-in-law Logan Pearsall

1 Edward Weeks, Editor of the *Atlantic Monthly*.

Smith sent the Placci portrait to the *Atlantic,* warmly recommending it to Mr. Weeks, who turned it down.

Ora parliamo delle cose allegre. But first let me tell you that we discovered an article of yrs. in an Italian magazine & read it with interest. But you are going to be more of a poet than critic. Now I want to know what Russian book Anya is bringing out. I do wish you could remain at Harvard but I understand why you may have to leave it. Luckily our smaller colleges provide more leisure, more quiet — *es bildet ein Talent sich in der Stille.*

You ask whether Santayana does not write too well for a philosopher. No philosopher can write too well. Who wrote better than Plato! But Santayana thinks too much *à faire du style* & the result tends to put one off, perhaps.

No end of love to all of you, you blessed trinity of flesh & blood & life & thought.

With Nicky's love besides

Yours

B.B.

To John Walker

Settignano

20 February 1947

Dear Johnnie:

Yrs. of the 7th — although air-mailed — arrived only yesterday. I will not bring a charge of *De Haeretico Comburendo* against you if you publish yr. conclusions about Titian's possible retouching of the figures in the Bacchanal. *Tutto può darsi* say the Italians, & you may be right. Who am I to set up my

senile opinion ag. you in the vigorous flower of yr. years. But
I could discuss the details you bring in proof of yr. theories if
both of us work in presence of the *corpus delicti.* Meanwhile
publish, & a day will come when a *cand. phil.* will make a name
for himself by demolishing you, as they are demolishing me.
Please take all this as lovingly as I mean it.

To come to my own affairs, I wish you could persuade Kurt
Wolff to print my book as Constable and we have settled upon.
I have made all the concessions I can, omitting all repetitions, &
points that even a British publisher thought might give offence.
To go further would emasculate the book. Nor do I understand
the re-arranging as proposed by K.W. of a diary where the day-
by-day succession is an *integral* contribution to the effect.

My heartiest & loving congratulations on the 10th anniversary
of yr. wedding. My best to Marghie.

Ever affectionately,

B.B.

To PHILIP HOFER

Settignano
17 March 1947

Dear Philip,

. . .

A couple of months ago I received as a free gift from Stan-
islaus Joyce the MSS of a clean & meticulous autograph of his
famous brother James' book of verse known as "Chamber
Music."

As he is a very poor man working hard at Trieste as teacher of
English, I wrote to ask him whether he was aware that the MSS
might have a certain monetary value. For various reasons the

reply was delayed & I expecting every day to receive it put off writing to you till the following day. Just now I have had word from him & I gather that he would not be indisposed to cash it in. In case he consents to part with it to his profit instead of insisting on my keeping it would you allow me to submit it to you either for you to acquire, or to propose it to others? You would have to decide on what it is worth for neither S. Joyce [nor I] have an idea of its monetary value.

The MSS is on a slightly glazed ivory coloured paper & has 34 poems, one on each leaf. Except for the last it is in perfect state. Page 34 has a pale coffee-coloured stain, which however is not disfiguring. The measurements are 21 by 17 cm.

If you want me to send the MSS tell me what is the safest way. Or if you really are coming over soon, we could discuss the matter when you are here. Please incline yr. heart to coming very soon & to staying with me while you are here in Florence.

In one of yr. letters you mention Isham. Can't he be induced to bring out editions of his Boswell loot at prices more accessible & in less cumbrous *format?*

Forgive a curt letter & believe that it carries affection to both of you.

Yours

B.B.

To Miss Beryl de Zoete[1]

I Tatti

9 April 1947

Dearest Beryl,

I am sorry that you had such a rough time at Madrid. *Est-ce-que je voyage Moi?* It is apparently the common lot for anyone

---

[1] Miss Beryl de Zoete is the author of well-known books on the ballet and Eastern dances.

who ventures abroad. Happily you now are basking in the shadow of the Giralda. I had no idea that the Botticellian Nastagio degli Onesti panels were now in the Madrid gallery. When I last saw them they were at Barcelona. They are fascinating and the hunt of the stripped young thing is as cruel as great art can tolerate.

Here we are enjoying the flowers of the spring, so lush, so gorgeous, such a delight for the eye and a joy for the senses.

Roger Hinks has just left after a short stay. Praz[1] arrived yesterday for a few days. The Trevys [Robert and Julian Trevelyan] are here for a fortnight. Bobby seemed alarmingly feeble after the journey but is recovering fast. . . . His brother George *nebst Frau* will be here in a minute for luncheon.

To Henry Coster

Casa al Dono
Vallombrosa
26 August 1947

Dear Harry,

It was good to read yr. delightful letter telling about your doings & thinking. It makes me more than ever regret that you are so far away. It would be so stimulating to discuss your work & what we were reading & what we thought about events. I wonder by the way whether you mean to lecture at Princeton or Yale. Byba did not seem to know. She must have told you how pleasant it was here. It has been an enchanting summer. Now it is more like Oct. than August & one has to write indoors & we leave fires in sitting & dining room.

I waste time reading dailies, weeklies, monthlies & quarter-

---

[1] Mario Praz, an Italian authority on English literature and the Editor of *English Miscellany* (Rome).

lies. They give me no satisfaction. On the contrary they make me feel dissipated, debauched. What I enjoyed was reading Tacitus, his style, his attitude, his judgments. I felt in touch with a world of values close to those of my too, too private universe. Now I am continuing something of the same mood reading Seneca. If I followed my deepest desire I should read nothing later than 1900 & then only the very best authors & stop reading of events that occurred since 1914. Instead I grab at books that attempt to interpret the recent past. A good one quite Tacitean in style was Trevor-Roper's *The End of Hitler*. We now are in the midst of Hassell's *Vom andren Deutschland* (Atlantis Verlag, Zürich). It is a diary kept by the man who was German Ambassador to the Quirinal. I knew him & his wife, the daughter of Von Tirpitz, one of the most genuine, integral, courageous women I ever met. The book speaks of Hassell's efforts from 1938 till his death by hanging in '44 to organize opposition against the Nazi régime & how it went on despite him & his friends. Nevertheless it is an important document testifying to the presence in high quarters in Germany of awareness what was going on & what should go on.

The prospects here are murky. If Italy goes Soviet then Europe is lost for decades, for generations perhaps. It would have to be reconquered from the Asiatics & their adherents. These seem to be growing in numbers & many well informed observers foresee their coming to power by constitutional means at the next election. We alone might prevent their triumph but we should have to do it in a pure crusading spirit & not only tactfully but without the least alloy of "dollar politics." I confess I begin to feel discouraged but still succeed in fighting it off. Not only in the field of politics but art, literature & thought as well.

Write again very soon. With love from Nicky & myself to you & Byba

Ever yours
B.B.

To HENRY COSTER

[I Tatti
Settignano
Florence]
13 December 1947

Dear Harry,

Yrs. of Nov. 27 deserves a more detailed & interesting answer than I can give it, partly because I am a poor writer but also that this is the time when one has to write so many conventional letters.

Reading P.L.'s [Percy Lubbock's] book [about Edith Wharton] as if I did not know her. I admired it, enjoyed it & thought it adequate. Yet when I recalled all I knew about her it became a good literary achievement based on her life, but oh! so skin-deep! Foreseeing it would be, I got out of contributing any pages toward it. I could write as I did about Carlo Placci but in much more detailed way & at greater length. I never shall.

But for accumulating fatigue Rome was delightful. We saw a fair number of old Italian friends, some more recent ones like the Orlandos & Sforzas & many Anglo-Saxons as well as continental acquaintances. The Dunns[1] turn out to be a cultivated couple & very sensitive & receptive, so that I enjoyed sight-seeing with both of them. Another worth-while couple now heads our Academy & I hope that I may make you acquainted with them next time you come over. I dream of getting you to lecture there on late Roman — miscalled "Early Xian" history. We got back less than 3 weeks ago & enjoy & suffer from a steady stream of "house-guests." I Tatti has become an inn for acquaintances going to & from Rome. Some of them are good enough to make up for the less welcome.

Now "shop." What is happening to *Byzantion?* Where & when is the vol. for 1947 to appear? Then can you find the time

---

[1] Mr. James Dunn was at the time American Ambassador to Italy.

to inquire about *Metabyzantina* published by the Society for the promotion of Byzantine & Modern Greek Studies, New York. First vol. appeared in '46. If worth while, please send it.

Every good wishes to Byba & yourself for 1948 & may it bring you back soon. There is still so much we can discuss.

Ever affectionately

B.B.

TO PHILIP HOFER

Settignano

31 January 1948

Dear Philip,

. . .

I am all agog to know who will be the new Foggocrat. "A Youngster" you say. I hope no passionate surrealist, abstractist, iconologist, pseudopsychiatrist, or any other ist. I hope it will be somebody who takes an interest in the work of art as DING AN SICH, & not all the subtile, whopping, profound, shallow, toothsome, tasteless things that can be said about it. In short I hope & PRAY that it will be neither a Picassinière nor a German-minded person.[1]

Ever yrs.

B.B.

[1] It proved in fact to be Mr. John Coolidge. B.B.'s interest even in later life in such matters — one might say, the gossip of the art world — was striking.

To Professor Paul J. Sachs

Settignano
19 May 1948

Dear Paul,

It makes me happy to hear fr. you again after so long an interruption of our correspondence. I must tell you at once that I had not heard how ill you have been last winter or I should have written to give you my sympathy. For my part I cannot boast of rude health although I should not complain seeing I am within a month of 83. I have little energy left for work & still less for play. I have to waste greater part of each 24 hours in care for my body & resting. Correspondence takes too much time & despite myself I have become an institution. My chief regret is that I get so little work done.

I hear nothing but good of Coolidge & I should be free from all prejudice but for two matters in which I do not agree with the inanimistic tendencies of the day: 1. It seems to me a council of despair to discard experience & to tell the young "We have made a botch of things. Try your hand & God help you." 2. Rather from the same source of despairing empiricism comes the idea of appointing a person with overwhelmingly architectural interest to head an institution like the Fogg dedicated overwhelmingly to the figure arts.

How I wish you could come over, both of you. We have ripened all around since we last met & it would be useful to talk over matters serenely as we now could & delightful to recall the enchanting past. How distant it seems as reflected in the minds of people under 50 to whom 1887 — my class year — is as remote emotionally as Ancient Egypt. I had counted on revisiting home, i.e. America & it was a bitter disappointment to give it up. How I should enjoy seeing you all & the marvellous collections. For these reasons I am forbidden to undertake it. I should not survive a month of such excitement.

Love to you both & remembrances to Edward in all of which Nicky joins me.

Affectionately
B.B.

To MISS BERYL DE ZOETE

I Tatti
29 March 1948

. . . I wonder how Montale[1] felt in London and what you highbrows made of him. And by the way, who now are your highbrows? Who in the British council of imperfection decides what foreigners to invite like so many baboons in the light of the moon? The strength of a chain depends on its weakest link.

Who published Judith Gautier's "Journal"? The lady interests me because of her father's sake, because of her opium-fiend of a Chinese husband and in gratitude for her translations from the Chinese. When I was a student in Paris more than 60 years ago I kept hearing all sorts of absurdities about both of them.

I look forward to your book and to Waley's next, whatever it may be about. Only beg him from me to avoid learning-larning for its own sake even in the Celestial world.

[1] Eugenio Montale, poet and literary critic.

To Professor Paul J. Sachs

Settignano

5 July 1948

My dear Paul,

Thanks for your remembering my birthday & sending me the volume on Lawrence Lowell. It certainly belongs to a library that is to be a Harvard institution.

I hope you are not as ill as alarming reports that have reached me. Even if they were true months ago. I wish they were so no longer.

My own news is that I enter my 84th year with diminished capacity for work & increased desire for writing more books & articles. Quite a few preoccupy me. I have to waste so much time resting that I doubt how much more I shall get done.

The Italian version of my *Aesthetics & History*[1] is out already & the English one should be out soon. A copy will reach you directly any are available. In London my Sketch for a *Self-Portrait* is in the press. . . .

Let me hear from you when you feel disposed to write & give my love to Meta.

Affectionately,

B.B.

To Henry Coster

Vallombrosa

30 July 1948

Dear Harry,

. . .

Kept hearing sickening accounts of Caliban's behaviour for some days after the attempt on Togliatti. Same Caliban boasts it was nothing compared to what he means to do toward Nov.

1 *Aesthetics and History in the Visual Arts.*

All that happens elsewhere, excepting of course "acts of God," are as nothing compared with what is going on between eternal East & West when they meet, now in Berlin. "Stalin" behaves exactly as did Attila or Hulagu, or Suleiman. We forget that till Peter the Great, Russia was integrally the East & that only a Franco-Germanised small ruling class become Westernized & under Alexander I till Nicholas II seemed "for external use only" to be a Western nation. She now is acting the Oriental one whose sovereign refuses everything — "obstacle tout" — until he gets his way or sees that he can't.

But you know all this. So let us come down to ourselves & let me tell you that I hope you will return months earlier & that when you do we must arrange for a weekly meeting to gossip & talk shop. I must give up reading so much about the events of today & of the last 30 years & devote more time to real reading. Scores of books brought here. And I still want to write two books, the next on Man as Work of Art.

The season seems to be out for being a wet one. It rains every day, but babbling brooks make a pleasant music & trees & fields are ever so green.

With love from Nicky as well as myself to both of you

Affectionately

B.B.

To HENRY COSTER

Lucerne

22 October 1948

Dear Harry,

I am happy to receive yrs. of 13th telling me among other things how in my book you did not always understand the issue. It is entirely my fault. I write as if appealing to any cultivated reader & yet I take for granted that he knows like a specialist what is at stake. Chief reason perhaps why as a writer I am such a failure.

You end with a postscript to the effect that the present muddle is not Truman's fault but Roosevelt's. You are right & wrong. Roosevelt could see but one thing ahead, to defeat Hitler. How blame him & not Churchill together! What could one do after the Nazi challenge but concentrate on smashing them although the more clear-sighted never failed to see that it meant levelling the barrier, the dyke that kept the Tartar hordes out of the West. It is an American trait to want *one* thing & damn the expense & the consequence. Therein as in much else Churchill is more American than British, as indeed I always have realized. Now there is nothing left but to rebuild the barrier against the Soviets & to make sure it has neither holes nor leaks. *À rideau de fer rideau de fer et demi.*

We have been in Geneva for six days, now here for three, three in Zürich & then I Tatti again. Travelling is fascinating but I am getting too old for it. I shall be glad to get back to my sedentary habits & creature comforts.

Love to you both from Nicky as well as myself

Affectionately
B.B.

To Professor Paul J. Sachs

Settignano
1 November 1948

Dear Paul,

I have just returned fr. Switzerland & find your letter of the 15 *ult.*

You say nothing of your own health about which I have been

sympathetically anxious. May I venture to conclude that it is greatly improved?

Thanks for the books you have sent. I look forward to receiving & reading them, in particular Rosenberg's *Rembrandt*.

In Switzerland I had a good look at the Liechtenstein pictures which were on exhibition at Lucerne; & at Zürich before it opened a show of nearly every old Master worth seeing in Lombardy excepting those in the Brera. This is so important that I shall try to return for ten days before it closes at the end of March.

I hope you received my last book. Others will follow.

Nicky's & my love to you both

B.B.

To Professor Paul J. Sachs

Settignano
19 November 1948

My dear Paul,

Ever so many thanks for the four books you sent that have just arrived. I shall peruse them all & Rosenberg's *Rembrandt* is a pleasure.

I hope my *Aesthetics and History* has reached you. It has had unexpected success in the Italian translation. I fear it will be less appreciated over the water.

I fervently hope that you are well out of all your troubles & may expect to enjoy fair health for many a year. Mine has become capricious & precarious. I may last for ever on? Aches, pains, every kind of physical self disgust assail me & there are moments when one questions whether they are worth while. If only I can manage to write a couple of books still in my head.

Love to you & Meta

B.B.

To Professor Paul J. Sachs

Settignano

7 December 1948

My dear Paul,

Accounts keep coming in of your 70th birthday celebration. It seems to have been as cordial, as affectionate, as enthusiastic & appreciative as your career deserves. You & Edward working together have achieved a great school & a great museum. May both continue to flourish for many years under your guidance if no longer under your direction.

It is a great pity that age has overtaken me & I no longer desire to encounter such activities & excitements as I should if I returned home. It would be hard to exaggerate my longing to see you all again at work in your own domain & to see all the drawings you have accumulated & to discuss the future. I have little energy left & much of that goes waste even here on the calls made on me.

Every good wish for 1949 & love to you both

B.B.

To Henry Coster

Settignano

Florence

19 December 1948

Dear Harry,

This is no attempt to write a letter worthy of the one I received from you a few days ago. It is to thank you for it & to wish you both a Happy New Year. It is the best of news that you mean to be back here soon. I look forward to many talks. Just now I had a wrangle with a Communist who claimed that his religion would do for the world what Christianity did to the decaying Greco-Roman world: that it did barbarise it for a 1000 years but produced in the end something finer than Greece or Rome had been. He ejected this jejune proposition as a parallel to what Communism was after, but I should like to investigate the question with you as a partner. Our civilization is of course the product of Xianity but what would it have become had Xianity not intervened. I suspect at times that it was Goethe's *Stirb und Werde* or indeed the infusion of physically hardier blood poured in by the Nordics that brought about renovation.

I am reading Leland Baldwin's *Best Hope of Earth: A Grammar of Democracy,* decidedly suggestive & stimulating.

Affectionately

B.B.

To Professor Paul J. Sachs

Settignano

5 February 1949

Dear Paul,

I hope this will find you well enough not to feel too overburdened by my begging you to read the enclosed. I know well enough how over-worked & how under financed even Harvard is. I know most of the difficulties in the way. Nevertheless if means could be found to invite Yashiro[1] for some years as teacher of a seminar where he communicates his methods & conclusions while himself at work on a given problem, it would put

---

[1] Yukio Yashiro, Japanese art historian, the author of an authoritative work on Botticelli (3 vols., London, 1925).

the study of Far Eastern art on a level it has not yet had in any Western land. Could not among so many lovers of Chinese & Japanese art, people be found to endow a chair for a number of years with the hope that later on it may be extended indefinitely? I appeal to you, dear Paul, because I know nobody else to whom I can turn in this matter. I have it at heart not only on Yashiro's account. Far Eastern studies are as all other art-historical subjects being pursued in a way that makes me despair of the subject & wish often that the teaching of art history should be altogether abandoned. Yashiro would be a corrective.

I have just had a charming letter from Coolidge & look forward to seeing him in the summer.

Every good wish to you & Meta

Affectionately

B.B.

To Professor Paul J. Sachs

Settignano

4 April 1949

Dear Paul,

Yes I have been minutely informed by various participants of all done in yr. honour & I heartily wished I had been one of them. I hope it will end in an adequately illustrated vol. reproducing the drawings exhibited.

In re Yashiro — the ideal would be to find him a research fellowship. Why should he not succeed to Coomaraswamy at B.M.F.A. Yashiro to be sure is a Sino-Japologist & not an Indianist but he is what I should suppose we want most. I repeat that nobody else has yet lived who combines as Yashiro does knowledge of Sino-Japanese languages, literature, myths & iconologies with an acquaintance unsurpassed of Far Eastern art products & our methods of studying them. It is a pity to lose such a chance of putting Far Eastern art study on its real footing & in its real frame.

I hope your health is restored enough to enable you to work with zest. There is always plenty to do provided there is pleasure in doing it.

I still am writing bits although I have little energy remaining.

Ever affectionately
B.B.

To Professor Paul J. Sachs

Settignano
13 July 1949

Dear Paul,

Yrs. of March 27th was long in coming, & since it arrived I have been away in Rome over-busy there & returning have been over-tired for even letter writing. In fact the three weeks spent there where I had not a tenth to do that I should have to at home gives me great qualms about the visit I was hoping to make. The fact is I am in 83rd year & my flesh knows it if my spirit does not.

Now for yr. letter. I am cheered by yr. declaration that yr. student body is so satisfactory. I hope they realize that art is not merely a matter for classification & exhibition but a revelation of the human soul through the ages. Thacher came to see us the other day & I thoroughly enjoyed his visit. We disagreed on no subject touched on & I do not recall avoiding subjects. Yesterday I had a long confab with Rich of the Chicago Art Institute. There is a man & I chided him for not going to Harvard. I fear we are in the shade just now. Princeton carries everything, nor should I mind if they carried what was worth while and what is worth while. I am too old to bother & besides I have confidence that Harvard will recover.

I am busy writing or rather rewriting & completing the library. I want to leave it with (as it were) paths laid out so that my successors will need but to follow & pace them.

You speak of a catalogue of Maurice Wertheim's "French Painting Since 1870." It has not reached us. Perhaps you could send another copy. All the other things you so kindly sent have arrived.

Affectionate greetings to you both.

Yours

B.B.

To Henry Coster

S. Maria la Bruna
(Napoli)
14 October 1949

Dear Harry,

Your so sympathetically thoughtful & delightful letter finds me here staying with Clotilde Marghieri. The very comfy house is placed in the midst of a Pompeian landscape & the scenery reaches the utmost bounds of what I can enjoy. No human mind could conceive greater beauty than is here; the whole gulf from horn to horn & all that between lies, the long drawn lines of mountains stretching to their bases & these covered with a powder of human habitations. As you know it can be violent, beside itself, but for the most part it is radiant, encouraging, joyous. And Clotilde is a perfect hostess.

Pompeii & Herculaneum are at a stone's throw & they never cease fascinating me. We go to one or the other each forenoon. Sorrento is a short hour away & there we have dear friends, the Ruffinos. Donna Titina[1] must be my age.

But we must be back by the 19th because on the 20th the Walter Lippmanns are coming for a couple of days *en route* for India & way stations. Otherwise I should be tempted to linger here & enjoy as rarely elsewhere immediate contact with things. And that, as you truly imply, is the mystical state. You have divined what is the realest thing in me. As I look back on 75 years of consciousness I realize that from earliest years until now my *tropism* has always been toward immediate contact with things of every nature but most of all with persons. That often has been difficult & disastrous but on the whole I never grew discouraged. Perhaps I could not *function* in any other way.

You have put yr. finger on my present trouble. Never has my mind been more active but all in vain when I try to put it down in black & white. Fruitful ideas fly away like teasing *diabletons* & leave me staring, abandoned with pen in hand on the unwritten page. An illusion no doubt but to me it seems as if still I had so much to say. Indeed when alone I think of nothing else & all sorts of ideas come to beg friendly reception.

You are aware no doubt that Egypt is now in a dangerously anti-foreign humor. I hope you will not linger but return to Florence early in 1950. I long to see you. . . .

Write again as soon as you feel like it & give my best to Byba, & Nicky's to both of you.

Ever affectionately

B.B.

---

[1] Titina, the daughter of the statesman Ferdinando Martini, married first to Count Benzoni and after Benzoni's death to Carlo Ruffino.

To Hugh Trevor-Roper

I Tatti
Settignano
Florence
7 December 1949

Dear Hugh,

I hope my wire reached you before you left. Of course you will be welcome & for as long as you can make it.

Do you know Norman Douglas? I don't. So if convenient do sample him for me. He is at Capri it seems. I greatly admire his writing.

Sylvia[1] is here attending rhetorical effusions which in Italy pass for politics. What we call politics is done but never talked of here.

If you go to Paestum try to see the near-by Foce del Selle with its diggings of c. 600 B.C.

Affectionately
B.B.

To Judge Learned Hand

28 December 1949

. . . Fifty years ago to a day we moved into this house.[2]

---

[1] Sylvia Sprigge is the author of a biography of Berenson. She and her husband Cecil Sprigge were at that time representing the *Manchester Guardian* and the *Economist* in Rome.

[2] B.B. here makes a mistake. He and Mary Costelloe were married on December 28, 1900, and moved into I Tatti at the same date. See B.B.'s letter to R. C. Trevelyan from Poggio Gherardo December 1900.

To Walter Lippmann

Settignano
New Year's Day 1950

Dear Walter,

Thanks for the letter just received, the longest & most interesting ever had from you. I am delighted that your conclusions about the countries you have visited confirms what I feel about them. They are for the most part totalitarian because all human societies as societies have been totalitarian. I for instance spent my first ten years in one & I have vivid recollections of what it is like. Untotalitarian societies may have been a byproduct of mediaeval feudalism & of English in particular. *Liberty is an aristocratic postulate;* the others care only for welfare. By the way, one of my reasons for in the long run expecting more from Pakistan than from Hindustan is that the Moslem gentry of the latter are genuine country squires.

I share yr. horror of India not only for its squalour & inertia but as the most estranging mentality on our globe. I took the trouble to learn Sanskrit. I read everything I could lay hold of. I saw numberless Anglo-Indians & some Hindoos. I studied their art through all the ages & always with increasing loathing & *terror,* positive terror that such trains of thought & such feelings should exist.

To return to yr. conclusion that Asia is totalitarian. I want to include in "Asia" all of Russia & now that the gentry has gone from Poland, Hungary & Rumania those countries as well, as naturally totalitarian & totally indifferent to individual liberty & cosily satisfied from the point of view of welfare.

Do not feel obliged to decipher the above.

Love to all of you & may 1950 be satisfactory & bring you back here.

Ever affectionately
B.B.

To Miss Beryl de Zoete

Casa al Dono
24 August 1950

. . .

Please tell Arthur[1] that Nicky has been reading his *Po-Chu-I* aloud to me. How I envy the Chinese writers and their interpreters. They take me back to a world where it is so delicious to sit together with friends so sensitive, so trusted that one can be communicatively, happily silent together.

Just finishing *Chekov in My Life.*[2] [One] could believe it was a novel by Chekov himself.

Love to Arthur and your dear self

To Beryl de Zoete

20 November 1950

How good of you and dear Arthur [Waley] to send me his translation of the Ainu epic. It is fifty years, sixty years, sixty-five years since I read translations of the *Kalewala*. Yet the Ainu poem seems to recall the great Finnish one. Doubtless Arthur is aware of this. Ask him if he has the leisure to tell me what kind of language Ainu is, monosyllabic, agglutinative or inflectional. Agglutinative perhaps and in that case of the same family as Finnish.

I could envy your autumn wanderings in France, the more so as I fear my travelling days cost me too much. They use me up to an alarming degree and I have to make a serious effort to recover from every effort. Even the month in Rome has almost wrecked me. But how I did enjoy it. Mine eyes did see the

[1] Arthur Waley.
[2] By Lydia Cirilova, London, 1950.

glory of the greatest of all artifacts, the Catholic Church. The pilgrimages are the acme of its ritual and the choreography surpasses all that lay ballet masters dream of. Perhaps choreography is not quite the word. Yet scenography is far too inadequate.

Now we are back and I am too fagged out to do any real writing. When I don't I feel distressingly *minderwertig*.

Love to you both

To WILLIAM PHILLIPS

Settignano
11 December 1950

Dear William,

It is a year at least since I have had direct news of you & I can delay no more, & ask you to write & tell me about Caroline, about yourself, your offspring & your occupations. As for me, I spent two months in Paris . . . October we spent in Rome. . . . Now I am here worrying over events which seem to me darker than [any] since French Revolutionary & Napoleonic times, but worse far. There seems to be no fighting the Soviet. You might as well hurl a bomb at the ocean. I am sure that their menace will pass in the course of time as so many others have, but how soon? Perhaps not in generations, not in centuries. Meanwhile I should not complain. Being 85 & a half I still am fairly well, still enjoy working (when I can) still delight in good talk & good books. Only periodicals take up most of my leisure. Getting old & yet keeping alive is a whole time job.

With affectionate remembrances
B.B.

To Professor Paul J. Sachs

Settignano
18 March 1951

Dear Paul,

. . . What little energy I retain goes in doing my utmost for the library. That and that alone I feel proud of, & Stalin permitting, may survive me.

My love to you both
B.B.

To Professor Paul J. Sachs

Settignano
6 May 1951

Dear Paul,

. . . I am proud of the library as of nothing else I have achieved.

Affectionately
B.B.

To Lawrence Berenson

Casamicciola
Ischia
3 June 1951

I have just received and read the round-robin you wrote from Jerusalem May 1st. It is delightful reading, well observed and well written. Optimistic to a degree! I see snags ahead, the most alarming being the rabbinical zealots. If they get the upper hand Israel will become a mere Yeshiba supporting drones who shake backward and forward mumbling prayers like Tibetan Lamas.

Israel must, in my opinion, first and foremost become the most powerful organization in the Near East. That alone will render the Jew the self-respect that he suffers from lacking. That will procure him respect from OTHERS the world over and of his neighbours in particular. Then in good time Israel must conquer Transjordania of which *perfide Albion* needlessly treacherously deprived it the very moment it promised the Jews a "National home." [1] With Trans-Jordania Israel could support millions and make her authority felt in Cairo as well as Baghdad and Damascus and be a state even ex-Great Britain would want to be allied with.

Of course this is a wild program and could be realised only with American money and American-Jewish pull on top of the iron determination of the Israelis.

To Lawrence Berenson

Settignano
22 January 1952

Dear Lawrence,

. . .

I envy you Cuba. It is, by the way, the only part of the Spanish American world about whose art I know next to nothing. They must have published in recent years books on the architecture & sculpture of post-Colombian as well as pre-Colombian days. Get your friend to process & send me what there is & give him my regards. I should love to know him.

---

[1] In view of Berenson's habitual Anglophilia, it is interesting to note his prejudice *in this instance* and the rather commonplace nationalism of his scheme for the aggrandizement of Israel through the conquest of lands belonging to others.

I am deeply grateful for all you do for me on my finances, but as I cannot have any judgment of my own I am happy to rely on yours.

Ever affectionately
B.B.

To Roger Hinks[1]

Santa Cesarea Terme (Lecce)
19 June 1952

. . .

Apulia is full of churches with grand Romanesque proportions and space. French sculpture and chiselling as nowhere else in Italy but with much that is Byzantine and a touch of Arabo-Sicilian.

Lecce — I don't enjoy its superfluities of ornament on buildings of commonplace design. The unique thing in Lecce is the cathedral close. Nothing like it elsewhere in Italy, perhaps not on the Continent. A perfect architectural unit and harmony — rather Spanish as architectural effect. By the way, the *campanili* in this region are very fine in every way and almost approach the Italianate one of Murcia. In a number of them one feels the Pharos[2] of Alexandria.

1 English art historian and man of letters, author of *Greek and Roman Portraiture and Myth* and *Allegory in Ancient Art,* at present head of British Council in Paris. He was doubtless working at the time of this letter on his book on Michelangelo (London, 1930).
2 The famous light-house of antiquity, from which the minarets of North Africa and the Giralda of Seville also derive.

To Miss Jacqueline Bouvier

Settignano
6 July 1952

Dear Jacqueline

Thank you for most unsatisfactory photos. Please get anybody to snapshot you and send me the result.

You write about Lee as if she had got tangle-footed on flypaper. I fervently hope it is not so. American girls should marry American boys. They wear and wash better. It would life-enhance me to see either or both of you — even if honeymooning — although that would make me jealous and envious.

You would find me at Vallombrosa till October. *Souviens-toi* of our first and only but so enchanting encounter? We go there in a few days.

Have just returned from the tip of Italy's toe — glorious.

Love,
B.B.

To Professor Paul J. Sachs

Settignano
11 July 1952

Dear Paul,

A fortnight ago Agnes Mongan asked me whether it was true that I had willed I Tatti away from Harvard. She did not know when the rumour started. Today Offner[1] asked the same question & added that "everybody" was talking about it. I simply cannot imagine who & why such rumours are spread abroad. Needless to say that never has any such intention passed

1 Richard Offner.

through my head, much as I may deplore much that Harvard
fails to do in our field. Please deny this nonsense whenever you
can & above all to Edward. . . .

Affectionately

B.B.

To Walter Lippmann

Vallombrosa

(Firenze)

20 August 1952

Dear Walter,

I know that my writing is getting more illegible yet I cannot
dictate or type. That is why I do not write oftener, why I have
not answered your good letter of June 16.

Johnnie Walker is here & told us today that before leaving he
heard from you something about yourself & my leaving of I
Tatti to Harvard. Could you take the time to tell me what it
was you heard? The petty welkin of the minuscule world concerned with such matters seem to be ringing with gossip about
me, Harvard & I Tatti. I cannot imagine where & why these
rumours. I made my will 20 years ago leaving my entire estate
to Harvard & never thought of changing it — unless indeed Harvard refused it.

I need not tell you that though I never thought of burthen-
ing you with it, I should feel happier about the future if I could
count on you as defender of my purpose, hopes & ideals for Harvard at I Tatti.

Perhaps you will come over after the elections & give me a
chance to talk about I Tatti.

In a month or so you will receive "Rumours and Reflexions"

in all but unabridged bulk & perhaps you will find a passage here & there to arrest yr. attention.

Affectionate greetings to you both from Nicky &

B.B.

To LAWRENCE BERENSON

Casa al Dono
Vallombrosa
21 September 1952

. . .

The difficulty I foresee is that my ideas for I Tatti's future are so unpopular at present. I want to form scholars and gentlemen, not brainless hacks of petty learning, such as our Ph.D.'s, turned out as postgraduates even by our best universities.

Conant was in Rome a few months ago but never thought of coming to I Tatti. This shocked people so much that they kept his visit to Rome a secret from me. Indeed I learnt it as a fact only a few days ago.

To LAWRENCE BERENSON

Settignano
24 December 1952

Dear Lawrence,

. . .

I worry over yr. connection with Batista.[1] He is almost sure

[1] Mr. Lawrence Berenson was the attorney of Fulgencio Batista, the former President of Cuba.

to be assassinated & I don't want you with him at the moment. Then I fear the air accident that may over-take you going & coming to Cuba. . . .

Your gratefully affectionate
B.B.

To John Walker

Settignano
5 January 1953

Dear Johnnie:

I enjoy and love Hoffmann's, & Strauss's and Cole Porter's fancies, waltzes, tunes, but I do not place them along with the sublime music of Bach, Beethoven and Brahms. I love the Lanckoroński St. George, a pretty super-Xmas card — never an Uccello. I should love to own it, & I am sure it would attract "the people" if you put it in yr. N.G. But I cannot place it remotely on a level with the Mantegna St. Jerome you mention. I don't know why I let myself express disapproval of the price asked for the pretty picture. When I think of all that could be done with money, it raises my gorge to see it wasted.

By the way, what exercised me more is that I have not yet received the Murray Crane Clemenza book nor your second colored N.G. picture book. Were they really sent?

Nicky, Thank Heaven, is making good recovery. It was touch & go.

Every good wish, dear Johnnie,

With love,
B.B.

To Arthur McComb

Eden Hotel
Rome
25 January 1953

Dear McComb,

Yrs. of Jan. 3 finds me here too busy almost to write. Yet I do not want to delay telling you that . . . I like yr. idea of a book on Veduta painting & find the opening pages entirely to my taste & therefore admirable.

Why don't you apply for a Guggenheim fellowship for this work? You could refer them to me & you can rest assured that I would back you. Or better still a Fulbright to come abroad with a view to prepare yourself & carry through this job. There also are Rockefeller & Ford scholarships.

I fear you have been too un-sensational hitherto in yr. teaching & writing to satisfy the demands of academic salesmanship.

With every good wish

Sincerely yrs.
B.B.

To Lawrence Berenson

Settignano
29 January 1953

Dear Lawrence,

. . .

It was an unexpected blow to be told all of a sudden after so many talks between you, Conant, Metcalf, etc., etc., that Harvard was likely to refuse I Tatti. I realised how much the thought of Harvard was in my mind & it was always with a view to future Harvard scholars that I zestfully was building up a library almost unique for its purpose.

If Harvard refuses — then what? I want advice about that. It would be logical perhaps that having lived in Italy for over 60 years devoting myself to Italian art [and given] American refusal to accept I Tatti & my capital, I should bequeath it to an Italian institution or the town of Florence.

So I scarcely worry any more.

Affectionately
B.B.

To Roger Hinks

Hotel Villa Igea
Palermo
14 May 1953

My dear Roger,

Thanks for one of the most delightful letters I ever received. It followed me from place to place and finally reached me at Girgenti ten days ago. I have been turning it over my palate ever since. It tastes so good.

You have had a radiant time in the States and it makes me happy that you appreciated it as you have and that cis-Atlantic, even English people so rarely do nowadays. I agree with all you say about places, museums, persons. Yes, New England (especially as I knew it in my formative years) was perhaps more English (being still colonially nostalgic for the culture of the mother-country) than England itself. I knew villages in Western Massachusetts that hark back to early 18th century, still untouched by "modernism." In so far as I feel myself to be anything it is not [so much] an American as a New Englander.

One of my real regrets is that New England has been (as it were) snowed under by America. I am glad you liked the two great Bellinis, the Feast of the Gods and the Saint Francis. You do not mention the Gardner Mausoleum. Did you not see it while in Boston?

. . . I am stopping over in Rome to see the Picasso exhibition. I do it to get material and detail for the verbal war I am carrying on and shall continue [to carry on] against that Satan, that fallen Angel of the arts.

To Henry Coster

Vallombrosa
10 September 1953

Dear Harry,

Thank you for yours of the 2nd & the enclosed photos & films of I Tatti & good advice about using them for effective reproduction in post-cards.

I am delighted to read that you mean to return in November. I look forward to seeing you often & to stimulating talks.

Your *tour d'horizon politique* is so identical with what I should make that there is little to discuss. I am inclined to regret Acheson & Truman. I fear Mr. Dulles could scarcely be worse advised & that our President should have remained in the army. Yet given universal suffrage & government by the masses & their hysteria we are doing tolerably. Our cis-Atlantic friends, the British particularly, are nearly at the end of their patience.

By the time we meet much will be clarified, at least this side of the Atlantic. Indeed, while I do not the least expect it, I should not be overwhelmed with surprise if the Soviet hold on

Europe did not collapse. As for Asia, we may have to help defend Russia against them, not today nor tomorrow, but some day if the Chinese get sufficiently industrialized & armed.

We have been living our usual life up here but less crowded than former years. My brother-in-law Perry's visit for the whole of August was delightful. Most other visitors & callers have been museum & art people. The 23rd inst. we begin autumn wanderings, first to the Friuli, then Venice followed by the Milanese & finally the first half of November in Rome. This is our program but I am not sure my health will let me carry it through. Suddenly I have begun to feel and act old. I dare say my health is good for one in his 89th year but positively it is but indifferent.

I do a bit of work every day, now on the insoluble Giorgione problem.

With love to you both

Affectionately

B.B.

To Hugh Trevor-Roper

I Tatti
Settignano
Florence
21 February 1954

My dear Hugh,

May the Lord grant a Happy Issue to your troubles. What more can a sympathizer like myself do; than to — shall I say "pray for you."

What a paean to Brenan![1] Yes I received the book & of

1 Gerald Brenan, the author of *South from Granada* and other books on Spanish topics.

course I shall read it & his Spanish literature. He is no stranger to me. . . . Tell Brenan how glad I should be to know him in the flesh. I hope he will come here soon enough for me. I hope he is not like Chandler Post a Harvard professor who already has published a dozen or more volumes on the history of Spanish painting & only reached the very beginning of the 16th century. A few years ago he came to Naples to study Spanish influence there. He wrote to ask me to explain how it was that everything in Italy repelled while everything in Spain captivated him. . . .

I write articles for the *Corriere de la Sera,* superintend the printing of my new *Lotto* & a small book on Sicily, translations into "foreign" tongues & am preparing a new edition of the catalogue of Italian Paintings. An undertaking for years & I am nearly 89.

Ever yours

B.B.

To HUGH TREVOR-ROPER

Hotel Europa e Britannia

Venezia

25 June 1954

My dear Hugh,

Nearly a month since I received the last of your ribald & fascinating epistles. Since then I have had a letter confirming yr. optimistic prospect from Xandra. The solution must be approaching — or has it come already, & as I hope turned out to the desire of both your hearts?

I came here expecting more leisure than at I Tatti. Not at all! For after every hour that I pass looking I have to waste more than as much time resting in the dark, dozing, sleeping.

Likewise when I see people. The result is that I find no time at all for reading & scarcely any for writing. Hence my silence of a month almost.

We came here to get away from the madding crowd that in summer time mills about I Tatti & to work on the new catalogue we are preparing of Venetian pictures. . . .

The "Biennale" is an encyclopedia give-away of *Unkunst*. Sheer infantilism or impudent bluff. All the exploiters of that heavy industry have been here from every part of this shrunken little earth.

We leave the 29th for I Tatti. So address there & let it be soon & with good news

Ever yrs.
B.B.

To Professor Paul J. Sachs

Settignano
11 November 1954

Dear Paul,

Thanks for your *Modern Prints and Drawings*. I have enjoyed every page & the admirably worded interpretation you have given to each reproduction. To me the book is a revelation. Of course I always have known Goya's & Daumier's graphic work, but little or nothing of the Modern. Picasso comes out as the best of the group & Matisse next. I congratulate you on this splendid & valuable achievement.

I hope you received a volume of facsimiles of Florentine drawings in the Uffizi. Some of those I should have reproduced are suffering from *Exhibitionitis* which removes works of art for years from their legal domicile. It is an alarming disease, against which I am trying to fight. An article of mine to that effect has appeared in the *Corriere della Sera* as well as in the *Manchester Guardian*.

How are you all, you & Meta & the daughter of whom I had a glimpse in Rome?

Affectionately
B.B.

To AXEL BOETHIUS[1]

I Tatti
17 February 1955

. . . Do you recall what Wilamowitz says at the end of his book on the Alexandrian poets?

I have always loved Catullus and since 1885 the *Pervigilium* to which Walter Pater in Marius introduced me. Very few years later J. K. Huysmans' *À rebours* led me to read Ausonius and Claudian and all sorts of late Latins. How I used to enjoy browsing among poets in many languages. Now I have to spend so much time sleeping, dozing, resting that I have leisure only for the little work I still dare to undertake.

To WALTER LIPPMANN

Settignano
5 March 1955

Dear Walter,

Thank you for *The Public Philosophy*. I have read it & most heartily approve of your aim, admire your way of putting the problem & thoroughly enjoyed your dialectic.

---

[1] The distinguished Swedish scholar, for many years director of the Swedish Institute in Rome.

BUT — the remedy would be — Ferrero proposed a return to LEGITIMACY & you if your discourse were carried to its logical conclusion, to the Mediaeval polity of Dante, etc., etc. Something of that leads me to stand by the Catholic Church as the one powerful defence, the one solid barrier against Sovietism.

I fear that there is no remedy for the situation where we are & getting worse unless we return to a graduated, a pyramidal, i.e. hierarchical & even oligarchical society, despite all their drawbacks, of which I am so painfully aware.

Universal suffrage can only lead to ochlocracy, to satisfying the mob, "the PEOPLE." Now the real *arcana regni* is that the people now as hitherto care only for *panem et circenses,* are indifferent to our ideals & our values & will not listen to us. Those of us who stoop to conquer them find that they are a quicksand that swallows them up & reduces them[1] to their mouthpieces.

The return to a Public Philosophy would be conceivable in an aristocratic community that temporarily had got off the rails or lost its North Star but scarcely in the kind of community to which we now are being reduced.

The response to yr. book is immediate & would be hopeful if those who read & understand had the power & authority.

I am recovering from my fall but not from my 90 years. More demands are being made on my diminishing energies than can be fulfilled & keep me agitated & driven. Yet I have no right to complain. Given *la condition humaine,* I am still enjoying life.

I long to see you & discuss many things, even eschatological.

Love to you both
B.B.

---

1 Berenson must mean "reduces *us*" (i.e., "those of us who stoop to being their mouthpieces").

To Lawrence Berenson

> Grand Hotel & San Domenico
> Taormina
> 25 May 1953

Dear Lawrence,

. . .

I have recommendations to make to Harvard with regard to my hope for the future of I Tatti, but nothing to go into a will. I shall discuss them with Coolidge before putting them in writing.

What you tell me about Batista[1] is very interesting. I wish him well, but I don't want you to be assassinated at his side.

> Love to you all
> B.B.

To Lawrence Berenson

> Settignano
> 19 February 1955

Dear Lawrence,

I have just read yours of the 16th & can assure you that I seldom have had a more beautiful one addressed to me. I am sorry that the leisure was bought at the price of a *grippe*. If reading the "Sketch" helped to cure you it is the best recommendation possible. A sedative yet stimulating & comforting! What more can be said of a writing that is not informative.

You confuse me in my conviction that I have failed of my

[1] This refers to Lawrence Berenson's letter of 18 May 1953. It is historically of great interest and as the reader's curiosity may have been aroused by Berenson's comment, he is referred to the Appendix where it is given in full.

mission. I should have been a poet, a novelist, an essayist & not an art-historian & *horrible dictu* an expert. Others can do that as well as I; but I was born with a message & have failed to deliver it.

Your letter betrays extraordinary gifts as a writer. You could have been one had you turned your mind & efforts toward it. It is so rich in thought & feeling & so well expressed. Perhaps some day, years from now, when you feel like retiring & I hope [can] afford it, you will take to the pen & write, write your memoirs for instance. . . .

Affectionately
B.B.

To Miss Natalie Barney

Casa al Dono
Vallombrosa
(Prov. di Firenze)
16 August 1955

Dear Natalie,

Thanks for the Preface. It is a wonderful and beautiful piece of writing, far away the best I have seen from your pen.

Do you want it back? If so I'll address it to Paris.

The last visit, short as it was, brought back the Natalie I was so much in love with nearly 40 years ago. Thank you for letting me recapture a glimpse of those bitter-sweet days of intense living.

Love,
B.B.

To Walter Lippmann[1]

I Tatti
Settignano
Florence
23 November 1955

Dear Walter,

Let me thank you for the good note of the 19th. I envy your spending a night with Adlai Stevenson on his farm, do tell me about it if you can without being too indiscreet.

Delighted that you have been given an Honorary Degree by the University of Chicago. Boast for boast I can outdo you altogether; on the 4th of this month, *in absentia,* I was given an Honorary Degree at the Sorbonne. *Item,* I was offered one last May in Oxford but as they will only give it to those who come and take it I had to refuse. In a few days a committee of the University of Florence is coming to bring me the diploma of the Florence University.

I have just had a delightful letter from Hazel Albertson from West Newbury, Mass., with photos of the farm that I knew so well 75 years ago.

Rumor reaches me that it is Huntington Cairns who has kicked up the rumpus at the N.G., wishing to replace David Finley. From my point of view it would be a disaster. Therefore *absit omen!*

Out walking yesterday dear Nicky stumbled and broke her ankle-bone. The first ten minutes were horrible, she suffered so. She was taken at once to the hospital, put in plaster and brought back. She is fairly comfortable now but will not be able to accompany me on my walks for some time.

Love to you and Helen.

Ever,
B.B.

[1] A typed letter.

To Walter Lippmann[1]

I Tatti
Settignano
Florence
9 December 1955

Dear Walter,

Thank you for yours of December 3rd.

Yes, Nicky has had a nasty accident, a double fracture of her ankle which is still in plaster and I fear will have to be so for two or three weeks to come. The house is sunless without her.

What you tell me about Adlai Stevenson excites and delights me. It would be a wonderful thing to have that kind and quality of man as President of our country.

If Nixon is to be the Republican candidate for the next election and by bad luck gets in, he might turn out to be another Harding. *Absit Omen.*

I fear Johnny [Johnnie Walker] has very small chance of being made director of the N[ational] G[allery]. The dice seem loaded heavily in favor of Huntington Cairns. I am against him, Cairns, on entirely impersonal grounds. . . . I understand that the Mellon lectureships up to date, nearly all of which I disapprove deeply, were dictated by him.

The third of my articles on Calabria will appear in a few days and I will send all three addressed to Helen. I hope she will give you the gist of them and I hope further that, as promised, she will repay me with the more significant articles that you are printing in the Herald Tribune.

Love to both of you from Nicky as well as myself.

Yours,
B.B.

1 A typed letter.

To Axel Boethius

I Tatti

19 December 1955

. . . I envy you [exploring] Saint Peter's underworld in [Adriano] Prandi's company. The coming of Christianity to Rome is a subject that has fascinated and troubled me ever since I first came there myself in 1888/89. I hesitate to be too sceptical, yet to accept the Catholic interpretation is more than I can do. I should like to discuss the problem with you. Do have it in mind for our next meeting.

To Gisela Richter[1]

I Tatti

Settignano

Florence

16 January 1956

Dear Gisela,

Thanks for an altogether admirable paper on "The Origin of Verism in Roman Portraits."

The possible influence of Egyptian portraiture on late Hellenistic sculptors is far from unlikely. Be that as it may, I can assure you that in Aegean lands, in Asia Minor, in continental Greece, in the Islands I've seen portraits as veristic, although far from being as crude and vulgar as some of the products found on the Italian soil. The theory that they were all portraits of Romans who happened to find themselves in Aegean lands can scarcely be taken into serious consideration.

1 A letter from Berenson to Miss Richter's father will be found under the date 5 January 1905. It is interesting that both letters are congratulatory and concern pieces of work done by J. P. Richter and his daughter, respectively, at a distance of half a century.

In this connection I wish you would see a portrait head belonging to the British Ambassador. It was bought many years ago by His Excellency's father-in-law at Smyrna and as found in Asia Minor. It is extraordinarily sensitive, as much almost as a Desiderio da Settignano. If authentic it is the kind of head that may even have been the model for the official portraits of Augustus and many Augustan heads.

Again my very best thanks for this admirable paper.

Affectionately

B.B.

To LAWRENCE BERENSON

I Tatti
31 May 1956

. . . I have had a message I venture to ask you to communicate to Batista. It is no more nor less than to get out while the going is good. If he hangs on they will either kill him or end by kicking him out ignominiously. So he should get busy selecting and forming a *junta* to take over and leave Cuba to it for better or worse. Let us hope for better. I know I am recommending something heroic and seldom performed. The only case I can recall offhand is Sulla early in the first century B.C. in Rome.

To Hugh Trevor-Roper

I Tatti
Settignano
Florence
18 November 1956

Dear Hugh,

At last, thanks to yours of the 13th I begin to understand Eden's mistake — the consequent hue & cry against his policy in the Near East. Strange that I should not have had it explained before by any of the periodicals that I con. Now it is Eisenhower who is forbidding you to touch a hair of Nasser's head. I am too disgusted, too sick. What a welter!

D.C. is only a picker-up of what forty & more years ago a certain Langton Douglas (father of Air Marshal Lord Sholto Douglas) art-critic, art-dealer did in Irish collections. He took the then dictator in Old Master matters, Bode, director of Berlin galleries, through most of them & picked out the very best to throw them on the market.

I look forward to yr. article on "Communism" even if Americanized.

The Swedes were here for a week — not only H.M. but one of the dearest bipeds now on the earth, Axel Boethius, archaeologist & bosom friend of H.M. Axel is the best read man I have ever known & intellectually the most generous. *Item,* he almost competes with you as a letter writer.

What now? Other Coreas or *Ragnarak Götterdämmerung?*

Dear Hugh, it was delightful to have you & Xandra here. Give her my love & I pray to all the gods that be that we may see you here again.

Yours
B.B.

To Hugh Trevor-Roper

I Tatti
Settignano
Florence
28 December 1956

My dear Hugh,

Thank you for the most fascinating letter yet addressed to me through all the precious years of our friendship. Unfortunately it ends with the distressing news that you jammed your right hand in the car. Let me hope that when you read this you will have forgotten the accident and be ready to give me a full account of Xandra's attendance at Wind's lecture.

The reason I am dictating this letter is that I was alarmingly and wretchedly ill when yours reached me and, although I am already on the mend, my handwriting is so shaky that even you, master as you are in decoding my chicken tracks, would fail this time.

Back to your letter.[1] I simply have never read anything more clarifying and more illuminating on a passing political situation. It is hard for me to believe that the Soviets threatened to bomb London and, if Bohlen really was urging Washington to behave as nastily to you as it did, he must have lost his nerve and taken the Russian threat seriously.

I cannot exaggerate my distress, my misery over the conduct of Washington in this affair. I feel ashamed as well as sorrowful that a great power as we now are should be so unprepared to meet a crisis like this one and obliged to mask its submission to oil interests by pretending that the world's peace should be guaranteed by that dangerous myth, the ONU [UNO] in their glass palace in New York.

If only your government hadn't lost nerve in July and gone

[1] The following paragraphs refer of course (without naming it) to the celebrated "Suez affair" of November 1956.

straight forward! *"Cosa fatta capo ha"* would have prevailed. Now I do not see how this disgusting and alarming muddle is going to clarify itself.

I feel tempted to ask you whether you would mind if I lent your letter to Walter Lippmann? I have not seen his latest articles but I strongly suspect he is as unhappy as you and I are. By the way, His Holiness the Pope in his last message *urbi et orbi* has said exactly what I think both of us would say to the world at large about the present moment.

My last illness all but had me and if I recover completely, as I still hope to, it will be on a lower level of vitality. I had little enough to spare before.

Our best wishes to you both for a personally satisfactory 1957, and hopes that we shall see you here again long before it is over.

With love to you both from Nicky as well as myself,

B.B.

To Axel Boethius

I Tatti
29 December 1956

My dear Axel,

Thanks for one of your most delightful letters and for your daughter's sketch. It promises well and she should be encouraged.

How I wish I could have been with you wandering about disinterestedly but not aimlessly in the heart of Rome. You make me feel poignantly how much I miss Rome.

Hirn — the name calls up a writer I read long long ago. He speculated and metaphysisized.

Art is the development of the building constructing impulses in all animals, bees, wasps, termites, birds, seals. In man this instinct ends by becoming conscious and reflective and ultimately intellectualized as is the case with all of man's activities. To-day we no longer know whither away. Once the almost physiological call for *otherness* gets the upper hand as it does in man, art undergoes changes ending ultimately in *Unkunst*.

Dear Axel, dearest of friends; take mine and Nicky's best wishes for 1957 to yourself and to all that is yours.

To JOHN WALKER

Settignano
[Received 31/12/56]

Dear Johnnie:

Congratulations on your achievement. It is an unsurpassed masterpiece of impersonal, serene, detailed, philological writing about a work of art. At the same time its study of change in taste as exemplified by subject of your work and its various phases and vicissitudes is done with an unsurpassable delicacy and precision. Indeed I know of no study of a single work of Italian art treated as exhaustively or subtly from as many points of view as you have in this essay on the Bellini-Titian "Feast of Gods." It overwhelms, delights and instructs me. Indeed it is in every sense of the word a valuable contribution to our pursuits.

How enchanting they would be if you and I could pursue them together! Let me thank you for the copious illustrative reproductions. True, I have them, but scattered, and it is ever so useful to have them together and so easy to lay hands on.

I feel very proud of you and am deeply touched by your

glowingly generous recognition of what you believe I have done for you.

You encourage me to work on. There is so much I still could do, if only!

With love and joy

Devotedly,

B.B.

To Walter Lippmann

I Tatti
Settignano
Florence
19 February 1957

Dear Walter,

. . .

I have no doubt you are as indifferent to press cuttings as possible, yet I enclose a long article about your last book in the *Corriere della Sera*.

I recall William James occasionally pulling press cuttings about himself out of his pocket and shyly showing them to me saying, "Naturally I don't care a bit but you know my wife enjoys them." . . .

Yours,

B.B.

To Axel Boethius

I Tatti

3 March 1957

My dear Axel,

Let me hope that you remain carefree to enjoy your convalescence and that it will not be long before you return to your activities.

I enclose a review of a book on the eternal Homer. What else but a past could he describe of which memory was still vivid.

Apart from all artistic qualities the *Iliad* would seem to me the epic of the conquest of the Aegean and the Southern shores of the Black Sea. The *Odyssey* on the contrary [the epic account] of the hazardous exploration of the West.

The comparison with the Old Testament — its historical part — holds. I find both Homer and the O.T. inexhaustible in exciting interest. I brood over them constantly, have flashes of revelation and turn to the text for confirmation.

Is it true that sensational finds are being made that may lead to the discovery of a key to Etruscan?

As you see I am reviving. If only I did not fear another blow!

To H.M. the King of Sweden

I Tatti

15 March 1957

. . . Here we are enjoying spring in all its glory. *Le fond de l'air* is still chilly and crisp but the sun already very strong.

I shall envy you all you will be seeing in London, not only

new things but all the wonders and marvels of the past. I fear I now can count on memory only. I can not look forward to much travelling and shall be grateful if I still can go as far as Rome, Naples and Venice. It is not the transport but seeing people and sights that are too much for my 92 years.

So "gather roses while you may."

To Axel Boethius

I Tatti
15 March 1957

. . . All my life I have been reading about Homer, philological, historical, archaeological, geographical, etc. Now I want to read him as pure art only, as commensurate with the heart and mind while humanity retains both.

There appeared recently a book about the *Odyssey* which talked of it as a sociological document only. It had a fabulous success and the American author was at once offered chairs in Oxford as well as in Cambridge.

Awareness of our lot, pity, friendship — humanization — is what seems to have come between 800 and 600 to Greece, to Israel, to India, to China as a final stage in our growth. Shall it now give place to the nuclear man and his in-human interests? *Absit omen!*

To Axel Boethius

I Tatti

24 May 1957

Never have I received a more wonderful letter than yours of the 18th, so redolent of deep and human scholarship, of universal interest, of fascinating information.

What you say about Linnaeus comes home to me because I have followed exactly the same empirical method as he did in my attempt to group the Italian painters of 14th-16th century. I say so in the new edition of my lists that is to appear soon.

How much like his is my lot! I too now forget names almost entirely as Linnaeus did. To recover a name I have to circumambulate it and try to conjure it up as the witch of Endor did to the Ghost of Samuel. Frequently I give up in despair and then in the middle of the following night I wake up with it on my lips.

To Francis Taylor[1]

17 October 1957

Dear Francis,

Thank you for yours of the 17th. I have received offprints of your article and with them a note from Weeks.

Meanwhile I have read your *Pierpont Morgan*. Before you stuff it with quotations, it is beautifully written. If you were here I could talk by the hour about P.M. In Italy he became a legend. I could scarcely look at a church treasure without being assured that *Birbo Morgo* had offered *cento mila* lire for it.

---

[1] Director of the Metropolitan Museum 1903-1954, and subsequently of the Worcester Museum.

That there was something cyclopic, demoniac about him I do not question but I doubt if his relation to works of art was in any way specifically aesthetic. I was in a position to know because of my friendship with Belle Greene. She adored him but through her hagiology I learnt a lot.

All gone with the wind. So many who battened on P.M. who curried for his favour, who howled when disappointed.

Please thank Pamela for her dear letter. What a jewel of a woman! *Life* is to bring out an article about me. The script is tolerable. I wonder what will remain of it when in print.

Dear Francis, I am devoted to you both and fervently hope to see you again before I am completely blind and deaf.

To HAROLD ACTON

> I Tatti
> 2 February 1958

Dear Harold,

I am happy to hear that you are preparing a new edition of your *Last Medici*. It is a work of art and not a mere chronicle of irrelevant events. I beg you not to alter a jot or tittle except of course for purely stylistic reasons. Do not dream of sticking on rags and tags of petty little documents that may have been discovered since the first edition appeared.

Hoping to see you back in Florence before long

> affectionately yours
> B.B.

Bernard Berenson's health began to fail, as is indeed indicated in the last sentence of his letter to Francis Taylor in 1957. He died on 6 October 1959 at Villa I Tatti, of which he was so fond and which he had occupied almost exactly sixty years.

Epilogue

BETWEEN the date of the next to last letter (17 October, 1957) in this volume and the spring of 1958, when B.B. fell seriously ill, he did keep up the correspondence with his friends but more by writing notes than real letters or by asking me to write in his name. "I have reached the point," he would say, "when to recognize the handwriting of a friend on an envelope and to know that he or she is still alive satisfies my appetite for news." During the last eighteen months of his life and up to a few days before his death I was always able to find moments when his mind was clear and receptive enough to take in what I could tell him about friends far and near who had either written or called.

In his introduction Arthur McComb says that the earliest group of letters has more life and freshness than the later ones, and from his point of view he is perfectly right. For me everything has a special significance from 1919 on. That was the year during which my life became linked up with I Tatti. Almost every letter wakes up some resonance not only of the voices of friends to whom the letters are addressed but of life at I Tatti or at Vallombrosa, of our trips to foreign lands, of my anxieties before and during the war, of B.B.'s and Mary's intense "post consciousness," of their eagerness to receive news from family and friends, of their indignation when during our journeys the mail failed to appear at the places where they expected it.

B.B. was very sceptical as to what permanent value his letters might have and I wonder what he would say to this selection? Perhaps he would be as surprised as I am to find in it a clear and consistent reflection of his personality, of his thoughts on events and books and human beings, combined with the recurrent themes of his aesthetic convictions and of his scholarly pursuits and curiosities. It re-creates for me the image I used to have of him, seeing him as it were at the centre of a huge web with threads spun out in every direction.

When the proposition of publishing a selection of B.B.'s letters was first made to me by Sydney Freedberg I felt a certain reluctance towards it. Familiar as I was with B.B.'s habit of swiftly covering several pages with his large sprawling handwriting, more as a relaxation from his usual work than as a literary achievement, I could not help being somewhat doubtful as to what the final result would be like. All the more grateful am I now to Arthur McComb for his attentive and sensitive choice of relevant letters or passages and for his excellent annotations. Our only point of divergence has been over the inclusion of the unfortunate exchange of letters between B.B. and Vernon Lee, (pp. 55-60). It does no service to the memory of either of them. Had Mary been near B.B. at that time, his letter might have been written in an impulse of resentment but it would not have been posted. Mary was devoted to Miss Paget and the estrangement following the clash made her very unhappy. I well remember Mary's deep satisfaction when in the autumn of 1922 peace was established and regular relations resumed with the Palmerino. Sometime in the spring of 1923 Miss Paget wrote a letter to Mary in which she admitted that looking through Miss Anstruther-Thomson's annotations made during B.B.'s talks with them she had realized that his accusation of plagiarism was not wholly unjustified.

I regret that letters written through many years by B.B. to friends, as for instance those to Belle Greene or Katie Lewis or W. G. Constable or Frank J. Mather or Billy Ivins should have been either destroyed (in the case of the letters to Constable, by fire) or not made available to the editor. But even in its present form, less varied than it could have been, this selection helps to fill out the mosaic of B.B.'s complex and unusual personality.

NICKY MARIANO

San Martino a Mensola
April 1963

Appendix and Index

Appendix

LAWRENCE BERENSON TO BERNARD BERENSON
18 May 1953

Dear B.B.:

I hope you are off enjoying a complete rest, and that you are both entirely free of callers. For me, nothing is more exhausting than seeing vast numbers of people. You have always amazed me with your patience.

I have just completed several weeks in Cuba seeing large numbers of government officials and other people, and nothing fatigues me as much as these interviews.

Batista too amazes me with the numbers of people he has to see, but he has the saving grace of comparative youth and physical strength. He arranges appointments from about 2:00 P.M. to 10:00 P.M. and then works until about 4:00 A.M. and sleeps and rests until about noon. In that way he manages to carry on.

I usually dine with him two or three times a week at the Presidential Palace from 10:00 P.M. until 1 or 2 A.M. reviewing all of his problems. The miserable part of it is that his Ministers and other high officials in the Government believe that I have a great amount of influence with him with the result that they interview me constantly day and night to persuade me about the correctness of their positions and their claims. The truth of the matter is that he is extremely alert, keen, incisive and with excellent balance of judgment. Really, all that he uses me for is to unload his inner heart and confidences and the conflicts which arise among his Ministers, only because he cannot divulge his inner thoughts to any of his Cuban associates. My only real help to him is to enable him to ventilate his emotions and problems and that in turn enables him to make his decisions. Rarely do I find him blundering in his final decisions. Sometimes the discussions are heated and I find the politicians wasting much of his time on politics. His viewpoint is that he needs the politicians for the votes whereas mine is that he should employ that time toward accomplishing visible results for the people, such as roads, aqueducts, drainage, sewage, etc. The politicians have retarded his progress so much that he has had to postpone the elections for another year. This has brought very considerable adverse publicity from the opposition. He must hold the elections as promptly as possible because Cuba is different from most South American countries in that the Cuban people are accustomed to having elections.

Notwithstanding the delays, Batista has made excellent progress and is establishing himself more firmly and solidly with the people each day. I am confident that by the time the elections are held, he will win by an overwhelming majority because of what he is accomplishing for them. He will show tremendous accomplishments by election time.

He expects me to spend long periods of time with him in the future. It is impossible for me to do so because of the work here, but I have promised to come and spend as much time as I can. . . .

Affectionately,

Index